DESIGNING OUR WAY TO A BETTER WORLD

DESIGNING OUR WAY TO A BETTER WORLD

THOMAS FISHER

UNIVERSITY OF MINNESOTA PRESS
MINNEAPOLIS • LONDON

The publication of this book was supported by the Imagine Fund for the arts, design, and humanities, an annual award from the University of Minnesota Provost's Office.

Published by the University of Minnesota Press
111 Third Avenue South, Suite 290, Minneapolis, MN 55401–2520
http://www.upress.umn.edu

Printed in the United States of America on acid-free paper
The University of Minnesota is an equal-opportunity educator and employer.

22 21 20 19 18 17 16
10 9 8 7 6 5 4 3 2 1

Library of Congress Cataloging-in-Publication Data
Names: Fisher, Thomas, author.
Title: Designing our way to a better world / Thomas Fisher.
Description: Minneapolis : University of Minnesota Press, 2016. | Includes bibliographical references and index.
Identifiers: LCCN 2015049868 | ISBN 978-0-8166-9887-5 (hc) | ISBN 978-0-8166-9888-2 (pb) | ISBN 978-1-4529-5163-8 (epub)
Subjects: LCSH: Design—Human factors. | Quality of life. | Social systems. | BISAC: ARCHITECTURE / Urban & Land Use Planning. | SOCIAL SCIENCE / Sociology / Urban. | ARCHITECTURE / Criticism.
Classification: LCC NK1520 .F565 2016 | DDC 745.4—dc23
LC record available at http://lccn.loc.gov/2015049868

CONTENTS

VII **Introduction**

  1 **PART I Invisible Systems**
  3 **1** The Design of the Invisible
13 **2** Design Thinking
21 **3** The Logic of Creativity

33 **PART II Education**
35 **4** Creative Education
47 **5** Schools and Communities
55 **6** Reconstructing Design
     Education

65 **PART III Infrastructure**
67 **7** Fracture-Critical Failures
75 **8** Overextended Infrastructure
87 **9** Designed Disasters

97 **PART IV Public Health**
99 **10** The Infrastructure of Health
107 **11** Healthy Landscapes
117 **12** Viral Cities

129 **PART V Politics**
131 **13** Designer Politics
141 **14** The Politics of No
149 **15** Left, Right, and Wrong

159 **PART VI Economics**
161 **16** An Opposable Economy
169 **17** A Third Industrial Revolution
181 **18** Metadesign

191 **PART VII Beliefs**
193 **19** Community Resilience
201 **20** Evolutionary Transformation
209 **21** Spatializing Knowledge

221 **Postscript**
     A Past and Possible Future

229 **Index**

INTRODUCTION

VII   Never has one species—ours—so dominated the planet. We can traverse and communicate around the globe at unprecedented speed, command and control natural resources almost at will, and affect or alter ecosystems anywhere on earth. And yet, at the very moment when we seem unstoppable and invincible, humanity is facing new threats, with rising global temperatures, a rapidly growing human population, and increasing economic inequality, at least in the United States. Like our technology, which moves bits and bodies around the world at an ever faster pace, humanity has started to career rapidly toward some sort of breaking point.

To understand what this means for us and what life might look like after we reach that point, we could start with the idea of "panarchy," developed by the ecologists Lance Gunderson and C. S. Holling.[1] They have shown how ecosystems change in dynamic, adaptive ways as a series of interlocking "figure eight" cycles happening at various scales and at different speeds. The same pattern that occurs in nature's ecosystems seems to occur in human systems as well. Over time, systems tend to become highly productive, efficient, and interconnected, with relatively few dominant actors. But in this process, a system can lose its resilience, flexibility, and adaptability to change, making it highly vulnerable to collapse and reorganization, which leads to an increase in the system's diversity, a decrease in its interconnectedness, and a reduction in the dominance of one part of the system over others. The system returns to a more balanced state—until the process starts all over again.

We humans may like to think that we can elude the processes of nature because of our knowledge and technological prowess, but we cannot avoid the fact that human systems remain an inseparable part of the natural ecosystems that surround and support us. We know that businesses and organizations fail and reorganize all the time, but panarchy suggests that this happens at larger scales as well—to entire systems and possibly to the global human ecosystem. I explore how this might happen across a range of systems in my book *Designing to Avoid Disaster,* in which I try to look ahead to what reorganized systems might be like and how we might think about them (and ourselves) differently as a result.[2] I see these possible futures not as something to fear but instead as tremendous opportunities to create human ecosystems more in harmony with those of nature and with how most people would probably prefer to live, with less stress and greater security.

VIII   These opportunities will, in turn, demand a considerable amount of creative "design thinking" on our part as we envision new ways of doing things. Enabling us to imagine what does not yet exist, design becomes especially valuable in situations characterized by dramatic or unprecedented change, when we need innovative ways of addressing a problem. As the human and natural systems that we depend on face rapidly approaching tipping points, we need novel ways of thinking and acting, now more than ever, and design thinking has much to offer in that regard. It provides not just a useful and rigorous process of coming up with creative ideas but also a synthesizing, holistic way of looking at the world around us, making connections and seeing relationships among things we often treat as separate and distinct.

We tend to think of design in terms of the visible world around us: the buildings we occupy and the products we use. But the "invisible" systems that we depend on in our daily lives—the infrastructure buried beneath our feet or in our walls, the educational and health systems that we all experience as we age or become ill, and the economic and political systems that affect us in myriad ways over time—remain just as much designed as anything that we inhabit or use. Many of us may not think of them this way. Because we cannot "see" or "touch" them, our political, economic, health, education, and infrastructure systems may appear to lie beyond anyone's ability to change them, even though they all arose from some sort of design process. Because of the scale of these systems, as seemingly vast as the invisible "dark matter" and "dark energy" that constitute 96 percent of the universe, they may appear too difficult to move.[3] But we can shift them if we think of them as a whole and look for the levers that can lead to the greatest transformation.

Let me explain what I mean with a story. Several years ago, local county authorities asked some of my colleagues to help redesign the waiting rooms of the county's juvenile detention facilities because fights had begun to break out among the people waiting there. My colleagues agreed to take on this project and started by doing what all designers do: documenting the rooms, making observations about their use, and listening to the people who used the waiting rooms as well as to those who worked in the detention system. The county had hoped that my colleagues, all designers, would come back with waiting-room plans and recommendations for moving furniture, changing the lighting, and maybe putting up a few dividers to separate people and discourage fighting.

Instead, my colleagues recommended that the county redesign its juvenile detention process, since no amount of reorganization and redecoration of the waiting rooms would end the fighting, which remained the most visible symptom of a dysfunctional system that frustrated almost everyone involved—those who worked in it as well as those served by it. In making this recommendation, the design team diagrammed the current system, showing where the communication gaps and process breakdowns were occurring. The county had not seen the system visualized in this way, and the designers' diagram led to conversations among people who had not understood how they fit as part of a larger whole and how they connected to the work of others in ways not immediately apparent.

The design team did not just analyze the situation and help the county visualize its system; it also suggested strategies that would begin to repair the dysfunction. My colleagues proposed, for instance, engaging the youth and their families, who had experienced things not well understood by those in charge of the system, in the system's redesign as well as in its ongoing operation as mentors to young people who, with guidance, might avoid the same path. Design arises out of empathy for the real needs of others and often reveals things about a circumstance that those in the midst of it may not see.

This does not always please those in power or those who have a stake in the status quo. The county did not appreciate my colleagues' doing something other than what they had been asked to do, and as a result nothing happened at first. After a while, though, the county's leadership acknowledged the problems with the system and began to act on aspects of the designers' proposal. To their credit, the county leaders overcame their initial annoyance and engaged my colleagues in the redesign of other county systems that were also not working as they should.

This story holds several lessons. First, it shows how much professionals need to tell the truth as they see it about a situation and recommend what they believe to be in a client's best interest, rather than simply giving the client what they think the client needs or wants to hear. As patients, we would not go to doctors who would do whatever we told them to do, whether medically sound or not. Nor should we want other professionals

X

(in this case, designers) to do strictly what we ask of them; we should trust in their ability to analyze a situation and recommend what we most need, rather than what we think we want.

Second, the story demonstrates the power of creative insight and problem solving. We often associate creativity with artists and think of it in terms of particular outcomes, like works of art or pieces of music. This overly narrow interpretation of creativity misses the role that it can play in improving our lives and those of other people, future generations, and the other species with whom we share the planet. The ability to make connections among disparate entities and activities, such as those in the juvenile detention system; to distinguish between the symptoms and the causes of a problem, such as fights in waiting rooms; and to diagram a circumstance as the basis for understanding and recommending possible solutions to the problem—all characterize the real value that design and creativity bring to the challenges we face.

Third, the story reveals a new way of thinking about design. For most of their history, the design fields have focused on the creation of tangible or at least visible things: landscapes, buildings, interiors, products, and images. The reason seems obvious: we all live in the physical world, with bodies that need shelter and lives that need products, services, and information to survive and thrive. But that focus led the design community to overlook the enormous territory of designed systems that remains invisible to us but affects us every day—in some respects, even more powerfully than the world we can see. We can walk away from a fight in a waiting room or call security to break it up. But a juvenile detention system, as much a product of design as those waiting rooms, becomes much harder to avoid once we are in it, since from that vantage point we often cannot see its flaws. Such a system also becomes more difficult to correct if we do not recognize it as designed in the first place.

Finally, the dysfunction of that juvenile detention system shows what happens when discrete, hierarchical organizations become inflexible and unable to adapt to changing conditions. The fights in the waiting rooms represented what Gunderson and Holling might see as a system entering a panarchic collapse, in which the misalignment between the way in which the system functioned and the needs of the juveniles and their families had gotten so great that it demanded a rethinking and reorganization of the entire entity.

Too many systems have the same hierarchical rigidity and organizational inflexibility, and too many people suffer, needlessly, as a result of these invisible design failures. Design failures, of course, happen often enough among the visible and tangible designs that we use and inhabit. We have all experienced clothes that don't fit well, chairs that hit our backs or legs in the wrong way, graphics that are more confusing than clarifying, and cars that break down far too often through no fault of our own. But whatever these designs lack in terms of comfort or convenience, at least most of what we buy in the mainstream commercial world has met fairly stringent safety standards and has often undergone demanding product testing in order to be offered on the market for our use.

This does not apply to the vast amount of design that we do not see: the systems and strategies, policies and procedures, and organizations and operations on which we depend in our daily lives. That invisible world of design affects us all the time, but it rarely has to pass safety tests or meet performance standards, and we all suffer enormously as a result. Badly designed investment products have crashed the global economy, badly conceived policies have brought the U.S. government to a halt, badly implemented safety procedures have led to unnecessary deaths, and badly performed operations have killed too many people.

We can improve the performance of such systems. We first need to recognize them as designed, and second, we need to subject them to the same level of scrutiny that we apply to physical design. The intense, rigorous, and self-critical process applied to all designed products and environments works very well for identifying flaws and possible failures long before something becomes available to us to buy and use. While it does not always catch every shortcoming, a highly effective, iterative process has evolved in which a design proposal is run through a series of assessments by established experts as well as potential users until all of the people involved can no longer find a failing or suggest further improvements.

A third step involves getting past the common tendency to equate design with taste. Too many people view design as a subjective process or a matter of personal preference and so not worth paying much attention to or arguing about. That has resulted in design largely disappearing from the curricula of most primary and secondary schools and going unstudied by most students in higher education. If there's no accounting for taste, as the saying goes, then why study it?

This misguided dismissal of design and its absence from most curricula have led to the paradoxical situation in which we depend on the outcomes of the design process in the products we buy and the environments we occupy while knowing little or nothing about how the designs came about. In the case of physical design—cars, computers, clothing, and so on—that lack of understanding may not matter much, given that the rigorous process of its creation means that most physical design works relatively well. But when it comes to the design of the invisible, the almost complete absence of education about design matters a great deal. When we do not recognize the systems we depend on as designed, we often accept failures to an extent that we never would with the products and environments of our physical world. We would not endure structures that easily fall or products that readily fail, but we tend to treat events like the bursting of the housing bubble and the economic collapse that followed as acts of nature or as situations that no one could have anticipated—a faulty and overly fatalistic assumption.

Such fatalism plays into the hands of those who benefit enormously from system failures such as the investment bank collapse and the precipitous drop in home prices. They hedge their bets on bad design and win huge fortunes on the ill fortune of others, which may explain why those in positions of power have done so little to regulate the design of the invisible world. The design community has not helped here either. Most designers have paid relatively little attention to the design of what we cannot see and have continued to pursue work in, give awards to, and largely focus on the world of physical design, despite the increasingly competitive nature of traditional design practice.

As the competition for conventional design commissions has increased, the amount of work to do in the invisible world of design has continued to grow as well. Most designers have not seized the opportunity to address that work because they do not recognize dysfunctional systems as design problems and do not acknowledge that design has a great deal to offer in improving systems' performance. System dysfunctions often manifest themselves in inequities (not only among different people but also between humans and other species on the planet) and in the unsustainability of how our species has come to inhabit the earth, using up finite resources at

XIII unprecedented rates and setting in motion environmental changes that, paradoxically, threaten us as much as they do the many other plants and animals with whom we share this earth. The world deserves better design, and this represents the greatest challenge for the design community in this century.

The design community has said such things before, of course, and it has not worked out well. Modern architecture arose in the early twentieth century with grand ambitions to improve the world and to redesign not just individual buildings but entire cities in ways that architects like Le Corbusier and Frank Lloyd Wright saw as leading humankind to a better future. Though mostly well-intentioned, these designers made the crucial mistake of thinking that they knew what others needed and wanted, and that people would embrace their monoculture vision of what constituted a good life.

The postmodern reaction to that arrogance over the last three decades of the twentieth century led to a withdrawal of the architectural community from broader social, economic, and political discussions. Instead, many in the design community focused on formal or historical concerns of relatively little relevance to anyone outside the field. Postmodernists rightly rejected the presumptuousness of their predecessors but wrongly assumed that design had little to contribute to the larger discourse about the challenges and opportunities confronting humanity.

In the early twenty-first century, we have begun to move past that position to encourage designers to contribute to conversations about the future in ways that neither presume that we have the answers nor retreat from design's responsibility as a discipline to help others create better lives for themselves. Some call this "public-interest design," "social-impact design," or "design for good," and while I admire the approach for its empathy and humility in the face of complex, global problems, I must point out that much of it remains closely tied to the traditional output of the design community: environments, products, and communications.

In this book, I try to sketch a broader role for the design community along these lines, one that applies the empathetic and iterative methods of our discipline to the larger societal dilemmas we face to help people not only create a better physical world for themselves but also improve systems and services that have been badly designed by nondesigners. As with any sketch, *Designing Our Way to a Better World* provides a broad-brush look at this possibility, with little of the detail that experts or scholars might want or expect. Like any schematic design, this one will benefit from the input and ideas of many other people as it evolves, just as the measure of its success may lie in what it suggests rather than in what it tries to solve.

THE STRUCTURE AND ORIGIN OF THIS BOOK

This book has seven parts, each of which begins with a summary of the part's content; this is followed by three chapters related to the part's topic. After the first part explains in greater detail the idea of "invisible" design, why we need it, and how it works, each of the following parts explores a different designed system: education, infrastructure, public health, politics, economics, and beliefs. Each part stands on its own, and the order of the parts moves from systems that may seem more tangible, like education and our built infrastructure, to those that may appear more elusive, like our political, economic, or belief systems. The book ends with a concluding essay on the implications of this work for the future.

Thinking of such systems as designed may seem odd not only to the specialists in each of the fields addressed but to designers as well. Western culture has long associated design with the things that we see and hold, use and inhabit, and it has typically attributed design to individuals or groups of people who conceive of and then carry out the end results with particular goals in mind. The invisible design discussed in this book often has none of those features. Our political, economic, educational, and health care systems, which result from the work of myriad people over long periods, can sometimes seem like Rube Goldberg machines, with so many add-ons and make-dos that they appear barely functional. But that results from poor design, not the absence of design. I hope to suggest how we might begin to design such critically important systems as well as we do most of the products and environments we use in our daily lives, and how we might do so with an eye toward the dramatic social, economic, and environmental changes happening around us.

The range of topics here may seem overly ambitious, especially during a time when disciplinary specialization has made it seem as if no one without an advanced degree in a particular field has much to offer. I make no claims to specialized knowledge in any of the subject areas in this book, except for that of design, which applies to all of the topics here. Indeed, as many designers know, in addressing a specialized field from a design perspective we have the advantage of seeing it anew and from afar, which often leads to innovative ways of rethinking and reorganizing systems that elude those who are too familiar with and knowledgeable about them.

Much of the material in this book has been published previously, although in scattered locations among a diversity of magazines, journals, newspapers, and websites. Those venues range from the online *Huffington Post* and the digital journal *Places* to regional magazines like *Architecture Minnesota* and professional journals like *Progressive Architecture,* which I edited for almost fifteen years. Most of what I have written during the past fifteen years has remained largely invisible, given the variety of places that now publish my pieces, so this book represents an attempt to gather this material and weave it into a larger whole.

I wrote *Designing Our Way to a Better World* not just to make several disparate essays more readily available. I hope that, through this book, the invisibly designed world will become a more coherent and, perhaps para-doxically, more visible concept. That needs to happen among those of us who do not understand how much design affects our lives and how much bad design we endure unnecessarily. It also needs to become more prominent within the design community as a vast territory of new work and potentially new services, all worthy of exploration. If nothing else, I am glad that this book, whatever you think of it, has become visible to you.

[1] Lance H. Gunderson and C. S. Holling, eds., *Panarchy: Understanding Trans-formations in Human and Natural Systems* (Washington, D.C.: Island Press, 2002).
[2] Thomas Fisher, *Designing to Avoid Disaster: The Nature of Fracture-Critical Design* (New York: Routledge, 2013), 22–34.
[3] Richard Panek, *The 4 Percent Universe* (New York: Houghton Mifflin Harcourt, 2011).

PART I

INVISIBLE SYSTEMS

The following three chapters describe different aspects of "invisible" design: what it means, the motivation for it, and the reasoning behind it. The first chapter looks at how Albert Einstein and Sigmund Freud, as creative thinkers, used the spatial analogies and imaginative leaps common to design thinking to explore and explain the invisible design that they perceived in the world. The advances they made in science and social science in the twentieth century show the potential of their same methods to advance the design fields in the twenty-first century. Chapter 1 ends with a reference to one of the most troubling paradoxes we face in the modern world, the paradox of efficiency, to show how such thinking can help us understand and address dilemmas in new ways.

The second chapter looks at how many of the dilemmas we face arise from our "disaggregation" of the world, reflected in public policies and economic incentives that encourage us to take apart the world in order to analyze, understand, and ultimately control it. Design represents a contrary process of reintegrating the myriad broken relations, dysfunctions, and misconnections that result from this disaggregation by synthesizing our knowledge about the world into greater wholes. This chapter examines a set of strategies that designers use to reconnect the disjointed reality around us, ending with an example of how well-designed technology can help us all do the same.

Chapter 3 explores the "abductive" logic that underlies design. Often viewed as subjective and intuitive, design actually follows a rigorous process that complements other forms of reasoning and that underlies most creative activity. This chapter looks at design's lateral, connective ways of working through the insights of the American philosopher Charles Sanders Peirce, whose philosophy of pragmatism provides guidance for how best to judge the merits of a design, based not just on the design's intentions but also on its consequences.

1

THE DESIGN OF
THE INVISIBLE

Design has entered its invisible century. This does not mean that design itself has become invisible—quite the contrary. Designed images have become ever more pervasive in our increasingly visual culture, designed products ever more pertinent in a rapidly growing human population, and designed environments ever more important given the predominantly urban existence of our species. But the great discoveries in design in the twenty-first century will come not from the design we can see but rather from that which we cannot. Let me explain by means of an analogy.

In 2004, the science writer Richard Panek published *The Invisible Century: Einstein, Freud, and the Search for Hidden Universes,* in which he argues that the twentieth century constituted the "invisible century" of science.[1] As he explains, at the end of the nineteenth century many scientists believed that the great discoveries had all been made and that the future of scientific investigation would involve the refinement of existing knowledge. "Little remained to be done but to measure physical constants to the increased accuracy represented by another decimal place," as one physicist put it.[2] But as it happened, such confident predictions would soon prove wrong, for it was in the first decades of the twentieth century that Albert Einstein and Sigmund Freud made their pathbreaking discoveries, revealing what Panek calls "hidden universes" that opened up whole new areas of understanding and activity in the "invisible" worlds of the subatomic particle, the space–time continuum, and human consciousness.

What Einstein and Freud achieved bears directly on design practices. In fact, the two scientists had much in common with designers. Einstein and Freud were both spatial thinkers, using thought experiments as the basis for most of their discoveries. Einstein imagined being in an elevator traveling at thirty-two feet per second squared, which is the force of gravity, and he recognized that in such a situation a passenger could not tell whether the elevator was moving or at rest, which means that acceleration and gravity are the same thing. He then imagined that if a light beam entered the moving elevator on one side, it would strike the other side of the rising elevator at a slightly lower point, appearing to bend—which means that gravity bends light.

Freud used spatial analogies to describe the unconscious as well. He likened the subconscious to the submerged part of an iceberg or an island to convey the extent to which the subconscious lies below the surface, invisible to us. Freud also described how the physical world takes on metaphorical meaning in our dreams, representing connections we may not be conscious of while awake. The role of the psychoanalyst, like that of a designer or a critic, involves the interpretation of people's dreams in search of the meaning that the dreamers give to the world around them.

Like the best designers, Einstein and Freud each displayed deep empathy, imagining the world from the perspectives of others. Einstein's discovery of the equivalence of energy and matter when traveling at the speed of light squared came about from his ability to see himself not only as a physicist looking at a particle but also as the particle itself, imagining what the world would look like from that vantage point. Likewise, Freud's discovery of the subconscious repressions of his patients hinged on his willingness to sit and listen to them speak as they struggled to resist and ultimately opened up to his nonjudgmental questions about their lives.

Both Einstein and Freud made imaginative and metaphorical use of Wilhelm Röntgen's late nineteenth-century discovery of X-rays. Much as architects and designers have the ability to slice through objects conceptually to understand them in plan and section, Einstein and Freud analogized their accomplishments as the equivalent of seeing beneath the surface of things to perceive what had surrounded people all along but never before been visible. As Panek writes, what Einstein and Freud "wound up discovering wasn't new evidence but a new way of looking at old evidence . . . a shift not in perception . . . but in conception."[3]

And also like designers, who envision objects and environments that do not yet exist, Einstein and Freud took a speculative approach to their work. Unlike many scientists, they did not draw their ideas from experimentation; instead, as Panek writes, "they hypothesized, and then, as need be, depending on the evidence, they revised, until the hypothesis matched observations."[4] In other words, Einstein and Freud made creative leaps, as designers do, and then tested and adjusted ideas in iterative ways until they aligned with reality.

Einstein and Freud set out to explore their hidden universes because science some hundred years ago left too many paradoxes unexplained and too many ideas unchallenged. Einstein questioned the old assumption that while we can alter space, we cannot alter time, just as Freud overturned the accepted notion that to catalog the symptoms of mental illness would be to explain it. And in both cases, they wrestled with paradoxes that others ignored, such as how energy or ideas move without any intermediary substance or connections, like the ether or neurons, to carry them.

Like science at the beginning of the twentieth century, design now faces its own unchallenged assumptions and unquestioned paradoxes, and it too has its own hidden universes to explore. Why do we assume, for example, that design primarily involves the creation of physical products or environments, when we know that every human activity has been "designed" in some way? Why have the countless processes of design, which pervade and inform almost all that we encounter in our daily lives, remained so invisible to most people? And what does design have to contribute to the seemingly invisible systems, services, and flows that have begun to fail us because of their poor design?

Because they have had no education in design thinking, most people do not understand or know how to employ the design process—the iterative, critical examination of possible futures that has proven so effective in the physical world in anticipating likely failures and unintended consequences that need correction before a design becomes a reality. And because most designers rarely apply this process to the invisible world of processes and procedures, we all suffer.

Think of what we might have avoided in the sphere of economics had we subjected some of the hazardous financial products that have wrought so much personal and collective damage—the devastating subprime mortgages and highly leveraged corporate buyouts—to "design reviews," assessing all that could go wrong and requiring thorough redesign before exposing so many people to so much risk. Or imagine how the past decade might have differed had we scrutinized the overly optimistic assumptions behind our infrastructural systems and addressed the possibilities of airport security being too easily breached, major bridges collapsing, a category 5 hurricane hitting New Orleans, and a tsunami striking the Japanese coast.

Many of those responsible for the dramatically inadequate responses that have followed such catastrophic events have claimed that no one could have foreseen them, but in fact we should have foreseen these events. Our failure to do so speaks to the lack of design skill and creative imagination on the part of those in charge. Design thinking enables us not only to create things that work well but also to anticipate what could go wrong and

6

to prevent that from happening as much as humanly possible. These catastrophes also show how rarely designers get asked to participate in development processes outside the narrow confines of what the design community itself has traditionally thought of as designed.

Architects and planners often complain about the constraints of working within rules and frameworks set up by other professionals in law, finance, and government that can make it difficult for them to do the right thing. But by limiting its view of design to the giving of physical form to the visible things we use and inhabit, the design community implicitly concedes that design can do little to change the badly conceived or simply outdated laws, policies, and procedures that have helped create and perpetuate environments that have become inequitable, unsustainable, and dysfunctional.

To change this situation, we need to begin applying design thinking to the invisible universe of processes, policies, and procedures as thoroughly and as rigorously as we have applied it to the visible world. This will entail two fundamental shifts in how we think about design itself. First, it will require a change in education so that the design of physical products and environments becomes just one among several possible ways to use this knowledge—and just one among a range of careers for designers.

Legal education went through such a transformation in the twentieth century, when law schools began to emphasize not only trial law but also legal analysis and thinking, and in this way expanded the application of legal skills to encompass the fuller range of career paths now available to lawyers, many of whom never set foot in a courtroom. For design education, this means a much greater emphasis on the epistemology of design—on how designers think and on how the design process works—and a much greater acceptance among educators that applications of this knowledge will extend well beyond those currently emphasized in most design schools.

Second, it will require a rethinking of design so that it comes to be viewed as a fundamental skill with which all educated people should have some familiarity and even facility. We accept that this is true for other disciplines—for example, we are all expected to have some understanding of mathematical, scientific, and historical models of thinking—but design, the one form of thinking that assesses the world not as it is or was but as it could be, hardly exists in primary, secondary, or even postsecondary education. To address this lacuna, design educators and practitioners need to develop new structures for collaboration with teachers at all levels in preparing design curriculum modules for K–12 education and to intensify partnerships with other disciplines in applying design thinking to the many ill-defined and open-ended problems we face.

These two shifts might seem contradictory. If we educate everyone to think like designers, will we need designers anymore? The answer, of course, is yes. We still have mathematicians, scientists, and historians, even though most educated people have some ability to understand how these disciplines think and work. We also still have law schools, even though legal thinking has penetrated many aspects of our lives. The design disciplines, too, will remain important fields unto themselves, and many practitioners will continue to design objects in the physical world, just as many scientists since Einstein and Freud have continued to discover new things about the visible world. But as in these other realms, design thinking will become more powerful in its ability to improve the quality of our lives as it becomes more pervasive in our educational system and more prominent in the design of the invisible world.

The examples of Einstein and Freud suggest how we might do this. Just as their discoveries produced paradigm shifts in our understanding of reality, so too could designers apply that way of thinking and seeing—"with X-ray eyes," as Panek says of Einstein and Freud—to phenomena far beyond physical forms, spaces, and products. This shift will almost certainly lead to new discoveries, if for no other reason than that the invisible realm of design remains so largely unexplored by the design community itself. And with these discoveries will come whole new professional roles. Science's invisible century launched fields such as atomic physics, psychoanalysis, and human genomics, to name just a few, and the invisible century of design has already begun to spawn new career tracks with names like service design, experience design, public-interest design, and geodesign.

Design thinking, prototyping, and visualization skills will link all of these new activities. Just as Einstein and Freud made the invisible world visible, so too could designers help others envision what policies or processes might look like visually and spatially and how such systems perform functionally. This might include diagramming processes to reveal weak points, connecting seemingly unrelated phenomena and thus identifying potential unintended consequences, and illustrating the physical implications of policies in order to evaluate their ultimate effects. Systems often fail because of oversimplification in their conception and design; the application of traditional design methods could help those in power understand the true complexity of the networks (e.g., infrastructure, finance, and information) for which they are responsible.

Also, just as Einstein and Freud had empathetic vision, the ability to see things from multiple perspectives, so too could designers enable policy makers and other professionals to view their own work in terms of those most affected by it. By gathering user information at the very start of the design process rather than after the fact (as so often happens), showing what regulations or procedures might mean to particular people rather than to abstract "stakeholders" or "average" constituents, and communicating those effects in plain language and smart visuals rather than in obfuscating jargon, designers could have a transformative effect on the quality and efficacy of public and private decision making.

Finally, just as Einstein and Freud speculatively explored previously hidden universes, so too could designers show those in power how to prototype and test alternative scenarios and critically assess the possible consequences of projects and plans. With designers as regular participants in the development of policies and processes—much as lawyers and financial analysts are today—we would see much less of the linear, deductive, and reductionist thinking that has enabled so many design failures in the invisible world and much more of the iterative, abductive, and divergent thinking that has helped make the physical world, especially in the most developed countries, so much safer, healthier, and cleaner than in the past. The larger goal here is to make our environments and systems better and stronger still—the public should never be expected to tolerate financial "innovation" that could destroy the global economy or "austerity" measures that lead to deferred maintenance and collapsing roadways. We can no longer afford to neglect involving designers in these arenas.

Proof of the benefits of this way of thinking about design will ultimately rest with what design can accomplish. We continue to value Einstein and Freud because of their insights into the most difficult and perplexing problems of their day; the pathbreaking explorers of design's invisible century need to set their sights similarly high. The usefulness and value of design thinking lie in its ability to resolve pressing and persistent paradoxes, such as the Jevons paradox of efficiency.

The nineteenth-century British economist William Stanley Jevons recognized this paradox when he observed that greater efficiencies in the use of finite resources, such as coal, do not reduce consumption of those resources but instead increase it, contrary to expectations.[5] We can easily see why the Jevons paradox occurs: greater efficiency in the production and use of a resource can increase its quantity and reduce its price, which prompts more consumption and increases economic growth, which in turn fuels ever-greater use of the resource as more people have the means to purchase it. Thus Jevons argued that we should not rely solely on improvements in efficiency to reduce consumption of a finite resource.

This paradox raises profound problems for modern society in general and for the design professions in particular. In recent decades a great deal of work—designs, proposals, competitions, books, articles, and so on—has been directed toward reducing the demand for water, energy, and materials in everything from industrial processes to LEED-rated buildings. Yet the Jevons paradox states that even if we persist in becoming ever more efficient, consumption will only increase—a losing battle environmentally. Jevons did not believe that we should simply give up and continue to be wasteful or inefficient, but his observation implies that we cannot rely on technology to ensure that we do not overconsume resources necessary to our survival.

Some have argued that with the right policies and incentives we can counter this paradox: for instance, we can levy taxes on resources like water and fossil fuels, set quotas on use, and control availability to keep prices high.[6] Such tactics have proven hard to sell economically and politically, however; they strike some as "social engineering" that unwisely tampers with the free market drive toward the greater efficiency and lower cost of commodities. But as Jevons shows, unless we take some action, an unfettered marketplace will often work to decrease costs and increase consumption to the point where we will exhaust the supply of vital resources and in the process ultimately drive up their costs. And as we have seen in recent years, the increasing scarcity of essential resources like water can disrupt entire economies and devastate people's lives.[7]

THE DESIGN OF THE INVISIBLE

The Jevons paradox also suggests that we have designed incentives in contradictory and ultimately self-defeating ways, undervaluing what is most important so that we have become ever more efficient at heedless consumption. So let's assume, for the moment, that we want to avoid solutions that look like top-down social engineering (which almost guarantees political defeat); we then need to design incentives that encourage bottom-up, voluntary choices by individuals to do the right thing. This could include attaching social stigma to overconsumption (as has happened with obesity) and educating ourselves about the hazards of unhealthy products polluting the commons (as has happened with smoking).

It could also involve creating a network of easily used infrastructures around sharing resources (as has happened with ride-share programs) and generating a sense of community around the reduction of waste (as has happened with the widespread acceptance of recycling and with the voluntary simplicity movement). These are just some of the ways in which the design professions might take on new and hybrid roles—and not only in creating the messages, products, and environments to help make such ideas happen but also in helping identify the structural problems and in generating and testing diverse ideas to address them. We have designed our way into such dilemmas and we can design our way out of them—if we conceptualize the challenges with enough depth and vision.

As was true of the invisible worlds discovered by Einstein and Freud, the hidden universe of design surrounds us; we just need to develop the eyes to see it. All human artifacts and activities—not just our objects and architecture but also our organizations and operations, policies and procedures, systems and infrastructures—have been designed, and too many of the most critical have been designed badly by professionals and politicians who did not know the first thing about design. While we cannot blame them for what they didn't know or couldn't see, the stakes have gotten too high for us to continue in this way. The expansion of design into these invisible realms has practical value, both for the design professions, in which labor-intensive work is increasingly automated or outsourced, and for the entire human population and the planet as a whole, which is suffering from the unsustainability of badly designed systems.

11 This chapter first appeared as the essay "Design's Invisible Century" in the online journal Places (April 23, 2012), http://places.designobserver.com/feature/design-invisible-century/32858.

[1] Richard Panek, *The Invisible Century: Einstein, Freud, and the Search for Hidden Universes* (New York: Viking Press, 2004).

[2] Ibid., 64.

[3] Ibid., 168.

[4] Ibid., 175.

[5] John M. Polimeni, Kozo Mayumi, Mario Giampietro, and Blake Alcott, *The Jevons Paradox and the Myth of Resource Efficiency Improvements* (London: Earthscan, 2008).

[6] Paul Krugman, *The Great Unraveling: Losing Our Way in the New Century* (New York: W. W. Norton, 2003).

[7] United Nations Policy Development and Studies Branch, *Water Scarcity and Humanitarian Action: Key Emerging Trends and Challenges* (New York: United Nations Office for the Coordination of Humanitarian Affairs, September 2010).

2

DESIGN
THINKING

13   The poorly designed systems that we suffer from arise, in part, from our having spent the last few centuries disaggregating the world, taking it apart, both physically and conceptually, in order to understand and control it. That strategy has succeeded brilliantly on many levels. Never have we had so much command over nature, so much power at our disposal, and such dominance on the planet. This, in turn, has led us to feel as if we stand on top of the world and are nearly invincible as a civilization—which also means that we have never had farther to fall or faced so great a vulnerability as a species.

As the Greek and Shakespearean tragedies have taught us, the hubris of humanity comes from our not recognizing the full consequences of our actions and decisions. We have designed a food system, for example, that produces an abundance of calories at a relatively low cost, without seeing how we will all pay dearly for it as the tsunami of illness from an increasingly overweight population hits our health system in the years ahead. We have designed school systems that produce wildly uneven educational results, keeping whole sectors of our population locked in poverty, without recognizing that we will all pay for our neglect of these inequities with a less productive workforce and reduced economic prosperity overall. And we have designed infrastructure systems that have brought paved roads and utilities to the most far-flung locations, without realizing that most communities have nowhere near enough tax or utility revenue to pay for the maintenance of these systems.

The surest sign of the disaggregation of our world, where even well-intentioned actions can lead to unintended and self-defeating consequences, occurs in the monocultures that now surround us. Our food system has wiped out complex ecosystems and replaced them with vast acreage of the same crops amid slivers of uncultivated land, fragmenting the habitats of other species to such an extent that fewer and fewer of them can survive. Our educational system has become as socioeconomically segregated as our residential neighborhoods, to the point where we have ghettoized ourselves into communities of people just like ourselves, with the United States now having one of the lowest rates of upward mobility in the developed world. And the political system at the federal level has become so gerrymandered that many congressional districts have become ideologically pure, containing such large majorities of one party or the other that neither has much of a chance to win on the opponent's turf.

We ignore such disaggregation and dysfunction at our own peril. To move in a new direction, we first need to stop living under the illusion that we stand as the most intelligent and invincible species on the planet. Although we have extraordinary knowledge about the world, we also continue to do extraordinary damage to it and to ourselves in the process, extinguishing resources, species, and languages and cultures at record rates. Although the global economy has become amazingly efficient in its ability to move goods and information, it also remains remarkably vulnerable to disruptions of supply chains and fuel sources. And although the pace innovation has increased almost exponentially in recent decades, we also find ourselves in a race between a growing number of catastrophic collapses and a growing pressure to innovate our way out of them.[1]

Now more than ever, we need more creative ways of thinking—*design* thinking. At one level, design thinking is the way in which designers generate new ideas, which involves both a rigorous use of analogy to make new connections among seemingly disparate phenomena and an iterative, critical process of assessing the consequences of those connections to arrive at optimal solutions to complex problems. We tend to associate such thinking with the traditional design disciplines: graphic design, apparel design, product design, interior design, architecture, landscape architecture, and urban design and planning. And we tend to judge the success of such thinking according to how well its end results function or sell.

But design thinking can bring valuable insights to almost any discipline. The application of this comparative, iterative, and critical process can generate creative ideas and actionable solutions in ways that no other type of thinking can. It becomes especially valuable in situations involving unprecedented and highly complex challenges. While humanity has always faced such situations, their scale and potential impacts have grown with the power of our technology and the extent of our global connectedness. The design theorist Horst Rittel called these "wicked problems," characterized by incomplete, contradictory, and rapidly changing information or demands, and they have become the dominant characteristic of our time.[2]

After centuries of disaggregation, we have arrived at a point where we need to "reaggregate" the world, to put it back together, and to see the interconnectedness of its parts. Design thinking serves such holism well. By connecting disparate phenomena and evaluating the consequences of different ways of doing things, design thinking can reintegrate what we have too often seen as separate and distinct. How does design thinking do this? While many designers seem hesitant to talk about this thought process, as if doing so will make it less valuable or at least less mysterious, design thinking remains a process as rigorous—and as teachable—as the scientific process, for example. Different designers may place more or less emphasis on various aspects of this process, but they all use the following techniques in creative and integrative ways:

- **Analogy, which takes something that works in one area and applies it to another one**
- **Metaphor, which reinterprets a problem to see it and its possible solutions in a new way**
- **Juxtaposition, which combines seemingly unrelated things to discover new connections**
- **Improvisation, which appropriates things at hand and makes something useful from their combination**
- **Rescaling, which reuses something that works at a different scale or for a different purpose**
- **Rearranging, which pulls things apart and puts them back together in new and unexpected ways**
- **Reinterpreting, which seeks new ways of explaining a situation or applying a solution**
- **Reimagining, which looks at a problem from another, radically different perspective**
- **Diagramming, which tries to map relationships or give form to what may not be obvious**
- **Prototyping, which gives ideas form and enables testing them to quantify their performance against the desired goals**
- **Critiquing, which holds up prototypes to rigorous and often withering analysis from as many viewpoints as possible**
- **Iterating, which constitutes the repeated cycles of idea generation, prototyping, and testing, until a solution emerges that seems best suited to the problem**
- **Producing, which is the stage at which a design goes to scale and where additional design problems often emerge**

- Assessing, which involves evaluating the design while in use and feeding this information back into the design of subsequent projects
- Enjoying, which entails the pleasure of engaging with something so well designed, so beautifully suited to its purpose, that it seems almost inevitable

Such techniques, among many others that designers use, help us see things in new ways and encourage us to think about them differently. Not all of them work in every situation or for every person, but all have proven useful for finding new and often unconventional solutions to the problems that plague us.

INTEGRATIVE TECHNOLOGIES

The reaggregation of reality has underpinned some of the most successful companies in recent years. Consider Apple's mobile devices, which are popular not only because of the way they look, feel, and function but also because they bring together activities and resources—verbal and text communication, music and photography, and encyclopedic information at the touch of a screen—that we once saw as distinct and unrelated. The power of this integrating technology became amply evident in the days following the untimely death of Apple's visionary leader, Steve Jobs. Jobs recognized that humans respond to what good design brings to our lives: beauty, simplicity, clarity, and community. Designers have long argued this point, but there exists no more effective proof of it than the popularity of Apple's products and the profound sense of loss that Apple customers showed at Jobs's passing.

Writers about design such as Daniel Pink, Tim Brown, and Roger Martin have shown how better-designed products, environments, and services improve the quality of our lives, and how design-savvy companies regularly outperform their competitors. But the lessons of Steve Jobs's life go far beyond successful product design. Jobs showed how design represents an often overlooked and underappreciated form of leadership. We typically look to politicians and elected officials for leadership, something that we have seen far too little of in our capitals in recent years. Jobs embodied a different type of leadership, one that entails looking over the horizon to a future that others do not yet see, telling compelling stories about what

17 that means, and imagining appropriate responses to it—and then marshaling the forces, attracting the funding, and organizing the people necessary to make that future happen.

Steve Jobs did that incredibly well, as do good designers everywhere when they create things no one knew they needed or had ever imagined. What set Jobs apart, though, was not just his design and organizational skill but also the future that he envisioned and the products that he thought we needed in order to get there. The iPod, iPhone, and iPad are not just high-tech devices that enable us to do things better or more efficiently; those products almost compel us to own them because of what they embody—advanced technology that connects us to some of the most ancient and fundamental human activities.

In that sense, Apple's recent devices counter the sometimes-perverse aspects of modern technology. While most such technology allows us do things more quickly, safely, and efficiently than ever before, it also isolates us from each other and the world around us as never before. Some technologies, like cars, planes, and telephones, have held out the promise of reconnecting us to each other and to nature, but they have largely encouraged us to do just the opposite: to live even further apart and have even fewer face-to-face interactions. The iPod, iPhone, and iPad have reversed that disaggregation. The lightness, simplicity, and intuitiveness of these tools have made them less like other technologies, which tend to come between us, and more like extensions of ourselves, giving us the immediacy of expression, quickness of communication, and information-gathering ability that our human ancestors had when they lived in small tribal communities.

Just look at how we use these devices. The iPod provides us with the music that defines our tribal subcultures, the iPhone gives us close-ups of people as if we are talking with them face-to-face, and the iPad recalls the first slatelike tablets on which ancient people wrote and drew. These products, combined with search engines like Google and social media sites like Facebook, have helped achieve what media guru Marshall McLuhan called "the global village," unobtrusively shrinking our world in ways that more intrusive modern technologies have not.[3]

The passing of Steve Jobs serves as a kind of passing of the torch to the rest of us to continue working toward the future he saw, in which technology becomes so minimal, so energy efficient and resourceful, and so much an extension and support of ourselves that it almost disappears. And therein lies the perfect paradox of what Jobs accomplished. He showed us how the most sophisticated technology should not look like technology and that the use of media need not feel mediated at all. It isn't the loss of Steve Jobs, the person, that so many people mourn; after all, most of us never knew him. I think the grief surrounding his death shows, instead, how profoundly his vision of a reintegrated world affected us and how much work we still have to do to achieve that world.

Such digital tools not only result from design thinking, but they also facilitate it. While design thinking still utilizes some very old media—pen and paper, cardboard and glue, tape and sticky paper—it has benefited greatly from the integrative power of digital media. Through the use of these media, we can see relationships never before seen and locate problems in ways never before possible. Thus "big data," so much a part of our digital future, may lead to "big design" as we recognize and reimagine the reality that the data reveal.

This will become especially important as we seek creative solutions to the many wicked problems we face. While design thinking began in the private sector among companies under incredible pressure to innovate ever faster, it has begun to pervade the public and nonprofit sectors, equally challenged to work in new ways. In all sectors, such thinking has demonstrated that the best ideas often emerge in participatory processes that utilize all of the data available and engage a diversity of points of view.

The application of design thinking in areas far beyond the traditional realm of design also suggests a new role for the designer. Unlike the old and decidedly out-of-date image of the designer as some impractical aesthete, the real role of the designer in the age of reaggregation is to facilitate the creativity of the people most affected by a situation and help guide them toward solutions that they have the capacity to implement. The design community does not have all the answers, but it does have skill and experience with a process that can generate answers to some of our most pressing problems, and more and more businesses and organizations have begun to recognize the value of that contribution. Design should no longer be seen as an add-on; it is fundamental. And the reaggregation of the world should no longer be an option; it is essential.

19

Portions of this chapter were previously published in *Architecture Minnesota* (July/August 2014); "Citizen Designers," *Minnesota Journal* 29, no. 2 (March/April 2012); and "The Real Innovation of Steve Jobs," *Huffington Post* (October 11, 2011), http://www.huffingtonpost.com/thomas-fisher/steve-jobs-design_b_1004196.html.

[1] For more, see my book *Designing to Avoid Disaster*.

[2] Horst Rittel and Melvin M. Webber, "Dilemmas in a General Theory of Planning," *Policy Sciences* 4 (1973): 155–69.

[3] Marshall McLuhan, *Understanding Media: The Extensions of Man* (Cambridge: MIT Press, 1994).

3

THE LOGIC
OF CREATIVITY

The design process has not only its own kind of rigor but also its own form of logic, which anyone can learn and apply to almost any human endeavor. We all learn in school about inductive and deductive reasoning, the former deployed in the sciences and social sciences and the latter in mathematics and logic. Both forms of reasoning seek consistent ways of understanding or describing the world, and both have proven very powerful in our efforts to control the world, for better or worse. But design follows a third form of reasoning, abductive reasoning, that forms the very core of design thinking and making. This third type of logic emphasizes creativity more than consistency and consequential results more than control.

The nineteenth-century philosopher Charles Sanders Peirce gave us some of the best analyses of abductive thinking.[1] He saw the traditional division of reasoning, since Aristotle, into deductive and inductive modes as inadequate for describing how humans actually think.[2] Instead, Peirce saw abductive reasoning as the way we come up with new ideas that help us explain or deal with new facts and unexpected situations. "Deduction proves that something must be," he wrote. "Induction shows that something actually is operative; Abduction . . . suggests that something may be."[3]

At times, Peirce sounded condescending in his description of abductive thinking: "Abduction is no more nor less than guessing."[4] At other times, though, we can see the centrality of this mode of reasoning in Peirce's mind: "Abduction consists in studying facts and devising a theory to explain them. Its only justification is that if we are ever to understand things at all, it must be in that way."[5] "Abduction is Originary in respect to being the only kind of argument which starts a new idea."[6]

While Peirce believed that all inquiry regarding a new idea or new discovery involves abduction, he also knew what he was up against in challenging the prevailing view that thinking proceeds through either deduction (the drawing of conclusions from an agreed-upon premise) or induction (the proof of something based on experimentation or extensive observation). Peirce defined abduction as a mode of reasoning that "consists in examining a mass of facts and in allowing these facts to suggest a theory. In this way we gain new ideas; but there is no force in the reasoning"— no way, on other words, to falsify the claim, as Karl Popper would say.[7] While designers use inductive reasoning, for example, in the evaluation and selection of products and deductive reasoning in the application of proportioning systems, among other instances, the real value of design thinking lies in the use of abductive reasoning to generate new ideas and to suggest possibilities that the other two forms of reasoning often miss.

Abduction has received quite a lot of attention in areas such as logic, linguistics, and computer and cognitive science. But the design community, which uses abduction possibly even more than these other fields, has paid relatively little attention to Peirce's idea of it. Indeed, in his writings about abduction, he sounds like a designer when describing the way in which we arrive at new ideas.[8]

Consider these two descriptions by Peirce. First: "The abductive suggestion comes to us like a flash. It is an act of insight, although of extremely fallible insight. . . . It is the idea of putting together what we had never before dreamed of putting together which flashes the new suggestion before our contemplation."[9] Second:

> A mass of facts is before us. We go through them. We examine them. We find them a confused snarl, an impenetrable jungle. We are unable to hold them in our minds. We endeavor to set them down upon paper; but they seem so multiplex intricate that we can neither satisfy ourselves that what we have set down represents the facts, nor can we get any clear idea of what it is that we have set down. But suddenly, while we are poring over our digest of the facts and are endeavoring to set them into order, it occurs to us that if we were to assume something to be true that we do not know to be true, these facts would arrange themselves luminously. That is *abduction*.[10]

We don't spend much time, as designers, thinking about our thinking, but Peirce's writing comes as close as that of any philosopher to putting into words what designers frequently do intuitively. When confronted with the mass of facts in a project brief, for instance, we make certain assumptions or embrace certain organizing principles that help things "arrange themselves luminously" before our eyes. We see connections, make analogies, and invent paradigms about both the social and the material worlds, about how people might live and what they might live in.

Peirce also offered insight into what we do when he said that "abduction rests upon diagrammatic reasoning" and that it "furnishes all our ideas concerning real things."[11] Abduction, in other words, has a strong visualization component—it is a way of thinking diagrammatically, as designers so often do. It also has a strong focus on facts, on the "real things" that designers must constantly deal with.[12]

Likewise, the criteria for judging the merit of an idea arrived at abductively are the same as those we often use in judging a design idea. Peirce observed: "In all cases the leading consideration in Abduction . . . is the question of Economy—Economy of money, time, thought, and energy."[13] "The better abduction is the one which is likely to lead to the truth with the lesser expenditure of time, vitality, etc."[14] As in design, so in abduction an economy of means often leads to the most effective and elegant end result.

The challenge Peirce faced in getting others to value his ideas about abduction parallels the challenge designers face in getting others to value what we do. Modern thought arose with Descartes's emphasis on certainty and the elimination of all doubt, which induction and deduction can satisfy in ways that abduction cannot, through experimentation or definition. Abduction's "chief elements are its groundlessness, its ubiquity, and its trustworthiness," said Peirce.[15] The value of ideas reached abductively is not that they are certain but that they have useful or desirable consequences, as Peirce, the philosophical pragmatist, would say.

We might say the same about design ideas. We can never be absolutely certain about them, but their proof comes in accordance with how well they address the problem at hand, the needs of a particular type of client or community, program or site, fabrication material, or delivery method. For those who demand certainty, who insist that we know the full consequences of our work or that we can prove the rightness of our design solutions, the abductive quality of design thinking may seem doubtful or unreliable. What such people don't understand, and what we need to do a better job of explaining, is that, as Peirce said, "not the smallest advance can be made in knowledge beyond the stage of vacant staring, without making an abduction at every step."[16]

The Cartesian quest for certainty has not only privileged inductive and deductive logic over their more creative sibling, abduction, but it has also obscured the potential of a whole new area of design inquiry—research into abductive thinking itself—that has lain largely unexamined and yet has great potential for helping us understand the nature and value of what we do. The relative lack of attention to abduction on the part of designers may stem from the long-held prejudice in the larger culture and even within our own ranks that our creative leaps remain intuitive and inexplicable, even though the most cursory investigation of abduction shows that this is not the case. Abduction involves a highly disciplined way of discovering new knowledge and developing new ideas.

An example of that arises in an insightful paper written by educational psychologists Gary Shank and Donald J. Cunningham in the mid-1990s.[17] Shank and Cunningham draw from Peirce's theory of signs—the icons, forms, and symbols that populate the physical environment around us—to develop a more nuanced way of thinking about abduction, showing how abductive thinking proceeds in an orderly and methodical way toward the development of useful inferences.

The six modes of inference that Shank and Cunningham identify will sound familiar to designers, for they describe, in different words, the design process as we have come to practice it. But these authors' analysis of abduction also shows how the design process constitutes a type of discovery that can produce results as valuable as anything coming from a scientific lab or a mathematician's blackboard.

The value of Shank and Cunningham's work lies in its taking fairly abstract ideas and making them accessible and useful to our everyday lives, much as designers apply highly abstract concepts and theories to the solution of problems related to human activity. While we cannot know what Peirce, who died in 1914, would have thought about this, it does seem very much in line with his pragmatic temper, which embraced all thinking that helps us solve problems and get on with life. Indeed, Shank and Cunningham's work is, itself, abductive—it takes a creative leap to connect seemingly unrelated ideas to produce something new and useful.

The six classes of inferences—the six steps with which we develop new ideas—that Shank and Cunningham describe are as follows:

1. *Omen or hunch,* when we have an intuition about some possibility
2. *Symptom,* when we find in that intuition a resemblance to other things
3. *Metaphor or analogy,* when we see clear parallels to things we already know
4. *Clue,* when we relate the specifics of the particular case to more general solutions

5. *Diagnosis or scenario,* when we apply a prototype to more than the particular case

6. *Explanation,* when we evolve a theory from the particular case that can apply to all cases

For designers, the relationship of this list to what we do seems fairly obvious. When working on a project or problem, an experienced designer will often have a hunch that an idea will work to organize and make sense of the diversity of requirements. That hunch usually arises out of aspects of the problem that are symptomatic of other, similar problems the designer has faced, from which parallels are drawn. The design then typically evolves in an analogous or metaphorical way, in which ideas about what the designer already knows or has already solved are applied to the new situation, changing in the process. As the design proceeds, other clues emerge that suggest new applications of the ideas, beyond what has happened before, which eventually leads to more general scenarios and possibly to a broader theory that can be of use to others when they confront the same sort of problem.

Shank and Cunningham do more here than simply put into new words what designers already intuitively do. They help us see that the generation of creative ideas involves an abductive process. The design disciplines have long been accustomed to judging the value of what we do in terms of its consequences: Does a building or object function well, have strength and durability, and appeal to us aesthetically and intellectually? But rarely do we look at the consequences of what we do in terms of the inferences we make and the process we conduct.

What difference does it make, in others words, to work from a hunch, seek out an omen, look for a symptom, apply a metaphor, draw an analogy, respond to a clue, make a diagnosis, envision a scenario, or offer an explanation? Do certain starting points lend themselves better to some situations than to others? Do some of these steps produce better results than others? Are they all equally valid, with selection among them simply a matter of personal preference, or does each mode of inference have its own strengths and weaknesses?

Seeking answers to such questions remains a largely unexplored area of design. While some scholars have focused on the initial, sketch phase of the design process, and many have examined the origins of design ideas and their influences on particular designers, we have done very little to draw more general conclusions about the relations of particular types of inferences to specific kinds of results. Is the designer who seeks an omen of something never imagined before more or less likely to produce a desirable consequence than the one who methodically analyzes a situation looking for the symptoms of the underlying problem or the one who listens carefully for clues in what a client or users say that might uncover the most compelling solution? Does the designer who starts from a metaphor have a better result than one who sees a situation in terms of existing prototypes or as an opportunity to apply an existing theory? And are there certain clients, contexts, communities, or conditions that lend themselves to one mode of inference more than another? If so, how and why?

Such questions are not simply of academic interest. Research into the nature of designers' abductive forms of thinking can go a long way toward helping others understand the value of design and appreciate the importance of different approaches to design thinking. Abduction, as Peirce observed, serves as the prelude to all other research; without it, induction and deduction would not occur, for the latter would not have a reason to proceed. As Peirce put it: "Abduction [is] the inference which starts a scientific hypothesis."[18]

This, in turn, suggests that the design community has too narrowly defined what we do in terms of the products of our actions. We have legally determined that only people licensed to design buildings can call themselves architects, for example. But were we to understand the nature of the inferences we make as designers, we would see that our mode of thinking has applications far beyond the products and environments that we have associated with it for so long.

Our abductive reasoning gives us the capacity not only to solve problems in the physical world related to people's materials needs but also to see what Peirce called "firstness": the potentiality of things.[19] Every new design creates something that did not exist before and juxtaposes entities never before brought together in the same space and time. As such, it creates potential opportunities for us to be ourselves and to relate to others in new ways. It also generates the potential for research, the context within which we strive to understand the world or to answer questions that occur to us as we go about our lives, engage with the world, and pursue our disciplines.

But how might the design community expand its role in this way when others don't see the value of our abductive ways of thinking? Even if we can begin to connect the generation of ideas to particular consequences, can we ever prove for certain and beyond a doubt the merit of what we do? One answer entails not trying to justify abduction at all, and simply letting the results of the work speak for itself. As Peirce argued: "Abduction's . . . only justification is that from its suggestion deduction can draw a prediction which can be tested by induction, and that, if we are ever to learn anything or to understand phenomena at all, it must be by abduction that this is to be brought about. No reason whatsoever can be given for it . . . and it needs no reason, since it merely offers suggestions."[20]

Here, Peirce's pragmatism comes out. Unlike inductive or deductive reasoning, whose claims we can determine to be true or false, right or wrong, the value of abduction lies in the usefulness—or not—of the ideas it produces. We can teach abductive skills in order to improve students' ability to generate creative ideas, but we need to do so in a much more explicit way than we often do now, expecting students to learn creativity by reading about creative people. Abduction, like induction and deduction, requires practice for skillful use.

Another answer to those who might question the value of design and its creative idea generation lies in rethinking what we mean by the word research. Beyond its conventional meanings of investigation, exploration, and examination lies its literal meaning: to search again, to re-search.[21] We too rarely think of research in this way, and yet its literal meaning says a lot about what actually happens and how strongly it relates to what designers do.

Re-search involves an iterative process: testing and retesting results, explaining what happened and then challenging the explanation, proving something and then attempting to disprove it. Design is equally iterative. It, too, involves testing and then retesting ideas, explaining and then challenging a solution, proving and then critiquing the final product. If there is a weakness in Peirce's argument for abduction, it lies in the way that he presented it almost as if it always involves an epiphany, focusing on the creative moment and eliding the hard, iterative work that goes on both before and after. Peirce offered abduction as a kind of suggestion, something meant to inspire further investigation, but he left it to us to develop the means and methods of abductive research, to evolve processes as clear and compelling to others as those the sciences and mathematics have developed in relation to induction and deduction.

This is where abduction has great potential as a way of thinking about design and its responsibilities and consequences. Few areas of human activity have impacts as immediate and pervasive as design, which largely determines what we use and how we live our lives. As such, design offers one of the most fertile grounds on which to draw connections between the ways in which we develop creative ideas and the effects that they have on other people, other species, future generations, and the planet as a whole. It is one thing for people to say that they always operate according to their hunches; it is quite another when designers work that way and their hunches prove detrimental to those who must spend large amounts of time and money living with the results.

The link between designers' inferences and their consequences is never absolute or certain. As Peirce said: "An Abduction is a method of forming a general prediction without any positive assurance that it will succeed either in the special case or usually, its justification being that it is the only possible hope of regulating our future conduct rationally, and that induction from past experience gives us strong encouragement to hope that it will be successful in the future."[22] But through repeated experience, such as that gained through professional practice, we can begin to see which modes of inference have which consequences under which conditions. This suggests that, contrary to the notion that designers don't do much research, we engage in a kind of abductive research all the time, even if we don't think of our practice as such. Every time a designer has a creative insight or makes lateral connections among seemingly unrelated things, an abduction occurs that will have material results later in the process. What often does not occur is an analysis of different types of inferences and what effects they had on the outcome.

In part, this is because most of us never learned to think of our work in that way. Design education still remains largely focused on the end results of what we do—on the commodity, firmness, and delight of our designs— with very little time or attention given to the nature of design thinking and the consequences that different modes of reasoning actually have. Most designers are also not taught to think of research other than in its inductive and deductive forms—what occurs in labs and libraries and requires large amounts of money and equipment.

In that lies an irony in Peirce's use of the word *abduction*. The very idea of research has been abducted—whisked away—by those who have, for so long, equated it with the conducting of experiments and the drawing of conclusions from agreed-upon premises. Rather than seeing creative leaps of imagination as the subject of and basis for systematic inquiry, we have remained the intellectual captives of our abductors, accepting their view of what qualifies as research. This is not to diminish the importance of the sciences and social sciences, or to undermine the value of mathematics and computational work; the research that occurs in those areas is necessary, but it is simply not sufficient to encompass all of the ways in which we reason or know.

In our abducted state, we may find the idea of establishing a culture of design research like that of the sciences or engineering absolutely overwhelming. How could we ever make a case for design that would attract even close to the same kind of resources that our research colleagues in other disciplines have garnered? But given Peirce's idea of abduction, we don't have to; indeed, doing so would only show that we don't understand the nature of the research that is ours to do. Abductive research—research into the inferences we make and the consequences of our making them—does not demand a lot of money, or even a great deal of time; it mainly requires a change in perception about ourselves and the work that we do.

Rather than seeing our creative leaps as intuitive and unfathomable, we need to begin to systematically reflect upon them, the nature of the inferences we make, and the contexts within which we make them. To this end, the six modes of inference that Shank and Cunningham developed from Peirce's work offer one place to start. Rather than seeing our responsibility as ending with the delivery of a completed building or product, we need to evaluate the consequences of our ideas and decisions methodically over time: Where did our inferences lead, and what effects did they have, both positive and negative? And finally, rather than seeing ourselves as competing with each other and thus unwilling to share our discoveries in this process, we need to generalize from our inferences and their consequences and share that knowledge so that others can use and benefit from it.

Peirce once said that in "the study of Abduction . . . I was an explorer upon untrodden ground."[23] The same untrodden ground lies in front of every designer, and nothing is stopping us from exploring it other than our own self-imposed captivity in the halls of our abductors, those who have been so imbued with the logic of induction and deduction that they may be, ironically, less capable of abduction than we are. To begin the task before us, we have only to free ourselves intellectually from what we thought research was and start the search again for it in our own, abductive way.

This chapter first appeared as "The Abduction of Architecture" in the journal *Batture* (2008), published by Louisiana State University's School of Architecture.

[1] Charles Sanders Peirce also originated pragmatism as a philosophy and as a theory of meaning, arguing that the meaning of an action comprises all of the possible consequences of it. The significance of that for architecture is that, of all the arts, architecture is the most pragmatic, in the sense of having real consequences in our daily lives. Abduction is highly pragmatic in that we cannot claim an idea arrived at in this way to be "true"; rather, the consequence of our embracing the idea is that it works best in explaining the facts before us.

[2] Peirce claimed that Aristotle meant to include abduction as a third form of reasoning, along with deduction and induction: "Abduction [is] . . . what Aristotle's twenty-fifth chapter of the second Prior Analytics imperfectly described under the name of {apagögé}, until Apellicon substituted a single wrong word and thus disturbed the sense of the whole." Charles Sanders Peirce, "Reasoning" (1902; from Baldwin's *Dictionary of Philosophy and Psychology,* vol. 2), in *Collected Papers of Charles Sanders Peirce,* 8 vols. (Cambridge, Mass.: Harvard University Press, 1931–58) (hereafter CP), 2.776.

[3] Charles Sanders Peirce, Harvard Lectures on Pragmatism (1903), CP 5.171–72.

[4] Charles Sanders Peirce, "PAP (Prolegomena for an Apology to Pragmatism)" (MS 293; circa 1906), in *The New Elements of Mathematics by Charles S. Peirce,* ed. Carolyn Eisele (The Hague: Mouton, 1976) (hereafter NEM) 4:319–320.

[5] Peirce, Harvard Lectures on Pragmatism, CP 5.144–45.

[6] Charles Sanders Peirce, "Minute Logic" (circa 1902), CP 2.96.

[7] Charles Sanders Peirce, letter to Calderoni (circa 1905), CP 8.209.

[8] Peirce has received rather more attention from designers over the past few decades for his work in semiotics, where he developed one of the first theories of signs that played an influential part in postmodern architectural theory. There

has also been some work on the relation of his theory of logic to design. See Mike Linzey, "On the Secondness of Architectural Intuition," *Journal of Architectural Education* 55, no. 1 (September 2001): 43–50.

9 Peirce, Harvard Lectures on Pragmatism, CP 5.181.

10 Charles Sanders Peirce, Harvard Lectures on Pragmatism, deleted passage (1903), *in Pragmatism as a Principle and Method of Right Thinking: The 1903 Harvard "Lectures on Pragmatism,"* ed. Patricia Ann Turrisi (Albany: State University of New York Press, 1997) (hereafter PPM), 282.

11 Peirce, "PAP (Prolegomena for an Apology to Pragmatism)," NEM 4:319–20; Peirce, letter to Calderoni, CP 8.209.

12 "Abduction makes its start from the facts, without, at the outset, having any particular theory in view, though it is motivated by the feeling that a theory is needed to explain the surprising facts." Charles Sanders Peirce, "On the Logic of Drawing History from Ancient Documents Especially from Testimonies" (1901), CP 7.218.

13 Charles Sanders Peirce, Lowell Lectures (1903), CP 5.600.

14 Charles Sanders Peirce, Carnegie Application (L75; 1902), NEM 4:37–38.

15 Charles Sanders Peirce, "The Proper Treatment of Hypotheses: A Preliminary Chapter, toward an Examination of Hume's Argument against Miracles, in Its Logic and in Its History" (MS 692; 1901), in *Historical Perspectives on Peirce's Logic of Science: A History of Science,* 2 vols., ed. Carolyn Eisele (Berlin: Mouton, 1985), 2:898–99.

16 Ibid., 2:899–900.

17 Gary Shank and Donald J. Cunningham, "Modeling the Six Modes of Peircean Abduction for Educational Purposes" (paper presented at the Midwest AI and Cognitive Science conference, Bloomington, Ind., April 1996).

18 Peirce, Carnegie Application, NEM 4:62.

19 "Abduction, or the suggestion of an explanatory theory, is . . . thus connected with Firstness." Peirce, Harvard Lectures on Pragmatism, deleted passage, PPM 276–77.

20 Peirce, Harvard Lectures on Pragmatism, CP 5.171–72.

21 *Research* comprises a compound of the Latin prefix re-, meaning "again," and the Latin root word circare, meaning "to go around." *Concise Etymological Dictionary of the English Language* (Oxford, 1901).

22 Charles Sanders Peirce, "A Syllabus of Certain Topics of Logic" (1903), in *The Essential Peirce: Selected Philosophical Writings,* vol. 2, ed. Peirce Edition Project (Bloomington: Indiana University Press, 1998), 299.

23 Peirce, "Minute Logic," CP 2.102.

PART II

EDUCATION

Much of the designed world remains invisible to us not just perceptually but also conceptually, because very few educated people have had any instruction in the abductive logic of design thinking and creative problem solving, even though those skills remain key to success in a knowledge economy dependent on innovation. Indeed, we have designed an educational system so focused on our correctly identifying what is that we have neglected the equally important task of creatively imagining what could be. The following three chapters look at some of the wicked problems of modern education from this point of view.

Chapter 4 addresses the near absence of design education in K–12 schools and how this often reflects the myth of the creative genius in modern society. Looking at the work of a number of creative people and how they cultivated that creativity and the courage to deploy it, the chapter ends by sketching out what a redesigned K–12 education might look like, teaching to students' diverse intelligences and offering a more creative approach to the STEM fields (science, technology, engineering, and math).

Chapter 5 argues that one way to instill creative courage in students is by increasing their engagement in their own communities. This chapter looks at the role that schools can play in communities and how communities—especially those where poverty is entrenched—might demand different kinds of schools. Just as we have home schooling, we need to acknowledge the need for its opposite: school as a home for those who have none or whose homes interfere with their education.

The final chapter of this part extends the education and community argument from K–12 to higher education. At a time when colleges and universities face an unsustainable financial situation (falling support along with rising tuition and student debt) and disruption from the digital revolution, they need redesigning. This chapter looks at what that might mean, encouraging faculty to engage in this effort and to include in the process the real stakeholders of higher education: students.

4

CREATIVE
EDUCATION

Although creativity has become increasingly valued in the business world, creative problem solving rarely gets taught explicitly in our schools.[1] Too often education has contented itself with helping students understand the problems we face in ever-greater detail and with increasing precision. While we need that understanding in order to know how to deal with our wicked problems, we also need our schools to pay far more attention to teaching students how to address, more creatively, the grand challenges that confront us and how to imagine better, more sustainable, and more life-affirming ways of living on this planet. We need, in other words, education that addresses not only what was (as the humanities do) and what is (as the sciences and social sciences do) but also what could be (as design does).

With the focus in modern education on discovering and conveying knowledge about the world as it was and as it is, at least two things get lost. First, we too often lose sight of something that educators seem almost embarrassed to talk about: wisdom. It doesn't matter how much we know if we don't know what to do—and, more important, what not to do—with that knowledge. The wisdom that comes from understanding the limits of what we know and what we can and should do has become one of the missing pieces of education that we desperately need to rediscover.

Second, we too often forget that education should also involve imagining the world that we want and that we hope to achieve. Because we cannot know the future in the same way that we know the present and the past, and because empirical data and verifiable or falsifiable claims about the world have become the primary means through which we judge the truth of things, we largely neglect talking about the future. We relegate such thinking to science fiction or dismiss it as dystopian, and as a result, we have a hard time envisioning living in a world much different from the one we now occupy, at our loss.

With this impoverishment of the human imagination has come the belief that most of us lack the creativity needed to envisage better ways of doing things. That belief has, in turn, infected public education in many parts of the world, leading to a de-emphasis on creativity and a focus, instead, on competence and correctness. That may have served industrial capitalism well in the nineteenth and twentieth centuries, when companies needed a large workforce able to follow directions and willing to do repetitive tasks without complaint, but in the twenty-first century, dealing with the global economy and the grand challenges we face requires as much creativity and innovation as we can muster, as fast as we can. Our educational system, which has continued the old industrial model of competence building and repetitive exercises, has to change. And that will require a reappraisal of what creativity entails and how we teach it.

To conduct this reappraisal, we need to demystify creativity and reject the mistaken belief that it remains primarily the purview of artists or "geniuses." As a result of that genius myth, far too many people believe that they are not creative when in fact they have simply not been allowed, or allowed themselves, to use the creativity that they were born with. All human beings have a capacity for creativity because of how our brains work.

When we learn about an object, for instance, we store that knowledge in different parts of our brain. The object's name goes in one place, its shape and color in another, its weight and feel in yet another, and so on. When we next encounter that object, our brain almost instantaneously recombines the information, enabling us to identify, use, and think and talk about the object. Our educational system largely tests this recombinant ability. Pupils are graded on how well they retrieve the information they have learned, and they get marked down if they get some aspect of it wrong: misidentifying or misunderstanding something, or misspelling its name. Indeed, education has focused so closely on the correctness of our knowledge and the accuracy of our memory that it has almost completely repressed the complementary skill of creativity.

Creativity involves the intentional, systematic, and rigorous "miscom-bination" of what we know in order to generate something new. Because having too many variables makes the process hard to control, creative people frequently change just one or two aspects of something: shifting its size or scale, changing its function or context, altering its shape or color, and so on. Drawing an analogy or making a metaphor often helps move this process along.

To see how this creative process works, consider the work of the sculptor Janet Echelman, who creates site-specific art. Echelman began her series of netlike sculptures by suspending her own "correct" understanding of fishnets and changing her perception of them in a systematic way. She repurposed the fishnet as an artistic material rather than just a utilitarian one, recognized that nets form volumes when unfurled in water, and then reimagined nets floating and undulating in the air above us rather than in the ocean below.

Echelman held most of the other qualities of fishnets—their material, color, and fabrication method—constant and then began the hard work and constant practice that constitutes much of the creative process. She learned how to hand-tie fishnets, for example, and how to adapt industrial production methods to her work while collaborating with everyone from architects and structural and aeronautical engineers to fishermen and fishnet fabricators.

Her description of what she does debunks many of the myths about creativity: that a person has to be a loner or a genius to be creative, that creativity can't be taught and that only a few people can learn it, and that it demands artistic talent and the ability to draw. Echelman shows that what it really takes to be creative is the ability to remember what it feels like to be a youth: open to the world, full of play, and unafraid of where imagination might lead.

Her work also demonstrates why we need less correctness and more creativity in our education. By taking fishnets out of their context, Echelman causes us to see ourselves in new ways and to ask questions that lead to other ideas. What happens when we, the predators, see such nets from the point of view of our prey? How much does the beauty of traps contribute to their effectiveness? What other traps—seen or unseen—lie in wait for us? And how much do nets serve as a metaphor for life itself—its tangibility and ephemerality, its fixity and fluidity, its permeability and impermeability?

Echelman conveys such thoughts with a light touch and a sense of humor, as when she named her first piece, with its voluptuous form, *Wide Hips*. Creativity, like comedy, relies on such unexpected connections, and we laugh, in part, because of what they reveal about us. And that may be the funniest thing of all about creativity. It can begin anytime and happen anywhere, with anything, as soon as we start, as Echelman says, "taking imagination seriously."[2]

Echelman's work also captures another aspect of creativity: a willingness to be what Malcolm Gladwell has called an "outlier." In his book by that name, Gladwell argues that accomplished people have not only innate talent but also the capacity to work hard—to put in the ten thousand hours he sees as required to achieve proficiency—and supportive familial or social settings.[3] I would add one more characteristic: courage. It takes courage to envision something that has not existed before and to act on a creative insight and bring it to fruition despite the doubts of skeptics or the dismissals of competitors. Just as we need to integrate creativity in every aspect of education and stop suppressing the playfulness and imagination that come naturally to most people, so too do we need to teach courage, to help students believe in their imaginations and encourage them to pursue their passions regardless of what others say.

I saw that mix of creativity and courage at a conference that the founder of the TED conferences, Richard Saul Wurman, brought together on the campus of the software company ESRI in Redlands, California. He called it the "WWW conference," and while it did not have creative courage as its avowed theme, the event showed that creative people—from musicians (Yo-Yo Ma, Herbie Hancock, will.i.am) to scientists (E. O. Wilson, Craig Venter, Geoffrey West, Steven Pinker) to software developers (Jack Dangermond, Danny Hillis, Stephen Wolfram) to designers (Frank Gehry, Moshe Safdie, John Maeda, Todd Oldham) to members of the news and entertainment media (David Brooks, Jeffrey Brooks, Jeffrey Katzenberg, and Norman Lear)—all share one trait: relentlessness in the pursuit of a big idea or passion, regardless of what colleagues or critics think.

Cellist Ma engaged in a spontaneous performance with hip-hop artist will.i.am that combined classical music with rap, illustrating how creativity can come from the courage to mix things long thought of as separate. And architects Gehry and Safdie reflected on the ineffable aspects of buildings, on making stable structures look windblown (in Gehry's case) or solid structures look carved away by unseen forces (in Safdie's case), showing how creative people often act as if the impossible or the improbable were true.

Nor does creativity remain the purview only of artists and architects. Several of the scientists at the conference ventured far from conventional thought by combining seemingly unrelated fields in their work. Intersecting physics and biology, West talked about the constant relationship between the mass and the metabolism of all living things; mixing cognitive science and evolutionary psychology, Pinker argued that human violence has decreased in recent centuries despite the very different picture we get from the media; and overlaying computer science with landscape architecture,

39 Dangermond showed how mapping data reveals patterns and relationships that have long remained hidden.

The courage of creative people becomes most apparent when the combination of apparently divergent ideas or fields arrives at something that makes us uncomfortable. Wolfram's connection of biology and computer science has led him to ask, "Is the whole universe reducible to a few lines of [computer] code?" This question overthrows our long-held view of the universe as infinite and unimaginable. Likewise, Venter's discussion of how we can now computationally design new organisms by modifying their genetic information seems frightening at first, but, like so much science fiction, such insights have a history of coming true.

Another aspect of the genius myth has to do with our assumption that truly creative ideas lie beyond the comprehension of most people. The extraordinary outliers at the WWW conference came across as highly accessible, able to describe their ideas and work in simple and straight-forward ways. Which brings us back to Gladwell. While he rightly debunks the popular myth that only a few, innately talented people can ever achieve greatness, his emphasis on the need for supportive social settings makes it seem as if real accomplishment lies beyond an individual's control. At the same time, Gladwell's ten thousand–hour rule tends to conflate hard work with brilliance and proficiency in a field with its transformation.

As the WWW conference amply demonstrated, outliers do need talent, the willingness to work hard, and at least one supportive person in their lives. But without the creative urge to imagine something new and the courage to pursue that against all odds, we would have a world of very proficient people, all good at doing what we already know how to do. Unlike innate talent or supportive family, however, creativity and courage can be taught. We can instill in students these character traits that can increase their chances of great accomplishment. Not that our educational system recognizes this—we have become so focused on leaving no child behind and so wary of talking about character, lest it sound prejudicial, that the very traits we will need to thrive in the future, to transform our lives for the better, are hardly ever mentioned, let alone taught, in our schools.

This suggests that schools should equip students not only with the skills but also with the self-confidence to pursue their passions, regardless of what others may think. And educators should teach students not just what we already know about the world but also how to envision what we haven't yet imagined possible. We need to create many more outliers, many more visionary innovators, given the world's dire need of better ideas and more sustainable technologies. And we might start by thinking about education more as Wurman does, as what he calls "intellectual jazz."

We need to start promoting such intellectual jazz in primary and secondary schools, which, at least in the United States, seem outright hostile to the improvisation and invention embodied in jazz as a form of music. Modern education has a tremendous bias toward a couple of nonmusical forms of intelligence, linguistic and mathematical/logical intelligence, often to the exclusion of the other ways of knowing that educational psychologist Howard Gardner has identified in his theory of multiple intelligences.[4] Primary and secondary schools tend to view those other intelligences—musical, natural, kinesthetic, visual/spatial, interpersonal, intrapersonal—either as talents that only a few students have or as inborn traits that no amount of teaching can instill. The privileging of a few intelligences and the relative neglect of others leaves too many students behind and hampers our ability to foster the creativity that the world needs.

Colleges and universities know how to teach to multiple intelligences. Students who have musical intelligence gravitate to music schools, those with bodily-kinesthetic intelligence to dance departments or intercollegiate sports, those with spatial intelligence to art schools or design colleges, and so on. While these diverse departments in universities convey a lot of specialized knowledge and technical skill, they also do something equally profound: they recognize that people have *varied intelligences* and that people often learn best when content is conveyed in ways that match their intellectual strengths.

To understand the difference this makes, talk to almost any college student. Most will tell you how dreary much of their primary and secondary school education felt to them, with too much rote learning and too few opportunities for creativity, too many academic exercises with too little relevance to the world around them. Higher education has some of the same problems, especially in large lecture classes taken by nonmajors to fulfill graduation requirements. But once most college students find the majors that suit them, you can see in their faces and hear in their voices the excitement that comes from learning things that interest them and that play to their strengths.

41   Why do we make so many students wait until the last couple of years of college to finally find pleasure in learning? Why can't primary and secondary schools follow the model of colleges and teach to the intelligences of their students? Charter schools have tried to do this, with curricula that appeal to specific intelligences among the eight that Gardner has identified—language immersion schools for linguistically intelligent students, for example, and outdoor-oriented pedagogies for students with a nature intelligence. Still, these schools remain few in number and reach relatively few students.

Most public and private schools still march students through a standard curriculum, sorted by age groups rather than by intelligences. While such standardization may make it easier to test students to measure achievement, it comes at too high a price, making too many bright kids feel stupid in the process. As I hear from the talented students in my college, their visual and spatial intelligence and their natural creativity often went unappreciated and was sometimes completely stifled in grade school and high school. And they will tell you how hard it was for them to watch those students with abilities in language and math—the two forms of intelligence most valued in schools—being honored as the "smart" ones.

Critics of the theory of multiple intelligences have objected to its apparent lack of objective criteria, empirical evidence, and measurability, but if the theory has no merit, why do we sort students according to their intelligences in college? At the same time, some supporters of Gardner's ideas want every school to address all eight intelligences. While that may seem like an admirable goal, attempting to reach it would almost guarantee that every student feels equally frustrated, since very few are equally intelligent in every way.

Instead, we should consider expanding what works so well in higher education to primary and secondary schools. In my design college, for example, students learn a wide range of subject matter—science and social science, art and philosophy, math and technology—predominantly through their visual and spatial intelligence, and they apply that knowledge to projects in a hands-on way, making it immediately useful and relevant. Imagine elementary and secondary schools doing the same, with students grouped not by grade but by intellectual strength learning a diversity of content through linguistic, logical-mathematical, musical, bodily-kinesthetic, spatial, interpersonal, intrapersonal, or natural lens.

This would make K–12 teaching as creative and challenging as college teaching, attracting the best and brightest to education, and it would better prepare students for continuing their education in college. Most important, it would help students see that they are not dumb; rather, they are intelligent in different ways. School need not be such a drag—instead it can be, as college is for most students, a place that makes learning fun. Imagine that!

The need to make education more fun is particularly pertinent to the STEM fields (science, technology, engineering, and math), which rarely seem so. These fields play an important role in the twenty-first-century economy, with its need for rapid innovation. Students understand this as they flock to STEM fields, and so do funding agencies, which have continued to support these fields financially. This has led, however, to declining investment in many non-STEM disciplines, which does everyone a disservice. While we need STEM-educated graduates, we also need creative, well-educated generalists, many of them coming out of the humanities and social sciences, who can help ensure that the STEM fields produce the world we want and deserve rather than perpetuate the not-very-well-designed world that we now have.

This will, in turn, require a new kind of STEM. As Secretary of Education Arne Duncan stated in 2010, "Inspiring all our students to be capable in math and science will help them contribute in an increasingly technology-based economy, and will also help America prepare the next generation of STEM professionals—scientists, engineers, architects and technology professionals—to ensure our competitiveness."[5] The Obama administration followed suit by establishing the 100Kin10 program, intended to train one hundred thousand new STEM educators in ten years (with the goal date of 2021).[6] This came in response to an expected increase in the demand for STEM-related knowledge, "from about 6 million to 9 million jobs over the next decade," according to Anthony Carnevale, director of the Georgetown Center on Education and the Workforce.[7] We need to ask, though, what kind of STEM we want to grow. If we germinate it in the same soil that gave rise to post–World War II American industry, we will simply grow more of what we already cannot sustain.

We do not need more scientists creating more high-fat processed foods or more technologists devising more efficient ways of killing people. Nor do we need more engineers figuring out how to enlarge our already enormous ecological footprint or more mathematicians inventing increasingly eso-teric forms of financial arbitrage. The STEM fields do indeed contribute to our technology-based economy, but whether they do so for good or ill depends on how we grow these new educational shoots and to what end.

As an educator in a design college, I find it encouraging that Secretary Duncan mentioned architects along with scientists, engineers, and tech-nologists in his list of next-generation STEM professionals. This brings to mind the work of my colleague John Maeda, former president of the Rhode Island School of Design, who has led a national effort to turn STEM to STEAM, with the A expressing the need to add art and design to the mix.[8] He and his colleagues make the excellent point that we need more scientific, mathematical, and technological know-how, but we also need more creativity and innovation skills to enable the future workforce to imagine entirely new ways of thinking, seeing, and making, so that we can avoid simply going along our current self-destructive path faster or more efficiently.

The change in abbreviation from STEM to STEAM represents a trou-bling change in metaphor, however. STEM has a biological connotation that suggests growth and evolution, reflecting the ability of these fields to adapt to changing conditions, much as the stem of a plant does in response to external stimuli. STEAM, in contrast, carries a mechanistic connotation, bringing to mind not just the steam engines that helped prompt the nine-teenth-century industrial revolution but also the phase change in heated water, which can either be captured and used as a fuel or evaporate into thin air without much effect.

Such metaphorical differences matter. The arts and design can have the effect of moving the STEM fields in a more sustainable and constructive direction, or they can simply make the increasingly toxic and untenable world we have created for ourselves more attractive and thus more accept-able. STEAM can cloud our vision as much as clarify it, and I worry that simply adding the arts to STEM may not turn this educational initiative in a better direction, however much I applaud the idea behind STEAM.

Instead, let me suggest a metaphor more related to the biological con-notation of STEM and one that I think can help us ensure that the STEM fields take us in a better direction. Every STEM arises from a SEED, an abbreviation for *social, economic,* and *environmental design.*[9] The SEED Network consists of a group of architects and designers who argue that every decision we make in the future needs to contribute to the "triple bottom line," bringing social and environmental benefits as well as economic ones. Had we taken social and environmental impacts into account over the past two hundred years of our industrial development, we would, without question, have created a world more socially just, environmentally friendly, and economically balanced than the one we have now.

So, as we rightly push to increase the number of students in the STEM fields, we need to seed that growth with a set of assumptions different from the ones that have nourished those fields in the past. We should do all we can to encourage students to imagine science that enables us not only to understand nature but also to steward it, to innovate technology that helps us improve the quality of life not only of the wealthy but also of the world's poor, to engage in engineering that allows us to do things not only more efficiently but also in more culturally and climatically appropriate ways, and to devise mathematics that facilitates our ability to work not only smarter but also more sensibly and sustainably.

Some cynics may find these goals entirely too idealistic. But as one who works with the "millennial" generation in the classroom every day, I would argue that germinating STEM from this new SEED is precisely how we will get more students to study science, technology, engineering, and math. The current generation wants to improve the world and not just enrich the fat cats of finance or the captains of industry, and we will attract more students to the STEM disciplines by focusing not just on the lure of jobs but also on the idea that this work can have a meaningful and beneficial impact on their future. Millennials strike me as the most practical generation I have known, and there is nothing more pragmatic—and more pressing—than designing a more socially just, environmentally sustainable, and economically equitable future.

45 Portions of this chapter were previously published in "The Rigor of Creativity," *Huffington Post* (December 14, 2012), http://www.huffingtonpost.com/thomas-fisher/the-rigor-of-creativity_b_2280044.html; "A Conference in Creative Courage," *Huffington Post* (October 2, 2012), http://www.huffingtonpost.com/thomas-fisher/an-education-in-creative-_b_1932517.html; "Teach to Each Child's Intelligence," *Huffington Post* (December 6, 2012), http://www.huffingtonpost.com/thomas-fisher/teach-to-each-childs-inte_b_2251444.html; and "Seeding a New Kind of STEM," *Huffington Post* (May 8, 2012), http://www.huffingtonpost.com/thomas-fisher/seeding-a-new-kind-of-ste_b_1498579.html.

[1] Austin Carr, "The Most Important Leadership Quality for CEOs? Creativity," *Fast Company,* May 18, 2010.

[2] Janet Echelman, "Taking Imagination Seriously," TED Talk, March 2011, https://www.ted.com.

[3] Malcolm Gladwell, *Outliers: The Story of Success* (New York: Little, Brown, 2008).

[4] Howard Gardner, *Frames of Mind: The Theory of Multiple Intelligences* (New York: Basic Books, 1983).

[5] Quoted in "STEM Sparks Interest in Students," OrthoWorx eNewsletter, May 2011, http://orthoworxindiana.com/enewsletter-articles/2011/05/530.

[6] See the program's website at http://www.100kin10.org.

[7] Quoted in James Arkin, "Ed Secretary Arne Duncan Helps Launch Ambitious Teacher Training Plan," Medill on the Hill, February 21, 2012, http://medillonthehill.net.

[8] See Rhode Island School of Design, "About: STEM to STEAM," https://www.risd.edu.

[9] See the SEED Initiative's website at https://www.seed.uno.

5

SCHOOLS AND COMMUNITIES

We can design a better future for ourselves only in concert with the people and communities most affected by it, lest we end up with utopian—or, more often, dystopian—visions that end up never happening or doing more damage than what they set out to solve. To avoid the mistakes of the past, we need to stop thinking of education as something that happens mainly in schools, spatially separated from the communities in which they stand, and to stop partitioning off education in time, as something that happens mainly during our youth and early adulthood. This segregation of schooling from its context does have a dystopian aspect. I can remember from my last day of high school the number of my fellow students who seemed relieved that they were done with their education. One student announced triumphantly, "I will never have to read a book again," as he tore up the volume in his hands. I can't think of a more damning criticism of our educational system than that.

We need a system that not only teaches to the diverse intelligences of different students—as argued in chapter 4—but also makes education something that happens over our entire lives and is inseparable from the communities in which we live and work. While this approach recognizes the necessity of continually learning new skills as the economy changes with ever-greater frequency, it also acknowledges that communities need to reimagine themselves in creative new ways in an era of global competition for talent.

Establishing such a system will require an investment in our schools that is different from that of the past, one in which we calculate the costs and benefits in ways not always considered before. As part of his efforts to stimulate the slow economy during the Great Recession, President Obama called for $30 billion to rehabilitate public schools and community college facilities across the United States.[1] His opponents predictably denounced the proposal, but even those who might have been expected to advocate for such an investment, like major teachers' organizations, seemed skeptical that this part of President Obama's jobs plan would ever pass Congress, at least without some alteration. The educational community, long accustomed to underinvestment, seemed to give up on the idea of receiving an already inadequate sum to upgrade our schools.

That was too bad, because a major investment in our schools would have done a lot for us. Fixing leaky roofs and upgrading deteriorating windows

48   has immediate, pragmatic value, and the more we let such problems go unchecked in buildings, the more expensive the repairs, to the point where too much damage can make even the most expensive new construction less costly. The rehabilitation of school buildings would also have created more jobs than new construction, and certainly more than what Obama's opponents in Congress seemed ready to do. Finally, passing up a chance to fix our schools in a depressed economy represented a huge missed opportunity, since the downturn would have made every construction dollar go much further than it would in good times.

   We need not use such construction-related arguments, though, to make a case for investing in schools. We could pay for this work without another penny of federal money were we to see schools and the value they bring to communities more broadly. I cochaired a workshop in Washington, D.C., that brought together the school design community and public health workers focused on the childhood obesity epidemic to discuss how we could educate and encourage schoolkids to eat more healthily and burn more calories. Sponsored by the National Collaborative on Childhood Obesity Research, the National Academy of Environmental Design, and the U.S. Green Building Council, the gathering showed how much potential exists for schools to serve as centers for good health and exercise in our communities, not just for schoolchildren but also for adults of all ages.[2]

   Some might call this public emphasis on physical activity a form of communism, as if obesity were just another word for freedom. But how does learning good nutrition differ from learning proper English, and how does getting more exercise differ from getting more study time? We should instead recognize it as resourcefulness, a key element of design thinking. Consider the enormous savings we could achieve for society and for taxpayers by reducing the disease and the attendant health care costs we have already begun to experience with our increasingly obese population? We could more than pay for needed improvements to school buildings with a tiny fraction of the billions of dollars we would save on health care by using schools much more intensively as active recreation centers.

   That raises a second possible way of paying for school repairs. Both the Obama administration and its critics have mostly talked about schools as traditionally defined: places where teachers educate school-age children during the school day and over the school year. Largely missing from the discussion has been the role that schools can play in communities the rest of the time—evenings, weekends, and summers, when these facilities sit mostly empty and underutilized.

We could use our investment in school buildings not only to enhance the learning environment for school-age children but also to equip these structures for what they could become: places that can help revitalize local economies, upgrade people's skills, and increase community resilience and competitiveness. That, of course, already happens to some extent in communities where school buildings are used for continuing education classes and personal enrichment programs. But these remain at the margins in most places and generally engage only a small percentage of the population.

We need to envision how our local schools could serve as centers of extensive, lifelong teaching and learning on the part of almost all community members. We can no longer afford to have these buildings remain dark most of the time, nor can we afford to have so many Americans so ill equipped to compete in the global economy or to address the global challenges we face. Viewed this way, school rehabilitation provides not only short-term jobs for construction companies but also long-term career opportunities for the all community residents.

How might we pay for such an expansion of educational offerings, and how do we get people to take advantage of them? One answer: see everyone in the community as a possible teacher as well as a learner—from each according to ability and to each according to need, as Marx might say. Even the smallest and most impoverished communities have an incredible wealth of human assets, people with skills, knowledge, and talents that remain largely untapped. A community could, for example, institute a barter system for education in which everyone gets to take classes in subjects they don't know about if they volunteer to teach classes in areas where they are knowledgeable.

We could also tie school funding to the social and economic benefits that around-the-clock use of school facilities can bring to a community, reducing the cost of social dysfunction and economic decline in the process. We must invest in our schools, not just for the sake of our school-age children but also for the health, wealth, and well-being of everyone. And we do not have to fund this investment only through the federal government. A well-educated, highly skilled, fully employable population will save so much money in other areas and generate so much more income that funneling even a portion of that back to our schools will more than meet the need. Once we start down this road, we may well wonder why we waited so long.

As we think of schools relating to their communities in new ways, however, we also need to look at the negative impacts communities can have on the education of children. No amount of creatively rethinking the curriculum will amount to much if students—young and old—remain distracted, distressed, or discouraged by the events in their lives outside school. Education cannot succeed in environments hostile to education. The poverty, addictions, violence, and social and familial dysfunction that have become all too common in some places have also become major reasons students of all ages do not do well in school. Addressing such large social problems can seem daunting, but there are ways to help students in such situations.

In Haiti, after the 2010 earthquake that took many lives, a number of public boarding schools were established, in part because many children no longer had parents or homes to go to. These schools also created environments in which students could focus on their studies apart from the sometimes-chaotic conditions that existed around them. If a country as poor as Haiti can afford such boarding schools, why can't the United States?

If we in the United States were to take just a fraction of the $74 billion we spend annually on incarcerating criminals and put that into the creation of public boarding schools able to accommodate at-risk kids coming from terrible homes and dangerous neighborhoods, we would end up saving not only a great deal of public money but also—and more important—a lot of young people whose considerable potential we now squander.[3] That came home to me when my now-grown daughter told me of a boy named Jerome, who had attended elementary school with her; she remembered him as one of the brightest kids in the class. She had heard that Jerome, as a young adult, had gone to prison to serve a long sentence for some sort of violent crime. Jerome lived in a tough neighborhood, had an unstable home, and saw his own father go to prison, but he did not have to follow in his father's footsteps.

My father, a child and adolescent psychologist, treated many young people struggling in school or engaged in disruptive and self-destructive

51 behavior, often because of dysfunctional family or friend relationships, and he worked with the juvenile courts to take many children out of terrible home situations and place them in foster care. Fresh out of graduate school, he also worked as a psychologist at a boarding school for delinquent boys, a model that we need to make available, both for misbehaving youth and for children who simply need a stable place to live.

An unstable living situation can jeopardize any child's ability to learn. Across the United States, 1.168 million school-age children experienced homelessness in 2013, an increase of 10 percent over the previous year.[4] And research shows that housing instability affects the performance of students in school as well as their health and well-being generally.[5] Stable housing and safe neighborhoods, in other words, matter as much as good teaching and supportive schools in the education of our kids. The educational community knows this, and state governments have begun to respond, with increasing numbers appropriating money for affordable housing.

In cases like Jerome's, keeping kids in severely dysfunctional families or transporting them to school from homeless shelters or from living on the streets does not seem like a successful strategy. Affordable housing and school busing can do little to counter disruptive family lives and dangerous neighborhoods.

We need the alternative of public boarding schools. A few states (Maryland, Ohio, and Florida) and Washington, D.C., now allow "SEED schools"— public boarding schools for at-risk youth operated by the SEED Foundation.[6] Students have performed very well in these schools, with as many as 98 percent going on to attend college after graduation. So why hasn't this approach become more widespread?

The resistance to public boarding schools may be in part a reaction to the horror stories we have all heard about public orphanages. My grandfather, who spent several years in one before being adopted, recalled the orphanage director putting the older boys in charge of the younger ones and beating the former if the latter misbehaved. But I suspect ideology and economics also help explain why public boarding schools have yet to catch on in the United States.

The ideology rests on the reasonable belief, one that I often heard from my father, that children generally do better in family settings than in institutional ones. However, when family or neighborhood settings become so toxic that the children living there are at risk, a boarding school sure beats a jail cell.

And that brings us to the economic issue. The United States has a long tradition of private boarding schools where mostly wealthy children receive excellent educations in social settings that enable them to flourish. The cost of running such schools, generally much higher than the per student cost of public education, makes the public boarding school idea seem prohibitively expensive. The annual cost of room and board at a boarding school, however, averages roughly half that of incarceration, and when we include the indirect benefits of having the Jeromes of our society as productive citizens rather than incarcerated criminals, the economic—and moral—case for public boarding schools becomes compelling.[7]

The political case for such schools also seems convincing. While those on the political right might see them as an example of the "nanny state," public boarding schools would help us reach goals that people across the political spectrum should like: reducing the cost of government burdened with the highest percentage of incarcerated people in the developed world, closing the educational achievement gap that makes the United States less economically competitive, and increasing the number of productive, taxpaying citizens at a time when we need as many as possible.

My daughter remembered Jerome as an eager kid, obviously excited to learn, and I wonder what we might have done differently had we known then what we do now about what direction his life would take. If his school—or at least one nearby—had offered him room and board so that he could have escaped his disruptive home life to focus on his studies, I know he would be in a different, and much less costly, place than he is now. How many more Jeromes do we need to lose before we act?

53 Portions of this chapter were previously published in "What We Can Learn by Investing in Our Schools," *Huffington Post* (September 20, 2011), http://www. huffingtonpost.com/thomas-fisher/what-we-can-learn-by-inve_b_969707.html.

[1] Alyson Klein, "Obama Calls for $60 Billion to Save Teacher Jobs, Fix Schools," *Education Week,* September 8, 2011, http://blogs.edweek.org.

[2] National Collaborative on Childhood Obesity Research, "Green Health," accessed November 17, 2015, http://www.nccor.org.

[3] Brian Kincade, "The Economics of the American Prison System," SmartAsset, June 18, 2013, http://www.smartasset.com.

[4] Amy McConnell Schaarsmith, "Across U.S., a Record Number of Homeless School-Age Children," *Pittsburgh Post-Gazette,* October 30, 2013, http://www.post-gazette.com.

[5] Ellen Hart-Shegos, *Homelessness and Its Effects on Children* (Minneapolis: Family Housing Fund, 1999), http://www.fhfund.org/wp-content/uploads/ 2014/10/Homlessness_Effects_Children.pdf.

[6] See the foundation's website at http://www.seedfoundation.com.

[7] For a disturbing comparison of what U.S. states spend on education per child versus incarceration per prisoner, see CNN Money, "Education vs Prison Costs," accessed November 17, 2015, http://www.money.cnn.com/infographic/economy/ education-vs-prison-costs.

6

RECONSTRUCTING DESIGN EDUCATION

How might the design community, with its abductive form of reasoning, respond to the needs of the poor and disenfranchised? While the idea of public boarding schools utilizes the analogous way in which designers work—looking at something that works in one area and bringing it into another to test its relevance—the architectural community, in particular, has focused too much of its creative energy on form making and material assembly and too little on what may be the community's most important contribution: programmatic invention. Public boarding schools, lifelong-learning schools, community health schools—these just touch the surface of what design, rightly understood, has to offer, although the design community may have to reprogram itself to achieve such understanding.

This suggests, in turn, the need for a redesign of design education as well. Design has largely followed a medical model of practice, developing custom solutions to the particular needs of fee-paying clients, as physicians do with patients. While that practice works for those who have the ability to pay for such services, it leaves out most of the world's population, who need design as much as they do medical help but lack the money to pay for it. Medicine gave birth to the field of public health, which addresses the health needs of large populations, and design needs to do the same, developing a public health–related version of itself, with a new type of practice—and education—to make it happen.

A public health design field would remain grounded in communities, cocreating solutions in partnership with the people most affected by problems and with most at stake in their resolution. The design studio system seems well suited to this community-based approach, given its flexibility, fluidity, and exploratory nature, but a public health perspective would mark a real change in design education. Design instructors still largely expect students to address problems dreamed up by their professors. While there may be important pedagogical reasons for such studio problems, these academic exercises often divorce students from the communities in which they work and reinforce the design community's complicity with those who have the money to pay for design.

This also leads to one of the great paradoxes of our time, as our brightest and most talented students spend their time learning how to solve, often brilliantly, made-up problems. This became starkly apparent during the Great Recession, when there arose myriad condominiums for which there existed no market, high-end homes soon worth a fraction of their original cost, and office buildings that had too few tenants, all plugged into sprawling road systems that the public sector did not have enough money to maintain. The recession left behind a landscape littered with the well-intentioned work of designers doing what they had been commissioned to do by clients tempted by easy credit, fast money, and fantasies of quick profits. Never has so much talent gone into so much wasted effort while skirting the truly wicked situations that we face.

By reconnecting design education to communities we can help prevent such sad situations from recurring. Enabling students to work more often on projects with meaning for real people and ensuring that they apply themselves to relevant problems can also lead to what education should always do: prepare students to question the underlying reasons and the unspoken assumptions behind the problems they face. The idea of design focusing on programmatic invention reflects that change. Community-engaged studios quickly learn that the form of a design matters much less than what it does to meet people's needs and a community's aspirations. That doesn't make form irrelevant; it simply means that inventive programming remains the real foundation of inventive form.

Design education, in other words, needs to teach students how to *seek* problems in the reality of people's lives as much as how to help solve them. Every design student, like every physician, needs to embrace an oath to do no harm and to look for the least invasive, least destructive way of addressing each situation. In the case of design, that might mean finding a solution that addresses a problem with as little money, in as little time, and with as little effort as possible. Design students also need to learn how to look at the larger context and broader systems that surround a problem. Too often, we try to solve problems at the wrong scale and miss what may have caused the problems in the first place. Students need to understand— and question—the laws, codes, and regulations; networks, paths, and flows; and financial, material, and human resources that surround almost everything designers do.

This type of education will help students become more entrepreneurial and enterprising when they graduate. The more design educators can teach students to think laterally across different systems and vertically to address things at the right scale, the more likely real problems will be solved and the best designs will be implemented. Clients and communities should expect nothing less. That entrepreneurial spirit needs to extend to faculty as well. One of the more unfortunate characteristics of intellectual life over the past century has been the withdrawal of many academics from the larger public and political discourse, not just in the design fields but also across much of higher education.

The reasons that so many academics no longer speak to or engage with the public no doubt vary among individuals. The disappearance of many tenured faculty members from the public stage, however, threatens the very security that tenure affords. For evidence of this, look at the efforts in statehouses around the United States, most recently in Madison, Wisconsin, to abolish public employees' and K–12 teachers' collective bargaining rights. Such anti-unionism suggests that attacks on the tenure system, at least in public higher education, will not be far behind. To those who see everything in terms of the marketplace, tenure can seem anticompetitive and inefficient: If companies don't offer tenure, why should universities? Lost on most critics of tenure is the fact that universities are much more like municipalities than they are like companies, and tenured faculty are more like the property owners in a community than employees in a business.

It's not surprising that such arguments fall on deaf ears among governors and legislators trying to cut budgets and reduce the size of government. The public pressure to keep tuition increases down, the widespread misunderstanding of faculty workloads, and the growing anti-intellectualism in public discourse may further embolden those who see tenure as a costly and cushy deal, or who simply do not like or trust academics for whatever reason. So far, public universities have largely remained below the radar of those who have shown a startling animosity toward public-sector employees. Given what we have witnessed in Wisconsin, however, hoping that tenure will remain unchallenged and that universities can successfully fend off attacks on tenure as they largely have in the past does not seem like an effective strategy.

Instead, when it comes to tenure, faculty need to "use it or lose it." In other words, the best defense of tenure is a good offense: remembering why tenure exists in the first place and putting it to use in ways that the public and even skeptical politicians will recognize as valuable and worth protecting. One of the primary purposes of tenure is to protect faculty who speak out about potentially controversial subjects. As such, tenure largely serves the public interest by giving people access to pertinent facts and to the "truth" as currently understood by those with expertise in a specific area. Drawing attention to the public benefit that tenure provides seems essential at a time when some are inclined to portray tenure as an undeserved privilege.

With the receipt of tenure comes a responsibility to serve not just as an educator and researcher but also as a public commentator, addressing a broad audience about issues of general interest from the perspective of a particular discipline. In addition to publishing in academic journals, tenured faculty members need to communicate with the public by writing or speaking about their work in ways and through venues accessible to everyone. Faculty also need to demonstrate the value of tenure by taking stands on important topics for which they may require the protection tenure provides.

That may seem like a risky approach. It might seem safer for tenured faculty to keep a low profile and wait out the current wave of cost cutting, avoiding possibly controversial issues that might draw the attention of and even antagonize the very politicians who may look for reasons to go after tenure. I understand that sentiment, but while addressing controversial issues may anger a few, not doing so could disaffect a far greater number of people if speaking out would have made a difference in the public understanding of an issue or led to an improved outcome.

The time has come for tenured faculty to recognize their role and use the variety of tools at their disposal to reach out to a broad public before they lose that capability altogether. This seems especially important now, in an era in the which the future will differ markedly from the past, since the likely responses to the rapidly changing conditions we face will challenge those currently in power and benefiting from the rules as they stand. But in that circumstance lies a great opportunity for redesign. The more we can abductively rethink these rules in terms of the world we actually want to occupy in the future—one presumably less violent, less divided, and more sustainable than the one we have—the more likely it is that we will survive and thrive over the course of this century.

With the decline in academics serving as public intellectuals has come a related decline in public support for higher education. Indeed, this drop in support brings to mind the old Joni Mitchell line, "You don't know what you've got till it's gone."[1] The federal government and most state governments have dramatically cut financial support for research universities over the past several decades, to the point where public funding, as a percentage of most university budgets, now hovers in the single or low double digits. As a result, student tuition has also hit record highs, with student indebtedness becoming a major drag on the U.S. economy. Like K–12, higher education in the United States is in dire need of a redesign to put it on a more solid foundation and enable it to open its doors to more people.

In most U.S. states, the general public has little awareness of how much and how fast their governments have disinvested in higher education; most people seem to assume that state government remains a major—if not *the* major—funder of state universities. In fact, public funding has become such a small part of most state universities' revenue that it amounts to less than what either tuition or funded research brings into these institutions. As some observers like to say, the public research universities are now state located and state named but hardly state supported. The stately walls and serene campuses of such universities now seem more like false fronts, propped up by tuition dollars and donors' bequests, with state governments still having most of the control despite their small financial stake in these institutions.

This reflects a shift in thinking about higher education in the public at large. What we once saw as a common good has come to be viewed as a private benefit, and this perception is driving a rapid and almost continuous decline in financial support for most public universities. The assumption among many is that if individual students reap the financial rewards of their college education over their lifetimes, they should pay more for that education in the form of higher tuition. That this puts higher education out of the reach of many students doesn't seem to matter to those making this argument.

The decline in state support rests on other suspect assumptions as well. Some cash-strapped legislatures argue that universities have other sources of revenue to compensate for cuts in public funding, even though those other sources have limited capacity to absorb increases (in the case of tuition) or represent unpredictable and often quite variable revenue streams (in the case of funded research). Some legislators also argue that taxpayers should not subsidize well-off students who have the ability to pay more, even though tuition increases mainly affect middle-class kids whose parents' incomes are too high for them to qualify for needs-based scholarships but not high enough for them to afford the ever-rising tuition.

Such rationalizations for cutting government spending on public universities overlook something especially important. These institutions do not just educate students and conduct research. Most of them—particularly the large, land-grant universities—do an extraordinary amount of public service and outreach in exchange for the state and federal funding they receive. Working mostly in less affluent communities, public universities provide services that are often not affordable or even available in the private market.

While cuts in state support to universities have had the highly visible result of causing tuition—and student indebtedness—to rise, even more dire consequences may come from the much less visible reduction in the ability of universities to help people in need. As our economy becomes increasingly dependent on higher education to spur new growth, the diminished capability of universities to help communities maximize the potential of their youth and create opportunities for their entrepreneurs represents a tremendous loss, likely much greater than the money that states think they are saving by cutting their support of higher education.

Another negative economic impact of state cuts in funding to universities involves the private sector. While a lot of the funded research at universities depends on government support, much of this work greatly benefits businesses, large and small, through the creation of new technology, the generation of added jobs, and the production of increased profits. As governments cut back on their support of universities, reducing the ability of these institutions to support students, they diminish the ability of our best and brightest to help our economy and our communities thrive.

In part because most people and most companies remain largely unaware of the drastic declines in state support of public universities, the natural constituents of these institutions have done relatively little to advocate for increased public support or increased government spending on research. And while alumni and donors continue to make generous gifts to these institutions, these come nowhere near compensating for the size of the cuts that governments have made. If the public wants to have affordable higher education and the private sector wants to maintain a flow of skilled graduates and profitable innovations, they need to speak up for the greater good that public universities represent and step up the level of private support to defray the government's cuts.

This may also demand a new compact between universities and the public. Some 150 years ago, the Morrill Act established land-grant public research universities, initially paid for from the income of the land granted to each state for that purpose. Generations of further investments by public officials of all political stripes created some of the best institutions of their kind in the world, and yet now some politicians seem determined to undo all of that in a couple of generations. And once it is undone, there will be no going back: once the great public universities go "private," with so little public funding that they have become essentially indistinguishable from their elite private peers, states will never have the money or the political will to replace them.

Which brings us back to that Joni Mitchell song. We have begun to pave over—or, perhaps more fitting for the land-grant universities, plow under—the vast amount of investment already made in our public research institutions and are beginning to destroy what our ancestors worked for well over a century to create. And we likely won't know what we've got—or what we've lost—till it's gone.

All of this suggests the need for a paradigm shift in our thinking about higher education, something that the abductive methods of design seem particularly well suited to provide. If we think of higher education as a systems design problem, then we should begin its redesign by engaging the very people most affected by it—the students. The empathetic observation of the stakeholders in a redesign process often holds the key not only to the nature of the problem but also to the types of solutions most likely to work. Observe and listen to today's students, and the problems—and opportunities—of higher education become eminently clear.

Over the years, for example, I have watched students drift off if I lectured for more than the typical time span of a television program between commercial breaks, and I have witnessed students zoning out when I gave them a made-up situation, especially if it had little or no bearing on what they saw happening in the world around them. Of course, the students did the work I asked of them; they hadn't gotten into a competitive college in a major research university by shrugging off assignments, however bored they might be. I could tell, though, by the look in their eyes, that they had zero interest in doing pointless projects just to get a grade, and their assessments of my classes at the end of the semester reiterated what I already knew: the academic exercises had to go.

I decided to do two things with my classes as a result. First, I largely stopped lecturing, and in doing so, I found I no longer had to work so hard to keep students' attention in class. Instead, I now either video-record my lectures or use lectures and talks by other speakers, which my students watch online on their own time, allowing us to spend class time engaged in discussions and debate, with my students talking as much among themselves as with me and with them presenting to their classmates as much as I present to them. No one drifts off in my classes anymore—the level of interaction makes that impossible.

Second, I had my students working on actual projects in the local community, within the real constraints of each situation. They now work largely in teams, learning how to divvy up the assignment and work together in order to complete a project—skills they will need in the increasingly collaborative work world they will soon enter. And they present their work as concisely, clearly, and convincingly as possible to those members of the community responsible for or concerned about each project. The excitement I now see on my students' faces—and their obvious pleasure when their proposals are taken seriously by the community members reviewing their work—makes it hard for me to imagine ever going back to the old ways of teaching.

I realize that such reality-based exercises come easier in my field—architecture—than they might in a less applied discipline, and I know that colleges like mine in large cities have the advantage of proximity to diverse communities, something much less likely in small college towns. Still, I think *actual exercises*—as opposed to academic ones—exist everywhere, and even the most recondite disciplines in the most remote locations can find ways of applying knowledge to real-world problems. And why wouldn't we want to connect the education of students with the needs of communities? Students appear to retain knowledge best when they have to apply it, and universities seem to demonstrate their value best when they make tangible differences in the communities in which they stand and for the constituencies on whom they depend.

Colleges and universities across the country have begun to make such public engagement a core part of the educational experience, with students from almost every discipline involved in off-campus projects, applying in communities what they have learned in the classroom. And such efforts simply scratch the surface of possibilities. The millennial generation does not just want to address real problems and engage in relevant projects; students today also seem eager to cocreate with faculty new ways of discovering and delivering knowledge.

The more educators harness this energy and direct it toward constructive ends, the more our students will learn and, ultimately, the more higher education—and its tenured faculty—will seem worth investing in. Instead of the win–lose mentality that so often characterizes our political economy these days, design finds win–win solutions, ways of achieving multiple and apparently conflicting goals at the same time. The redesign of higher education should aspire to nothing less.

Portions of this chapter were previously published in "Expanding Our Field," ACSA News (October 2009), http://www.acsa-arch.org/docs/acsa-news-back-issues/web-acsanewsoct09.pdf?sfvrsn=1; "Tenure: Use It or Lose It," *Huffington Post* (August 17, 2011), http://www.huffingtonpost.com/thomas-fisher/tenure-use-it-or-lose-it_b_929238.html; "They're Paving Paradise," *Huffington Post* (June 14, 2012), http://www.huffingtonpost.com/thomas-fisher/theyre-paving-paradise_b_1594772.html; and "The End of the Academic Exercise," *Huffington Post* (November 14, 2012), http://www.huffingtonpost.com/thomas-fisher/flipped-classroom_b_2122470.html.

[1] Joni Mitchell, "Big Yellow Taxi," 1970, http://jonimitchell.com.

PART III

INFRA-STRUCTURE

Of all the "invisible" design that we depend on, some of the most important involves infrastructure—the pipes and cables, sewers and tunnels, caissons and bridges, cell towers and satellites that we rely on to function in our daily lives. While much of that infrastructure remains buried beneath the ground, underneath the roadbed, or too high in the air for us to see it, at least it has a tangibility that we can easily imagine. The first chapter in this part provides an overview of a topic that eventually became a book of mine, *Designing to Avoid Disaster: The Nature of Fracture-Critical Design.* Fracture-critical problems occur in almost all aspects of the invisibly designed world, and this chapter shows how the pattern-recognition power of design thinking enables us to make useful connections among apparently disparate and disconnected phenomena, demonstrating the real value of abductive reasoning.

The second chapter in this part looks at quantity rather than the qualities of our infrastructure and asks, how much is enough? That question matters to municipalities, whose tax bases often cannot come close to maintaining all of the infrastructure put in place to serve low-density suburban development. It also matters to the federal government, which faces the wicked problem of increasingly cata-strophic weather events that can overpower and destroy infrastructure. We cannot solve the deficit in our infrastructure repair bill until we address the issue of where and how we should—and shouldn't—live.

Chapter 9 is devoted to a topic that has preoccupied public dis-cussion in recent years: protecting our infrastructure—and us—from terrorists. Terrorists engage in a kind of design by seeking out places where infrastructure is most susceptible to attack. We will defeat today's terrorists only by learning from them, seeing where they focus their attention, and outsmarting them, finding our vulnerabilities before they do and fixing them. The value of abductive thinking lies not just in envisioning possible futures but also in avoiding potential threats.

7

FRACTURE-CRITICAL FAILURES

At rush hour on August 1, 2007, the 1,907-foot I-35W bridge near downtown Minneapolis fell into the Mississippi River, killing 13 people, injuring 145 more, and severing a key link in the interstate highway system. The cost of the bridge failure, including damages and construction of a new bridge, was more than $300 million.[1] After more than a year of investigation, the National Transportation Safety Board concluded that the engineers who designed the bridge in the early 1960s had undersized the gusset plates that connected its steel segments. That error, compounded by the weight of extra lanes added over time and repaving equipment and materials placed on the bridge on the fatal day, caused 456 feet of roadway to collapse in seconds and drop 108 feet into the river, taking with it 111 vehicles.[2]

Experts estimate that some 465 U.S. bridges are similar in design to the I-35W span. Inspection and reinforcement of these structures are vitally important as the nation prepares to upgrade its infrastructure.[3] Just as crucial, we need to see the I-35W and similar spans not as isolated cases but instead as harbingers of a problem that plagues much infrastructure and development of the past sixty years, a problem that engineers call "fracture-critical design."

A fracture-critical design has four key characteristics. The first is a lack of redundancy, which makes a structure susceptible to collapse should any individual component fail. The I-35W's undersized gusset plates might not have brought down the span if additional members had carried the structural load. At the time of the bridge's design, such redundancy no doubt seemed expensive and wasteful. But given the extraordinary costs, financial and human, of collapse, the incremental expense of redundancy would have been cost-effective and wise. Engineers understand this and in recent years have increased the redundancy of bridge designs, but the pressure to reduce initial costs continues to threaten the durability of our infrastructure.

Other characteristics of fracture-critical design include a high degree of interconnectedness and efficiency. The I-35W bridge had both. When the gusset plate cracked near the bridge's southern end, it overstressed other truss members—all interconnected so efficiently that nothing could interrupt the structure's serial collapse. The Tenth Avenue Bridge adjacent to the I-35W span shows the advantage of less interconnection and less efficiency. Completed in 1929, that bridge consists of independent concrete arches separated by concrete pylons that divide the structure into discrete parts. The concrete columns supporting the road deck seem oversized, making the entire ensemble less than efficient but more than sufficient to compensate for the failure of any one element.[4] Even if one of the arches or several columns fail, the bridge would not collapse.

Sensitivity to stress is the final characteristic of fracture-critical systems. Had inspectors attached strain gauges to the gusset plate that cracked on the I-35W bridge, they would have detected a gradual increase in stress, with a rapid rise in strain just before the plate fractured and the bridge fell. Sudden, exponential increase in strain prior to failure is a well-known phenomenon, and a fracture-critical design magnifies its effect. What seems a localized, controllable problem can quickly become catastrophic because of the nature of exponential growth, which doubles with each increment of time.[5]

The collapse of the fracture-critical I-35W bridge highlights the need to replace such structures with less connected, less efficient, and more resilient designs. But we need to change more than our bridges. In retrospect, the fracture-critical structures of the 1950s and 1960s reflected the larger American culture of the time, one that John Kenneth Galbraith famously critiqued as one of private affluence and public squalor.[6] In an era when the United States could have afforded the best infrastructure in the world, we began instead to channel wealth into private hands and to impoverish the public realm. This echoed a deeper shift in American culture at the same time.

The United States emerged from World War II as the dominant global power, and, as many commentators have noted, dominance can easily lead to hubris, to the pride of Pax Americana in the 1950s and more recently to theories of American exceptionalism.[7] We now know that our wartime enemies as well as allies have become formidable competitors, and that we can no longer take American preeminence for granted. In this sense the I-35W span stood—and fell—not just as a physical bridge across the Mississippi but also as a symbol of postwar overconfidence and the vulnerability of much of the infrastructure created in that period. The I-35W bridge stood as both metaphor and omen of what lies ahead for us in other fracture-critical systems.

Look at our fracture-critical global financial system. Like the one cracked gusset plate that brought down the I-35W bridge, the failure of just two investment banks—Bear Stearns in March 2008 and Lehman Brothers a few months later—caused a chain-reaction collapse of other banks and their insurers, and then of credit and stock markets around the world.[8] Just as highway repair crews had piled on extra weight while resurfacing the I-35W roadway before the bridge failed, so too did the markets pile huge amounts of debt onto the financial system, overloading banks to the point of collapse. And just as government inspectors and engineering consultants failed to detect the bridge's weakening plates or to understand the risk of inaction, so too did government regulators and independent auditors fail to provide adequate oversight or public explanations about how mortgage-backed securities might endanger the global financial system.

Once we see the collapse of our fracture-critical financial system as an adaptive cycle, we can predict what will follow and how to prevent future catastrophes. Our global banking system needs to become less interconnected and less efficient, and thus more resilient. As in a resilient bridge, a transformed financial system should have more discrete, disconnected parts, with strong internal divisions so that even if one part fails, others will not. It should have more redundant parts, with checks and balances to ensure that inspectors and auditors catch calculation errors or outright fraud before they do systemic damage. And it should have built-in delays, allowing for extra time and added review to slow down processes and allow for more deliberation. Indeed, the very idea of a globally integrated financial system might disappear, as nations hurt by the recent collapse (over which they had little control) set up procedures and regulatory policies to prevent worldwide meltdowns that might adversely affect them again.

We can recognize fracture-critical designs after their failures, but what about catching them before they fail? How can we prevent or at least mitigate the collapse of these systems? Most such systems send warning signs before they collapse; the I-35W bridge's gusset plates bent long before one broke, just as prominent investors warned about the dangers of credit default swaps before the investment banks began to fail. The challenge comes in not only seeing the signs of imminent failure but also not ignoring them when we do.

An example of that challenge has occurred with the electrical grid in the United States. On August 15, 2003, an outage near Cleveland cascaded into the largest power failure in North American history, leaving fifty million people across the United States and Canada without power for days and causing an estimated $10 billion in damages.[9] Years after the blackout, industry experts remain worried that the situation has only worsened, with excess capacity declining and demand for electricity by 2030 expected to increase 29 percent from 2006 levels. The electrical grid represents a fracture-critical system needing immediate attention; a single failure can cause damages far costlier than the expense of adding capacity and building in firewalls. Further, a few key points in the electrical grid are especially vulnerable to sabotage, making the need for added resilience even more crucial.

Because the electrical grid constitutes a coordinated, nationwide system, we should be able to bolster its resilience. The more difficult challenges come with vulnerable systems that don't appear so, such as the thousands of suburban housing developments constructed in the United States in the postwar era. For most of American history, communities were built over time, with diverse building types to accommodate different kinds of households. This was a resilient model because of its physical, social, and economic diversity. After World War II, however, we began constructing different types of communities—mass-produced subdivisions consisting entirely of single-family houses all alike in design, size, and price. Usually built all at once by a single contractor, each such community housed families at roughly the same socioeconomic level. Developers found these subdivisions easier to finance, build, and market, and many home owners liked the idea of having neighbors much like themselves.[10]

But postwar suburbia has proven fracture-critical. When home owners default on mortgages and go through foreclosure, the banks holding the mortgages typically lower the prices of the houses to sell them quickly and recoup their losses. But if enough foreclosures happen in a development where the houses remain more or less interchangeable, the value of all the properties can drop, often to the point where many owe more on their mortgages than the sale price of their houses.[11] This, in turn, can push home owners to walk away and more banks to foreclose, intensifying a spiral that can destroy the value and morale of the neighborhood.

The oil-dependent transportation system that made suburbia possible remains just as fracture-critical as suburbia itself. We know that we are vulnerable to decreases in the U.S. petroleum supply, more than half of which comes from foreign sources, yet we continue to rely on oil as the major energy source for transportation, panicking when prices rise and relaxing when they fall back to "normal."[12] And we know that we need to develop alternative fuels to free ourselves from our dependence on a single source, although the sunk cost in the carbon economy has led to a lot of resistance and wishful thinking on the part of those who fantasize about cheap oil flowing forever. Energy resilience would involve as great a range of fuel sources as possible, not just oil and biofuel but also electricity and hydrogen as well as solar, wind, and the most dependable source of all: human pedal and pedestrian power.

Unlike its fracture-critical predecessor, the bridge that replaced the I-35W span represents the kind of constructive change that we need. The new bridge, designed by Linda Figg of Figg Engineering, has redundancy to spare.[13] The sheer size and depth of its post-tensioned, concrete box beams contrast with the weakness of the previous bridge and emphasize the benefit of building in redundancy at the start rather than having to rebuild after a collapse. As essentially two side-by-side, unconnected bridges, the new span factors in further redundancy: if one side were to fail for some reason, the other side could still function. The new bridge also accommodates multiple transit modes, with some lanes strengthened to support future light-rail and a pedestrian suspension bridge planned beneath the highway. The more alternatives a system offers, the more likely it will last. And the new bridge arose from local conditions, ranging from site-specific construction methods, using the closed-off highway as the construction yard for the new structure; to community concerns, engaging a diverse group of people in giving input on the design; to local job opportunities, employing mostly local construction workers and material suppliers. The new bridge exemplifies the deep advantages of fracture-resistant infrastructure. It also suggests what a resilient future might look like, with more of the ruggedness and durability that we know from systems of the past.

Our fracture-critical systems—infrastructure, finance, housing, and energy—all need attention, commitment, and investment. But of course we face still more basic challenges as well. In his book *Collapse,* Jared Diamond estimates that we have about fifty years before we experience the irreversible effects of exponential declines in natural habitats, fish populations, biological diversity, and farmable soil; of serious shortages of fossil fuels, freshwater, and plant growth per acre; and of increases in toxic chemicals in the air and water, invasive plant species devastating ecosystems, ozone-depleting atmospheric gases, impoverished human populations, and unsustainable consumption.[14] Climate scientists like James Hansen warn that we have even less time to counter global warming and ensure that the planet remains habitable.[15] It is no exaggeration to say that our species itself now faces a fracture-critical future. We have the capacity to envision and create a more resilient one, using approaches not unlike those humans have employed for most of our time on earth: husbanding finite resources for future generations, cultivating renewable resources to maintain quantity and diversity, and finding pleasure in the infinite resources of human community, creativity, and empathy. But first we need to heed the warnings right in front of us. The systems we have created may seem strong, even invincible, but we have let ourselves be fooled by appearances before, and we must not let that happen again.

73

This chapter first appeared in different form as "Fracture Critical," *Places* (October 20, 2009), http://places.designobserver.com/feature/fracture-critical/11477.

[1] Paul Levy, "4 Dead, 79 Injured, 20 Missing after Dozens of Vehicles Plummet into River," *Star Tribune,* August 2, 2007.

[2] National Transportation Safety Board, "NTSB Determines Inadequate Load Capacity Due to Design Errors of Gusset Plates Caused I-35W Bridge to Collapse," press release, November 14, 2008.

[3] Robert J. Connor, Robert Dexter, and Hussam Mahmoud, *Inspection and Management of Bridges with Fracture-Critical Details: A Synthesis of Highway Practice,* National Cooperative Highway Research Program Synthesis 354 (Washington, D.C.: Transportation Research Board, 2005).

[4] National Register of Historic Places, Hennepin County, Minnesota.

[5] Gunderson and Holling, *Panarchy.*

[6] John Kenneth Galbraith, *The Affluent Society* (New York: Houghton Mifflin, 1958).

[7] Theodore Draper, "American Hubris, from Truman to the Persian Gulf," *New York Review of Books,* July 16, 1987.

[8] Phillip Swagel, "Why Lehman Wasn't Rescued," *New York Times,* September 13, 2013.

[9] Mark Williams, "5 Years after a Giant Blackout, Concerns about Electrical Grid Linger," Associated Press, August 13, 2008.

[10] Andres Duany, Elizabeth Plater-Zyberk, and Jeff Speck, *Suburban Nation: The Rise of Suburban Sprawl and the Decline of the American Dream* (New York: North Point Press, 2000).

[11] James R. Hagerty and Ruth Simon, "Housing Pain Gauge: Nearly 1 in 6 Owners 'Under Water,'" *Wall Street Journal,* October 8, 2008.

[12] James Howard Kunstler, *The Long Emergency: Surviving the Converging Catastrophes of the Twenty-First Century* (New York: Atlantic Monthly Press, 2005).

[13] Figg Engineering, *Bridging the Mississippi: The New I-35W Bridge* (Minneapolis: Figg Engineering, 2008).

[14] Jared Diamond, *Collapse: How Societies Choose to Fail or Succeed* (New York: Viking Press, 2005).

[15] Elizabeth Kolbert, "The Catastrophist," *New Yorker,* June 29, 2009.

8

OVEREXTENDED INFRASTRUCTURE

Aside from having a lot of fracture-critical infrastructure across the United States, we have more infrastructure than we have the ability to maintain. Rather than just assuming that we need the same infrastructure everywhere, we must start asking, every time we repair a road or replace a pipe, whether we can do things differently to avoid continuing to maintain what we can no longer afford. The design community, including the civil engineers most responsible for our infrastructure, should pose that question not just out of professional responsibility but also as a way of reaching out to those on the political right who seem bent on reducing government spending at all costs. What better way to do so than to not replace infrastructure we no longer need?

Randal O'Toole, a senior fellow at the Cato Institute and a frequent critic of mass transit, demonstrates the difficulty in making this case when he equates low-density development with personal freedom, overlooking the extraordinary cost of maintaining the extensive infrastructure we have had to build to service so much of our suburban sprawl. In an essay critical of a regional planning report calling for more transit-oriented communities with denser development, he claims that the report's authors show a "lack of any understanding of the law of supply and demand" and the "relationship between prices and quantities." But he then makes an equally obvious blunder when he equates higher density with higher-priced housing and lower density with lower-priced housing. Supply and demand suggest the reverse. Large-lot, single-family development eventually limits the supply of housing because of the finite amount of land in a given municipality, driving up the cost when the supply can no longer meet the demand. In contrast, a higher-density mix of detached, attached, and multifamily housing enables a community to increase the supply to meet—or exceed—the demand, bringing prices down.

Increasing density does more than hold down the price of housing; it also helps keep taxes low. As engineer and planner Chuck Marohn of the nonprofit organization Strong Towns has shown, we have built far more infrastructure than the tax bases in most communities can maintain.[1] Facing that funding gap, fully built-out municipalities often have just two options: they can increase revenues in the form in higher taxes (which I doubt Mr. O'Toole would support), or they can increase the density around existing infrastructure, using it more efficiently while growing their tax bases.

Although some may equate low-density living with personal freedom, an imbalance between the cost of maintaining infrastructure and the intensity of its use represents a type of financial suicide for communities that have no hope of keeping up with the repair and replacement of their roads and utilities. The infrastructure maintenance bills will force communities to either densify or die.

That reveals one of the great paradoxes in the political right's support of low-density development. Mr. O'Toole has written elsewhere against big-government subsidies to local transit systems and tax incentives to encourage denser development. He ignores, however, one of the most obvious examples of big-government programs in American history: our highly subsidized post–World War II suburbs. For much of human history, people have largely lived relatively close together in villages, towns, and cities for reasons that include personal safety, social solidarity, and economic opportunity. It took a lot of social engineering—and a great deal of disinvestment in cities—after the war to counter that history and to incentivize the development of low-density sprawl.

Those incentives stemmed from a couple of large and expensive federal programs: the interstate highway system, which made it easier for people to commute long distances, and the mortgage-interest deduction from taxes, which prompted people who otherwise might not have owned homes to want to do so. The market responded to the opportunities that these programs created and built the suburbs that now ring every American city. But it remains disingenuous to portray our postwar suburbs as strictly the results of market forces and personal choice. While some people have always wanted—and will continue to want—to live outside cities, the suburban sprawl we now endure would never have happened without massive government intervention. This fact makes the Cato Institute's defense of low-density development truly ironic.

Rather than politicizing the issue of density, we should promote it where it makes sense and prohibit it where it doesn't. And we should not deny that, increasingly, members of the two largest demographic groups in America—the baby boomers and the millennials—want to live in higher-density cities, with more amenities and services an easy walk or transit ride away. The development community has energetically responded to that change, and the likes of Mr. O'Toole should applaud this market response and stop holding on to the unaffordable settlement patterns of the recent past.

Can we densify fast enough, though, to keep up with the mounting maintenance bills for our existing infrastructure? If we listen to the American Society of Civil Engineers (ASCE), the answer sounds like no. The ASCE periodically releases a "Report Card for America's Infrastructure," and in a recent report it gave the state of repair of our bridges a C and our roads a D–.[2] The ASCE estimates that our nation's infrastructure needs $2.2 trillion over five years to address its deterioration, an amount equal to roughly 15 percent of the gross domestic product.

The $2.2 trillion figure, however, is based on the assumption that we need to repair all that we have put in place, an approach that we should question. All too often, transportation planning models extrapolate from historic trends to predict future needs without factoring in social, economic, or technological transformations that can dramatically alter where infrastructure dollars should be spent. We cannot afford to repair and maintain infrastructure that we no longer need or to neglect investment in new types of infrastructure that we will need. Predicting where we can save money and where we can shift investments so they will do the most good demands that we take a much more holistic approach to transportation planning, answering the question of what kind of transportation we will need in a century very different from the last one. The following examples show how we can reduce expenditures in some areas in order to increase them in others.

REMOVE RURAL ROADS

Our system of rural roads arose in an era of small farms. Over time, the agricultural economy has consolidated into industrial-scale farms, and many rural roads now see very little traffic, yet local governments continue to maintain and repair them. Instead, we should consider removing the roads that see the least traffic and converting those rights-of-way to other, more productive uses, such as the production of biofuels, the cleansing of storm-water runoff, and the creation of habitat corridors. This would save taxpayers money and spare local governments unnecessary costs while creating new forms of revenue and reducing expenditures in areas unrelated to transportation.

78 MOVE BITS MORE THAN BODIES

The new economy of e-commerce and kick-started small businesses has all sorts of implications for how we will live and work in the future (as chapter 17 will explore in greater depth), but the digitally based economy that has already begun suggests that the old models of transportation planning built around rush-hour traffic into and out of a downtown core have become obsolete. We may already have more than enough urban road capacity for the emerging economy. The growing numbers of self-employed workers and telecommuting employees will likely move around less, and certainly not in a rush-hour pattern. The new economy also suggests that we may need to shift transportation expenditures from highways to high-band-width digital connections as we move more bits of information than human bodies.

SEEK HEALTHIER MODES OF TRANSPORTATION

Seeing the world from our disciplinary silos, we often miss connections among disparate and yet related phenomena, such as the connection between transportation and human health. That motor vehicle crashes remain the leading cause of death among Americans ages five to thirty-four seems not to affect public policies that encourage an automobile-dependent lifestyle or to alter public opinion that young people are safer in suburbs than in cities—which they often are not when driving deaths are taken into account.[3] Dependence on the automobile also contributes to sedentary lifestyles, which have been linked with an epidemic in obesity-related diabetes, costing the U.S. health care system $147 billion annually.[4] Getting people out of their cars and moving, on foot or bike, may be one of the most cost-effective transportation moves we can make, allowing us to reduce health care and road expenditures at the same time.

USE INFRASTRUCTURE MORE EFFICIENTLY

The United States has the most extensive transportation infrastructure, per capita, of any developed country in the world. This situation represents a drag on our economy and places us at a competitive disadvantage, in part because municipalities have to take on the costs of privately built infrastructure. Although the expense of the initial construction of infra-structure is absorbed in the financing and home sales of many suburban developments, local governments are burdened with high maintenance and repair costs over time. To defray these costs, they need to increase land-use mixes and densities and to utilize existing roadways as effectively as possible. We can no longer afford to be so profligate with our transportation infrastructure, and if we don't rein in these costs and rethink these systems creatively, the global economy will eventually force the issue. That's a bridge I don't think we want to cross.

The rebuilding of our infrastructure also depends on our taking into account the increasing incidence of catastrophic events, like hurricanes and droughts, driven by global climate change—a wicked problem if there ever was one. Climate change will demand that we reconsider the relationship between our industrial civilization and the natural environment as well as that between our private property rights and the greater public good. As we have learned from past recovery efforts following natural disasters, the government sometimes needs to step in to return former private property to public land uses, to protect everyone from the extraordinary cost and loss of life that can occur when too many people live in harm's way.

This need came to mind with two nearly simultaneous events: Hurricane Sandy's devastation along America's eastern seaboard and the public television broadcast of Ken Burns's documentary on the Dust Bowl of the 1930s.[5] Hurricane Sandy may seem almost the opposite of the Dust Bowl—after all, the former involved too much water and the latter too little. But the two disasters have more in common than first meets the eye, and as people are still recovering from Hurricane Sandy, by some accounts the second most expensive disaster in American history, after Hurricane Katrina, we could learn a lesson or two from the Dust Bowl.

THE NATURAL DISASTERS WE CREATE

Both Hurricane Sandy and the Dust Bowl were human-made disasters. In his documentary, Burns shows how excessive wheat production and poor tilling practices on Great Plains farms in the 1920s and early 1930s led to the loss of topsoil when drought arrived soon after the start of the Great Depression. Farmers' practice of deep plowing across so much of the prairie made the Dust Bowl almost inevitable. The disaster did not end until the federal government stepped in to convert large areas of land back to protected grassland, hire people to plant hundreds of miles of windbreaks, and educate farmers about how to till their fields in more sustainable ways. Humans created what many still view as the worst environmental disaster in American history, and humans responded to it by returning much of the landscape to its natural state.

Hurricane Sandy holds similar lessons. While some skeptics may still doubt that climate change played a role in turning that hurricane into a superstorm, no one can deny that development along low-lying coastal areas increased the numbers of buildings destroyed, people displaced, and lives disrupted by wind, flooding, and fire. The people who own property in these coastal areas understandably want to rebuild what the storm destroyed, but this raises the question of what kind of rebuilding should be permitted.

Just as prairie grasses are essential for keeping the soil of the southern plains from blowing away, the reefs, wetlands, and sandbars long the eastern and southern coasts of the United States play a role in buffering the effects of storms, and we would do well to restore them. Former New Jersey governors James J. Florio and Thomas H. Kean have said as much in calling for a kind of "Marshall Plan" in which "the key to reducing risk may be to avoid major investment in especially vulnerable areas," to "target those areas for restoration of green infrastructure that can protect the investments we do make," and "to incorporate the latest design practices and technologies into our buildings and communities . . . to protect the steadfastness of . . . residential and commercial development as well as public infrastructure."[6]

What might such a "Marshall Plan" look like? Improving resilience in the face of growing threats to our well-being demands, first, a change in our thinking. We need to get over our hubris and sense of invincibility and assume that bad things will happen, that our best intentions will go awry, and that our efforts to control nature through technology will ultimately fail. In that light, building a $6 billion sea barrier at the mouth of New York's harbor, as has been proposed, represents the very thing we should not do.[7] Such a project would waste money and might even make the effects of future storms worse. It would not stop tidal surges and flooding that could affect New York City from other directions—from Long Island Sound, for example, as happened during Hurricane Sandy. A surge barrier also wouldn't do anything to protect all of the coastal development outside it, which is where most of the damage from Hurricane Sandy occurred. Nor would it prevent the flooding that will occur as a result of an overall rise in sea levels, which will inundate low-lying areas regardless of what else we do.

Moreover, such a large-scale, singular solution to a complex problem would create the same kind of fracture-critical infrastructure that failed during the hurricane. The explosion in the electrical substation that blacked out lower Manhattan and the partial flooding of the city's subway system show how fracture-critical infrastructure makes people more vulnerable. We have to stop making so many people dependent on systems that are so easily breached and incapacitated. We can make these systems more resilient by "hardening" them with watertight barriers that can withstand the highest possible tidal surges; by breaking down their scale, so that a failure in one part of the system causes the least amount of damage or disruption; and by redesigning them so that critical systems lie above flood level. The builders of the elevated train line that is now the setting for the High Line park had the right idea.

But real resilience along U.S. coastal areas will require a shift in thinking as well. Extensive, interconnected systems, however carefully designed, will always remain vulnerable to failure; we can never stop falling tree limbs from bringing down electrical lines or tidal surges from flooding sewer systems or severing gas lines. The only real protection from such events will come with a dramatic dispersal of our infrastructure to the scale of individual structures or small clusters of buildings. The more every property or community along the coasts can generate its own power, store its own water, and serve to some extent as its own utility, the more we will prevent such large-scale catastrophes and extremely expensive disasters as those that resulted from two hurricanes—Katrina and Sandy—less than a decade apart.

The lessons from those hurricanes should also prompt a rethinking of how and where people live along the eastern and southern coasts of the United States. I live and work in Minneapolis and St. Paul, where almost all of the shoreline along the many lakes, creeks, and rivers remains in public ownership, providing one of the largest systems of linked open space in any city in the world. First proposed by nineteenth-century landscape architect H. W. S. Cleveland, these waterfront parks arose in part as a way of protecting private property from flooding, and they have had the additional benefit of enhancing the value of the property facing the publicly owned shores.[8] The governments of all U.S. coastal states would do well to consider such a model.

As a former resident of Connecticut, where almost all the shoreline is in private hands, I know the strength of property owners' attachment to living near the water. And I can just imagine the resistance to and expense of an enactment of eminent domain to return America's low-lying coastlines to public open space as a buffer against rising sea levels and storm surges. In an era so suspicious of government overreach, it seems unlikely that such a taking of private property for the public good—however justified—will ever happen.

It may happen organically, however. The insurance industry alone could significantly change the location and kind of development along exposed coastlines by either refusing to insure property there or making it so expensive that few could afford to build there. Local governments, too, could have an effect, depending on how much they reflect in their property assessments and planning policies the cost of protecting and responding to properties vulnerable to catastrophic events. Such financial impacts would almost inevitably lead property owners toward more resilient ways of living along the water.

Centuries ago, the Native peoples of North America understood the dangers of coastal living well. They lived along coastlines in lightweight dwellings that could be moved or easily rebuilt, reflecting their responsiveness to—and respect for—the forces of wind and waves. And almost everyone else who came to these shores, especially prior to the last century, had a similar humility when living in exposed coastal areas, building seaside cottages and rustic cabins easily rebuilt or replaced if lost because of tidal surges or hurricane-force winds. This points to one way of achieving a more resilient future for seaside communities: what we can't preserve as public open space, we should rebuild in ways that allow property owners to move quickly or to absorb damage at minimal cost.

If such willingness to retreat from or relinquish property to a storm sounds too un-American to some, the opposite tack of resistance also works, but it has to be done right. Here, the Coast Guard might serve as a model to emulate. Having long built structures intended to protect our coastlines— lighthouses, boathouses, barrier walls, and the like—the Coast Guard has learned to construct things that can withstand the strongest storms. When you visit such facilities—as I have a number of lighthouses as part of a former job—you see their toughness and sparseness; they are often built of concrete, with just about everything bolted down or built-in so as not to float or fly away.

That suggests another form of resilience, requiring that structures along our most exposed coastlines have the same solidity and durability, something that could be done through building codes and the leverage of insurance policies. Although such water-and-wind-resistant construction might be costly in the short term, the overall expenditure may well equal that of moving or rebuilding temporary structures. Either way, given the almost certain increase in the number and violence of coastal storms, the nature of coastal dwelling will—and indeed must—change.

We ended the Dust Bowl by returning much of the prairie landscape to its native state and changing how we treated the land we continue to occupy, and we will reduce the damage caused by disasters like Hurricane Sandy the same way. We need to take as much of our coastline as possible back to its presettlement state, using the applied environmental skills of landscape architects to ensure that we find the most effective—and cost-effective—ways of protecting ourselves from future superstorms. We also need to rebuild along our coasts in ways that are as resilient, temporary, or indestructible as possible, utilizing the knowledge of architects and engineers to create structures that can be moved easily or that can readily accommodate surges of wind and water. This may not sound like a "Marshall Plan," but it may be the only plan that, in the end, works.

Portions of this chapter were previously published in the Minneapolis–St. Paul *Star Tribune* (July 11, 2014, A11) in response to an opinion piece written by Randal O'Toole in the same paper (July 4, 2014, A7); "Our Political Bridges to Nowhere," *Huffington Post* (April 4, 2012), http://www.huffingtonpost.com/thomas-fisher/our-political-bridges-to-_b_1399767.html; and "Are Hurricanes Our Next Dust Bowl?," *Huffington Post* (December 5, 2012), http://www.huffingtonpost.com/thomas-fisher/hurricane-sandy_b_2207228.html.

[1] Charles L. Marohn Jr., *Thoughts on Building Strong Towns*, vol. 1 (Brainerd, Minn.: Strong Towns, 2012).

[2] American Society of Civil Engineers, "Report Card for America's Infrastructure," 2013, http://www.infrastructurereportcard.org.

[3] Bethany A. West and Rebecca B. Naumann, "Motor Vehicle-Related Deaths— United States, 2003–2007," *Morbidity and Mortality Weekly Report* 60, suppl. (January 14, 2011), http://www.cdc.gov/mmwr.

[4] Cynthia L. Ogden, Margaret D. Carroll, Brian K. Kit, and Katherine M. Flegal, *Prevalence of Obesity in the United States, 2009–2010*, NCHS Data Brief 82 (Hyattsville, Md.: National Center for Health Statistics, January 2012), http://www.cdc.gov.

[5] Ken Burns, dir., *The Dust Bowl* (2012), http://www.pbs.org.

[6] James J. Florio and Thomas H. Kean, "Hurricane Sandy Rebuilding Effort Is Opportunity to Confront Climate Change," *Star Ledger,* November 18, 2012, http://blog.nj.com.

[7] "Will New York Build $6 Billion Sea Barriers to Shield Itself from Another Superstorm Sandy?," Daily Mail, November 1, 2012, http://www.dailymail.co.uk.

[8] Hess Roise Consulting, "History of the Grand Rounds," Minneapolis Park and Recreation Board, 1999 http://www.minneapolisparks.org.

9

DESIGNED
DISASTERS

We put ourselves in harm's way not only by building cities in places where hurricanes can strike but also by making ourselves vulnerable to terrorism, a type of disaster by design. Terrorism has become such a global threat, and its opposition such a patriotic duty, that we have become blind to the lessons that terrorists have to offer. To compensate for their lack of military might and moral authority, terrorists exploit the often-unseen vulnerabilities in our systems as well as previously unimagined collisions among disparate things. The rest of the world can outsmart terrorists by thinking abductively, as they do, and looking for the gaps that exist in the designed environment.

In recent years, terrorist acts have been happening with increasing frequency around the world. In 2010 alone, more than thirty countries experienced a total of 103 terrorist attacks—mainly bombings and assassinations—that killed at least 1,368 people and injured at least 4,324.[1] While the world community has rightfully condemned such violence, these politically motivated assaults by nongovernmental assailants against unarmed civilians have also served to highlight our own vulnerabilities. Terrorism relies not only on the element of surprise but also on the ingenuity of its perpetrators in exploiting weaknesses in vital infrastructure and in imagining how different systems rarely thought of as interrelated can catastrophically fail when brought together. With perversely elegant efficiency, terrorists have learned how to spread maximum fear and leverage maximum responses from victims with minimum effort and expense— apart, of course, from the fact that terrorists often willingly lose their lives in the act of attacking.

Countries around the globe, but especially the United States, have responded to terrorism by doing precisely what the terrorists have no doubt wanted them to do. More often than not, nations have overreacted (it is useful to remember that we are more likely to be struck by lightning than to be attacked by a terrorist) and invested huge sums to defend against threats of terrorism. The U.S. General Accounting Office reported that in 2003 the United States spent $11 billion on nonmilitary efforts to combat terrorism overseas, and by 2006, the Department of Homeland Security's budget for security inside the United States amounted to $30.8 billion.[2] When we compare what just nineteen people spent to carry out the devastating September 11, 2001, attacks on the Pentagon and the World Trade

Center—on tuition for flight training school, household tools available at any
hardware store, and a few domestic airfares—with what the United States
has spent since then to combat terrorism, we can see how extraordinarily
effective a very small group of modestly funded terrorists can be in com-
manding the attention and sapping the resources of a superpower.

We have come to the point where nations fighting terrorists find it difficult
to know whether or not they have succeeded—or even what actually
constitutes a victory. As a 2007 Congressional Research Service report puts
it: "Among the various U.S. government agencies involved in anti-terrorism
efforts, there is currently no common set of criteria for measuring success."
The report likens terrorist activity to "a process which includes discrete,
quantum-like changes or jumps often underscoring its asymmetric and
nonlinear nature."[3]

If terrorism does, indeed, have a quantum-like character, then conventional defenses are likely to be ineffectual in fighting it—perhaps because
we have been thinking in terms of the wrong metaphor. Terrorists may be
our enemies, intent on doing us harm, but their ability to leap to new
tactics in unpredictable ways—as we saw on 9/11, when they moved from
the detonating of car bombs to the hijacking of fully loaded jets—requires
that we think in new ways. As the old military saying goes, we cannot win
the next war by fighting the last one. The intrusive and costly efforts we
devote to screening people and baggage at airports, for example, are based
on the assumption that what terrorists have tried once, they will try again.
While some level of passenger and baggage screening makes sense—
terrorism or not—it does little good when terrorists already seem to have
moved on to new tactics, such as shipping explosives overseas in printer
cartridges. Airport screening might even lull us into thinking that we are
safer than we are and distract us from the vital work of anticipating the
new formats and different locations of future attacks.

Rather than focusing so much on protecting ourselves against the last
type of attack, we should work to develop more creative strategies. For
example, undercover FBI agents provided a suspected terrorist in Portland,
Oregon, with a dummy bomb and waited to see how he planned to use it
before arresting him. Better yet, we should try to think like terrorists, to
imagine where and how they might attack before they do, acknowledging
the creative thinking they deploy in devising attacks and preempting them.

Why should we have been surprised that terrorists, stymied by passenger screening at airports, would instead send explosives in minimally screened packages in shipping containers?

Terrorism, in other words, serves as a kind of critique of the design flaws in our systems. These assailants have taken advantage of weaknesses we have often overlooked and have exploited gaps we have not considered carefully enough, and the more we can recognize those shortcomings and close those gaps before terrorists get there, the more we will succeed in stopping them, and at a much lower cost. If, for example, car bombs remain difficult to detect, then why do we even allow cars in crowded pedestrian districts that could become targets, such as New York's Times Square? Might we find that good urban design thinking—such as encouraging more car-free, pedestrian-oriented streets—also proves effective in thwarting terrorists?

Acknowledging the creative critique embedded in terrorist acts does not mean that we condone or even admire the acts or their politics. But thinking of terrorism as a form of design critique also seems far removed from our current approach to antiterrorism, which has focused on reactive tactics rather than on the creative speculation and scenario building that characterize design thinking. But these approaches are not mutually exclusive. We clearly need to keep our guard up, but we can achieve a much greater level of protection at much lower cost by beating the terrorists at their own game, using the same degree of low-cost innovation against them that they have used against us.

We might begin to out-imagine terrorists by looking, generically, at where they have struck and with what strategies in mind. For example, the 9/11 terrorists identified gaps between seemingly disconnected systems and then exploited those gaps by bringing the systems together, stressing them beyond their designed limits, and causing their catastrophic failure. They saw that we had designed highly efficient skyscrapers such as the Twin Towers and had developed an extensive and efficient airline system, with planes able to fly very fast, fully loaded with people and fuel. But in neither case did we design these two systems to withstand a direct, full-speed collision, even though their proximity in large cities has always made this a distinct possibility. The 9/11 terrorists recognized this blind spot and took advantage of it, to spectacular and diabolical effect.

Terrorists have targeted places where large concentrations of people congregate in relatively enclosed areas with few means of escape. In this way they have used the density and proximity of these environments to their advantage and against us, maximizing death and destruction. We saw this strategy at work on 9/11 not only at the World Trade Center but also in the attack on the Pentagon. However well the U.S. Department of Defense headquarters was defended from a ground attack, the terrorists saw its vulnerability from the air, given the proximity of two major airports and the frequency of commercial airline schedules. The presence of so many military people in the Pentagon—at 6.5 million square feet, the world's largest office building—made it visible and vulnerable, and almost impossible to defend fully.

Terrorists have also identified popular public gathering areas, places with easy access, diverse populations, and events or activities that distract attention. We have seen this tactic in operation in the car bombings that have plagued major cities like Baghdad and in the similar actions that almost occurred in New York's Times Square and Portland's Pioneer Square. Here the vulnerability arises not from a gap between systems or the density of people within a system but instead from the sheer number of people and systems intersecting in a given place. Karl Popper's *The Open Society and Its Enemies* comes to mind here.[4] Terrorists, who hold what Popper calls "the tribal ideal," use the sheer openness of modern society against us.

PRESERVING THE OPEN SOCIETY

We have seen how easily we can overreact to the threat of terrorism and relinquish our freedom. There is a fine line between appropriate caution and palpable paranoia, and aspects of our physical environment have come to reflect our fears, with bollards around buildings that hardly seem like terrorist targets and surveillance cameras in places that appear unlikely to harbor bomb carriers. Even more disturbing has been the rise of racial and ethnic profiling in public places, with vigilance against terrorism sometimes seeming like an excuse for people to act out their prejudices, be they religiously, ethnically, or politically motivated.

So how can we resist terrorism while also maintaining an open society that values political freedom and human rights? To answer that question, we first need to challenge some of our assumptions about antiterrorism.

To prevent the collision of two systems, like airplanes and skyscrapers, we should ask, for example: Why have we built a very tall building in an exposed location, near the water's edge, at 9/11's Ground Zero? While that action might have cathartic value, as evidence of undefeated national spirit and civic pride, and while it clearly has financial value to the owners and developers, it also shows, as some have observed, that we have not learned from the attack and have simply created a new, albeit more fortified, target. A city of buildings of more uniform height, with a mat-like urban form in which few, if any, structures stick up above the rest, makes the kind of aerial attack that happened in September 2001 much more difficult.

That may seem at odds with the way cities like New York have evolved, but other modern cities—Washington and Paris, for example—have much more uniform skylines, with central-city height limits in place for a long time, so these kinds of restrictions do not necessarily undercut the economic viability or livability of cities. Indeed, height limits can increase urban viability and livability by increasing density more uniformly. Just because we can build high doesn't mean we should, and the terrorists have given us a compelling reason not to.

One area in which the West seems to lack imagination is in our widespread inability to understand what skyscrapers mean to many people around the world. At a time when, as Branko Milanovic of the World Bank notes, the "total income of the richest 25 million Americans is equal to [the] total income of almost 2 billion poor people," tall towers, especially in financial capitals like New York, can become symbols of the profound inequities of the global economy and targets of people's rage.[5] Moderating the lust for building ever-taller towers becomes a matter not just of defense but also of deference to the billions of people for whom such structures are reminders of what they will never have a chance to achieve.

This may also help explain the frequency of terrorist attacks on trains and airplanes and the buildings associated with these modes of transportation. By offering concentrations of the kinds of people that terrorists like to target, such settings also symbolize the mobility of the world's wealthiest populations and the lack of it among the majority of people on the planet. Because of that symbolism, diversifying the types of transportation and moderating the concentrations of people represents not only self-protection but also the self-effacement that comes from imagining what mobility must look like to those who have very little. Multimodal transportation strategies, including mass transit, electric vehicles, and bicycles, downplay the differences between rich and poor and possibly even enhance empathy for the diverse ways in which people move around the world; at the same time, they increase travel options and decrease dependence on fossil fuels.

Understanding the symbolism of wealth and poverty should lead us, as well, to question the large concentrations of people working in politically charged places like the Pentagon. While necessary in the past, when coworkers had to interact face-to-face, transfer documents by hand, and so forth, such high populations in massive buildings have become not only less necessary in the digital age but also less wise. We know from the research on telecommuting that distributing work among digitally linked and physically dispersed networks of employees can offer people greater flexibility in how and where they work while enhancing their productivity and loyalty. Distributing employees has the added benefit of reducing the likelihood any one building will become a target for terrorism, since no one place has many people doing a particular type of work. In a sense, this turns terrorists' own strategy of operating in small, distributed cells against them. When under attack, terrorist organizations have often shown the resilience of distributed networks, becoming almost impossible to disrupt even with the capture of key individuals.

Such strategies may seem counter to what we have come to associate with our open society. Tall skyscrapers, high-speed transportation, large-scale office complexes—all have become symbols of modernity, with its emphasis on maximizing individual freedom. The "Freedom Tower" at Ground Zero reflects this often-unquestioned attitude, as if choosing to construct a tower taller than the fallen ones expresses something important about the United States. But what freedoms might we be losing in the process? Do such symbols of freedom trump the loss of actual liberties, such as the freedom to live without anxiety, ever-present surveillance, or invasions of personal privacy? Does it make sense to keep constructing obvious and easily identifiable targets for terrorists when we can design other ways of living, working, and traveling that would make attacks more difficult?

As long as we see antiterrorism in primarily defensive terms, we will not change the paradigm we have followed since 9/11. Keeping existing targets, like the Pentagon, in place or building new ones, like the Freedom Tower, as if to taunt the terrorists represents not a creative solution to the problem but a confused one. If we don't want another terrorist attack, having buildings that seem to dare terrorists to attack again seems foolhardy, a matter of our ignoring the real design problem—and opportunity—that terrorism presents.

WHAT DESIGN CAN DO

Once we see global terrorism as identifying the design flaws in our systems and infrastructures, we can start down a more sustainable and affordable path toward protecting ourselves. Design thinking can help in various ways.

Rather than continuing to do what has not worked very well, we can use design thinking to reevaluate how we live and work in order to make the most expensive security measures almost unnecessary. Good design achieves the greatest impact with the least expenditure, something that terrorists themselves have done quite effectively, and we can foil them if we become as creative as they have been, preventing them from disrupting our lives with the least expenditure on our part, not the most, as we are doing now. Ironically, the distributed networks of people, diverse modes of transportation, and modestly scaled buildings and neighborhoods that characterize cities in the countries from which many terrorists have come also offer models of how we can resist terrorist attacks. As a result of the threat of terrorism, we might all begin to live more community-oriented and less compulsive lives than many people now do in fast-paced, high-pressure Western cities.

Design thinking might also help us look not at what terrorists have already done but rather at where they might attack in the future. Applying that predictive aspect of design would involve understanding the nature of terrorists' strategies rather than focusing on defending against their effects. Were a design team given the charge of imagining how to create the maximum amount of death or destruction in a city with the least amount of money or effort, it would produce a useful road map for where we need to focus our attention and expend limited resources. We need less homeland security and more homeland creativity applied to the problem of terrorism, seeing it as a competitive strategy good at getting the maximum attention and having the maximum impact for a minimum of means.

If we view terrorism in this way, we might employ the wealth of entrepreneurial talent in our midst to begin to develop counterstrategies that can eliminate opportunities for terrorism and nullify its effects, as we might with any competing organization.

Finally, design thinking might help us envision a future other than one in which we forsake our freedoms out of fear. Might the creation of a police state and the bankrupting of our public coffers with security measures be just what some terrorists have in mind for us?[6] Instead, we might begin to conceive of a future in which we protect our freedoms as individuals and our liberty as a people with the least surveillance and lowest expenditure possible. What if, rather than the massive offices and ghettoized residential developments in which so many of the wealthy of the world now live and work, we imagine communities of people who know and watch out for each other, who have enough different options for living and working that they can avoid crowds and congestion, and who interact with such a diversity of fellow citizens that no one place will become a target?

We have tended, at least in the United States, to equate strength and security with a testosterone-laden, tough-guy deployment of force, ringing government buildings with barriers and our national borders with walls. That may have been effective when others fought by the same rules we did, but in the twenty-first century, when no amount of military force can counter the actions of a few individuals bent on destroying as much as they can in the process of destroying themselves, we need to change the image we have of strength and security. It will require not just force but also finesse; not just crushing blows but also creative foils; not just defensive intelligence but also design intelligence. The terrorists have shown us how this works. They have proven to be exceptionally inventive in their strategies, from shoe bombs to printer cartridge explosives, and yet equally incompetent in their execution, given the number of failed terrorist attacks we have seen lately. We can do much better than them on both counts, but we first have to stop being terrorized and start thinking in new ways.

Maybe the greatest failure of imagination in the fight against terrorism, however, lies in our addressing the symptoms rather than the underlying causes of the problem. Focusing on symptoms—the actual terrorist acts themselves—leads to an emphasis on security. Were we to focus instead on causes, we would be forced to deal with what many in the West do not want to face: the enormous and widening gap between the relatively few wealthy in the world and the vast majority of hopelessly poor. Ending terrorism may ultimately require not arms but alms.

This chapter was first published as "Terrorism as a Form of Design Critique," *Architectoni.ca* 2 (2013), http://www.ccaasmag.org/arch-issues/arch-vol2/ Fisher_terrorism.pdf.

[1] Worldwide Incidents Tracking System, https://wits.nctc.gov.

[2] U.S. General Accounting Office, *Combating Terrorism: Interagency Framework and Agency Programs to Address the Overseas Threat* (Washington, D.C.: U.S. GAO, 2003), http://www.gao.gov.

[3] Raphael Perl, *Combating Terrorism: The Challenge of Measuring Effectiveness,* CRS Report for Congress RL33160 (Washington, D.C.: Congressional Research Service, 2007), 2.

[4] Karl Popper, *The Open Society and Its Enemies,* 2 vols. (Princeton, N.J.: Princeton University Press, 1962).

[5] Branko Milanovic, "True World Income Distribution, 1988 and 1993: First Calculation Based on Household Surveys Alone," *Economic Journal* 112 (January 2002): 89.

[6] Charles Townshend, *Terrorism: A Very Short Introduction* (Oxford: Oxford University Press, 2002).

PART IV

PUBLIC HEALTH

Few fields have done more to give alms to the poor and the ill than public health. Like much of the designed world, public health remains relatively invisible to most of us; in the United States, at least, we take for granted access to clean water, fresh air, safe food, and working sanitary systems, and we do not think about these things until we encounter their absence. The same occurs with design: we don't notice it until its failures become apparent, and, like breakdowns in our public health system, design failures can have dire consequences.

The first chapter of this part recounts the early history of the American public health movement, which arose in the wake of myriad failures in the design of urban infrastructure. A designer, the noted landscape architect Frederick Law Olmsted, played a key role in that movement when he led the Sanitary Commission during the Civil War. He recognized the link between good planning and good health. Because many Americans have largely forgotten our more polluted past, too many politicians today feel free to demean the value of planning and parks—something that the design community needs to counter as forcefully as possible.

Chapter 11 expands on the connection between human and environmental health by considering the diverse ethical reasons for protecting open space and the natural environment. It reviews the various ways in which we conceive of nature and its value and looks at our responsibilities toward environmental health in an increasingly over-crowded world. If we don't accept these responsibilities, nature will force us to do so in ways that none of us would want.

The final chapter of this part envisions one of the greatest invisible threats to our health, a viral pandemic enabled by a designed system that we rarely see as a threat to public health: the transcontinental airline system. The chapter looks at how we have addressed disease transfer in the past and examines what we might learn from that to protect ourselves today, using abductive reasoning to suggest simple yet effective solutions.

10

THE
INFRASTRUCTURE
OF HEALTH

We tend to think of infrastructure in terms of the economy and the smooth functioning of our daily lives, but much of the impetus to construct the water, sanitary, and park systems in the United States arose out of public health concerns. The career of nineteenth-century landscape architect Frederick Law Olmsted reveals the importance of that connection between the built environment and the health of the general public. Although best known for his design of New York's Central Park, Olmsted served for two years during the Civil War as the general secretary of the United States Sanitary Commission, dedicated to improving the sanitation of the Union army's military camps and the health of Union soldiers.[1] This might seem like a detour in Olmsted's career, an admirable but nevertheless tangential interlude in his progress as a landscape architect. But when we examine Olmsted's Sanitary Commission work in light of the history of public health, it is clear that here—just as with his foundational work in public parks—Olmsted set an example for the future.

Consider the state of public health in the period just before the Civil War. Commencing in Germany in the 1840s, the public health movement arose out of concerns about the typhoid and typhus epidemics that had begun to endanger Europe's industrial slums and the cholera epidemic that had hit London years earlier.[2] German physician Rudolf Virchow, one of the founders of the social medicine movement, was among the first to see the connection between poor sanitation and disease. In the United States, in 1847, the American Medical Association, after studying the unhygienic conditions in American cities and aware of Virchow's work, called for improvements to sanitation systems and living quarters in order to avoid an epidemic; sanitary commissions were established in several states, where they advocated for measures such as the better venting of domestic water closets to disperse the noxious odors once considered a leading cause of disease.

THE DESIGNER AS PUBLIC INTELLECTUAL

Olmsted, then living in New York City and working as managing editor of Putnam's Monthly, was well aware of this transformation in the understanding of ill health.[3] He traversed the packed streets daily, passing by the crowded tenements of lower Manhattan on his way to and from his office, and he saw the effects of what came to be called the Great Fire of

1845, which destroyed three hundred buildings in New York and prompted the city to enact the nation's first comprehensive building code in 1850. He also heard the debates going on in the 1850s about the health effects of poor sanitation in tenements, which culminated in New York passing the nation's first tenement law in 1867 to control unhealthy housing conditions. The law regulated, among other things, the placement and drainage of outdoor latrines.

In 1857, several events propelled Olmsted away from his role as an editor and public intellectual, which required that he report and reflect on these conditions, to a new role that required him to play a central part in changing them. In the summer of 1857 his publishing venture failed (although his vision for *Putnam's Monthly* would live on in the *Atlantic Monthly* and *Harper's Magazine,* both founded that year). That same summer Manhattan erupted in riots as street gangs in overcrowded neighborhoods clashed with police, and the first public health convention convened in Philadelphia. Also that same year, Olmsted became the superintendent of Central Park, then being planned, and less than a year later, in April 1858, the Greensward Plan that he and architect Calvert Vaux had prepared won the design competition for the park.[4]

Echoing the miasma theory, still in popular circulation, Olmsted argued that great public parks such as his proposed Greensward would function as the "lungs of the city"—green open spaces where city dwellers could breathe clean air. More accurate, in hindsight, was the emphasis that Olmsted and Vaux placed on good sanitation—on well-drained land, well-circulating waterways, and well-designed sanitation facilities—which reflected their knowledge of the sanitary movement and the connection the nascent field of public health had made between polluted water and disease.

Olmsted served as the chief architect of Central Park up until 1861, when political tensions with the park's comptroller and board of commissioners led him to resign the position. Meanwhile, the reform-minded Unitarian minister Henry Whitney Bellows had observed and admired Olmsted's managerial skills in overseeing the construction of Central Park. Bellows, along with a group of prominent physicians, wanted to form an American sanitary commission patterned on one in Britain, with the intent of improving the sanitation of the Union army camps. Bellows asked Olmsted if he would serve as the general secretary and chief executive officer of the new U.S. Sanitary Commission, which had been authorized by the War Department and created by legislation signed by President Abraham Lincoln in June 1861, two months after the start of the Civil War. Olmsted agreed.

Amazingly, the federal government at first resisted the requests of the Sanitary Commission to be allowed to enter the military camps with the intent of improving living quarters. Some in the government worried that the commission's efforts would distract the military from the campaign then under way—a hesitancy that underscores that public health, as a discipline, had not yet had much impact on either the broader public or even the military establishment. Evidence of the military's lack of awareness was all too abundant, from the rudimentary army hospitals then in operation to the archaic operations of the government's military bureau. And military attitudes reflected the wider contemporary acceptance of chronic illness as a part of everyday urban life. Periodic epidemics of smallpox and yellow fever got people's attention, but in the mid-nineteenth century crowded housing and bad sanitation made killers of more common ailments such as tuberculosis, malaria, and respiratory and digestive diseases.

A turning point—an increase in awareness of the harmful effects of poor sanitation—came in the wake of the Union army's horrible defeat at the First Battle of Bull Run, in July 1861 in Manassas, Virginia. Beyond the military reasons for this defeat—including the inexperience of the new troops—the Sanitary Commission showed how the soldiers' poor living environs had contributed to the rout, and the U.S. government finally gave Olmsted and his medical colleagues access to the camps. In his September 1861 report on Bull Run, Olmsted showed how "excessive fatigue . . . heat, and . . . want of food and drink" led to the "demoralization" of the troops. Such observations may seem far removed from his experience in the design of public landscapes, but Olmsted viewed the field broadly and did not separate the quality of a person's life from the quality of the physical or natural environment. The Sanitary Commission inspected and made recommendations not just about the soldiers' exhaustion levels but also about design issues such as the location of camps, the provision of drainage and waste disposal, the ventilation of tents, and the storage and preparation of food.

Olmsted directed the Sanitary Commission through mid-1863, at which point conflicts with colleagues and his executive committee, combined with exhaustion from overwork, led him to resign. The commission continued to operate through the end of the Civil War along the lines Olmsted had established for it, and it became the core of the American Red Cross, founded twenty years later. Olmsted resumed his extraordinary career in landscape architecture, for which he is best known. Yet it now seems clear that with Olmsted's resignation from the Sanitary Commission a potentially vital connection was severed—the connection between physical design and public health. The disconnection would remain in place for more than a century, and only very recently have the ties begun to be restored.

DESIGN AND EPIDEMIOLOGY

This disconnection was not Olmsted's fault, nor can we attribute it to landscape architecture as a field. In the decades after the Civil War, public health, as a discipline, began to move in a very different direction, focusing less on the *physical,* on sanitary conditions, and more on the *medical,* on epidemiology. To be sure, this new emphasis resulted in part from the very success of the sanitation movement in the latter half of the nineteenth century, when dramatic improvements in city building standards led to the elimination of many of the sources of diseases that had once been widespread. Indoor plumbing and water closets eventually became required in housing, as did sewers that separated storm water and wastewater. And when New York City passed the Tenement Housing Act of 1901, features we now consider essential to basic livability, such as daylight, natural ventilation, sanitation, and security, became available to even the poorest people.

Public health entered an epidemiological phase after the Civil War for another reason as well: the growing efficacy of the medical and pharmaceutical fields in ameliorating chronic diseases and epidemic outbreaks. Through the development of new drugs, the public health community managed to control once-serious threats ranging from smallpox and measles to polio and diphtheria. And through the application of environmental chemicals, diseases such as malaria and yellow fever virtually disappeared from North America. Improved living standards certainly helped to curb such diseases, but the physical environment became, at best, a secondary concern for public health.

That has changed in recent years. The public health community continues to have success in curbing the incidence of diseases that respond to drug or chemical interventions, but today we face public health challenges very different in nature from those of earlier generations. Today millions of people on the planet, especially in the rapidly growing cities of the developing world, endure living conditions much worse than those Olmsted witnessed in lower Manhattan, and almost a billion lack easy access to clean water. We confront as well—perhaps for the first time in history— the public health challenges of prosperity.

We now identify diseases like cancer, heart failure, diabetes, emphysema, and even obesity as "lifestyle diseases"—that is, diseases resulting from individual and social behaviors, personal choices, and cultural patterns. Indeed, the Centers for Disease Control and Prevention has been studying "urban sprawl and public health" for several years now.[5] We understand the problem: the increasingly sedentary, high-calorie lifestyle that has become common in wealthier countries has made obesity an epidemic, with all of the attendant malignancies and infarctions that come with it. Here, the causes lie even closer, in the car-dominated cities we build and the corn-syrup-laced beverages and high-fat foods we produce and market so aggressively.

THE LANDSCAPE OF HEALTH

And so, almost a century and a half after Olmsted left the U.S. Sanitary Commission, we find ourselves once again in an era when the larger issues of public health intersect the practices of landscape architecture, architecture, and urbanism. And we might well wonder: What would Olmsted do were he alive today and facing such paradoxical threats, arising from scarcity in some places and abundance in others? We might hazard a few guesses as guides to what we might do now.

First, he would write and speak out about these issues. Olmsted achieved lasting fame as a landscape architect, but he began his career as a public intellectual, and he remained one to the very end of his career. As we can see from his collected papers, Olmsted wrote well and persuasively, and we need to do the same today. Landscape architecture, like all of the design disciplines, has become extremely dependent on what others—clients mostly, but also communities—deem important; for this reason landscape architects more often than not implement the visions or policies of others. In an era of great change, such as ours, we need to adapt the methods Olmsted used in another turbulent time: defining the discourse, identifying the problems, and proposing the strategies and policies needed to resolve them. Some of that can happen through design, but nothing can replace the power of persuasive writing and speaking. We need to put aside the mouse more often, and take to the keyboard.

Second, Olmsted would partner with a wider range of disciplines than designers typically do now. At the Sanitary Commission, Olmsted's colleagues included an architect, Alfred Bloor, and an engineer, Bridgham Curtis, but they also included physicians, theologians, philanthropists, and financial analysts. Olmsted needed such radically interdisciplinary teams to do the varied work required of the commission, and the same is true of public health today. The causes of homegrown lifestyle diseases and of global pandemics are complex and interwoven; it will take many disciplines, working together, to devise solutions.

And of course Olmsted's example suggests that the landscape architect can function not only as an expert in how we inhabit and steward the land but also as a manager of diverse teams of people. Olmsted knew something about sanitation, but, just as important, he knew how to organize and operate a complex commission and oversee the work of a large multidisciplinary staff. This may in fact be among the more important skills landscape architects can offer today, as the field studies how settlement patterns, transportation modes, water quality, and so on relate to the ramifying problems of public health in an urbanizing world.

Finally, Olmsted would bring a sense of high professional purpose to the work. Throughout his life he pursued larger social goals, regardless of cost, as opposed to the politically expedient or personally beneficial course. His conflicts with Central Park's board of commissioners and the Sanitary Commission's executive committee arose out of his insistence that they authorize the funding necessary to do the job right. To a lesser extent, the conflicts also followed from his resistance to playing political favorites, something that, particularly in the case of Central Park, alienated him from the New York political bosses.

Surely a similar politics is at least partly responsible for the environments we have created for ourselves. The low-density development that contributes to our obesity, the air and water pollution that contributes to our cancer rates, and the systemic impoverishment that contributes to our pandemics—all are traceable to political decisions and cultures that favor property owners, developers, and landlords, and the banks and shareholders who benefit as well. We will never confront our contemporary public health problems in any meaningful way unless we question the prevailing power structures—unless we make a powerful case for long-range social good and challenge those who skew the rules in favor of short-term gain for an increasingly remote elite. It will take professionalism and political will, but the price of ignoring our contemporary public health crises—pandemics that endanger billions, chronic diseases that damage lives and by extension the whole society—will be steep, and we will all pay it.

Frederick Law Olmsted's career as a landscape architect foretold where that field would go for its first century and a half in America. His career as the leader of the Sanitary Commission may foretell where the design fields need to go in the next century. The health of all of us may depend on it.

This chapter was originally published in slightly different form as "Frederick Law Olmsted and the Campaign for Public Health," Places (November 15, 2010), http://places.designobserver.com/feature/frederick-law-olmsted-and-the-campaign-for-public-health/15619.

[1] See Frederick Law Olmsted, *Defending the Union: The Civil War and the U.S. Sanitary Commission, 1861–1863,* ed. Jane Turner Censer (Baltimore: Johns Hopkins University Press, 1986). All quotations from Olmsted in this chapter are from this source.
[2] John Duffy, *The Sanitarians: A History of American Public Health* (Champaign: University of Illinois Press, 1990).
[3] Melvin Kalfus, *Frederick Law Olmsted: The Passion of a Public Artist* (New York: New York University Press, 1990).
[4] Witold Rybczynski, *A Clearing in the Distance: Frederick Law Olmsted and America in the 19th Century* (New York: Touchstone, 1999).
[5] Howard Frumkin, "Urban Sprawl and Public Health," *Public Health Reports* 117 (May/June 2002): 201–17.

11

HEALTHY
LANDSCAPES

As America's first landscape architect, Frederick Law Olmsted knew that we cannot separate human health from the health of the environment and that we can do nothing more to protect our own health than ensure the health of the ecosystems around us, not only conserving the natural world as much as possible but also adapting ourselves to it. The idea that we need to adapt to nature runs counter to the ethic that has dominated Western culture for many centuries; we have long viewed the natural world as ours to use and exploit for our ends. But that ethic must change if we hope to prevent the further collapse of planetary ecosystems and, with them, our own health and well-being.

What might this look like, our adapting to the natural world? Various cultures might answer that question differently, but in Western culture it seems particularly difficult to answer. Western ethics has long focused on the responsibilities that people have to each other as individuals and groups, with little attention to our obligations beyond that. And because the West has also maintained a sharp division between the human world and the natural world, the very notion of what we owe the landscape is, at first, hard to fathom.[1] A core concept of Western ethics, for example, revolves around the issue of reciprocity, of doing to others as you would want them to do to you, as stated in the Bible (Luke 6:31). While this is a useful principle to keep in mind, it assumes that ethics encompasses only those able to understand such a principle and to reciprocate, something that, with the possible exception of pets, most of the animal and plant world cannot do.

Attitudes have begun to change in recent decades, however. Philosophers such as Peter Singer have argued that because all animals have "sentience"— the ability to feel pain and thus to suffer—we, as sentient beings ourselves, have an ethical responsibility to reduce the pain and suffering of animals just as we have that responsibility toward other people.[2] Singer's argument gets us partway to the question of our ethical responsibility to the landscape, since damage to ecosystems and animal habitat causes the sentient beings that live there to suffer. But the landscape per se figures only indirectly, as a support for animal life, in Singer's ethics, and in that sense his thought still reflects the dominant Western idea that the nonsentient world of plants and natural resources generally exists to serve the needs of sentient beings.

That idea has led Western ethics to largely embrace our responsibility to the landscape in terms of how it serves the needs of humans. Most of the legal systems in Western countries, for example, recognize private property rights as a foundational principle and uphold the entitlement of property owners to do what they want with the land they own within certain constraints, such as zoning and environmental laws, that protect the rights and safety of other people.[3] While some environmental laws also protect other animal species or certain types of ecosystems, these regulations still exist within an ethical framework that privileges human interests over those of nonhumans.

Within that framework, however, there are at least three different approaches to the protection of—and, indirectly, our ethical responsibilities to—the landscape in Western culture. These three approaches differ in terms of the time frame within which they look at our relationship to the landscape, with one focused mainly on the past, another on the present, and a third on the future. And each of these three approaches aligns with a different type of ethics: duty ethics, contract ethics, and utilitarian ethics. And yet, while Western ethics has long had a sense of human responsibility toward the landscape, these three approaches have proven inadequate in protecting the landscape, necessitating a fourth approach that involves a reexamination of ourselves as much as a resetting of our relationship with the natural world around us.

THE DUTIFUL LANDSCAPE

In Western cultures, and indeed in most cultures around the world, the landscapes to which people seem most attracted and that receive the greatest care are those related to our ancestors and to our past. Such landscapes can range dramatically in type. On one extreme are the cemeteries where we bury and memorialize the dead. These landscapes typically remain cleared of their native habitat, as if we don't want many nonhuman "sentient beings" among the nonsentient human remains interred in such places. Cemeteries stand as idealized landscapes, carefully planted, tended, and maintained at great cost, in terms of both money and resources, to remind us of the open ground and occasional tree cover that characterized the African savannas in which we evolved as a species and from which we have spread across the globe.[4] In cemeteries, at the least in the West, we return our bodies to places that remind us of where the human genome began.

At the other extreme, we set aside wilderness areas, forest preserves, and "national parks" in which the natural world, at least as we define it, can flourish without much interference from people. These places, mostly cleared of human habitat, reflect the sense of responsibility most governments now have toward at least small parts of the landscape and the sense of loss most people have toward the world as it was before our species became so dominant and ever present on the planet. Some, such as the environmental historian William Cronon, have criticized the setting aside of wilderness areas as our attempt to assuage our guilt for the environmental damage we continue to do everywhere else.[5] Still, wilderness areas do represent some sense of our ethical duty to nature and our desire to carve out some part of the landscape so that it is available to everyone and not beholden to private property rights.

The care with which we tend to these landscapes that hold the remains of our ancestors or the memory of our species recalls the duty ethics most often associated with Immanuel Kant.[6] Kant argued that we should do what we know to be right, regardless of the consequences to us personally. He also argued that we all know what is the right thing to do in a situation, even if we don't act on that knowledge, because of what he called "categorical imperatives" such as treating others as ends and not means and acting as if everything we do holds as universal. Kant saw those categorical imperatives applying to other human beings, although taken at face value his ethics applies equally to our relationship with the natural world. We can take Kant's argument to mean that we have a duty to treat other species, as much as other people, as ends and not means, and to act with the laws of nature always in mind, regardless of the consequences this might have for us personally in terms of lost wealth or power.

Kant also saw a connection between ethics and aesthetics that relates to how we see these landscapes that memorialize our past. He argued that just as we need to do what is right in a disinterested or unselfish way, we should appreciate beautiful or sublime places not as something we own or possess but as something we share with others. We share with other humans, for example, a liking of the savanna landscape from which we all evolved and a fascination with the wildernesses in which we spent most of our history as a species, and because of that we care for these places and willingly take that on as our duty. The challenge comes, as Cronon argues, in applying that same sense of obligation not just to isolated bits of landscape but to the entire planet, something we have so far failed to do, in part because of the contractual approach to the landscape and to ethics.

THE CONTRACTUAL LANDSCAPE

We primarily take responsibility for the landscapes that we inhabit by dividing them up into either public or private ownership, available for our use within legal frameworks and regulatory constraints. This conversion of the landscape into property may work for modern human societies, but it has increasingly not worked for other species and for ecosystems as a whole. For example, most development of the landscape for human occupation involves the destruction of the habitat for other species, as if we cannot inhabit a piece of land without first evicting others already living there. After clearing a site of its native habitat, we then often replant the property with flora in combinations and compositions that we find aesthetically pleasing, as if we want the natural world to approximate as much as possible an artificial one.

Landscape architecture, as a term and as a discipline, captures this idea perfectly. Humans have become so dominant as a species that, as environmentalist Bill McKibben has argued, we have come to the "end of nature," where no part of the planet remains untouched or unaffected by our actions.[7] In that light, the earth has become a design problem, something that we have control over and responsibility for and something that we need to steward and maintain as carefully as we do the architecture we inhabit. Too few people understand or appreciate the important work that landscape architects do. But in the broadest sense, we have all become "architects" of the landscape, given our pervasive impact on the planet through the multiplying effects of technology.

How we handle that responsibility depends on how we see the "state of nature" embedded in contract ethics. One of the first contract ethicists, Thomas Hobbes, argued in the seventeenth century that human life in the state of nature is "nasty, brutish, and short" and that humans, living in constant conflict, enter into a "social contract," trading some degree of personal freedom for the peace and security of obeying the rules and regulations of governments.[8] Jean-Jacques Rousseau, in the eighteenth century, argued the contrary position, that life in the state of nature is peaceful and bountiful, and conflict arises only after we divide up the natural environment into private property and experience the corrupting influence of society.[9]

These two positions have guided the West's treatment of the natural world ever since. Romantics, in the tradition of Rousseau, see nature as a refuge from society and want the landscape to seem as "natural" as possible, while realists, in the shadow of Hobbes, see nature as something to control and want the landscape to reflect human rationality and social order as much as possible. We also see the tension between these two forms of contract ethics in our politics and economics, with the proponents of big government and central control of the economy facing off against the advocates for small government and laissez-faire economics. And we see the same tension in how we treat the land, with the artificial naturalism of the romantic landscape and the geometric orderliness of the rational landscape at odds with each other and at odds with native ecosystems and natural habitats. The resolution of those conflicts brings us to a consequentialist approach to the landscape and to ethics.

THE CONSEQUENTIAL LANDSCAPE

The landscapes around us endure and evolve so slowly that they often lull us into thinking we can expect them to remain largely unchanged in our lifetimes. But it has begun to dawn on us that nature doesn't always work that way: when conditions reach a certain tipping point, the natural world can change suddenly and sometimes violently, as we have started to see with the extreme weather events that many scientists attribute to climate change. Climate change will not only dramatically alter the landscapes we occupy but also demand that we alter how we see our relationship to and responsibility for the nonhuman world. We can no longer content ourselves with setting aside a few natural areas or convince ourselves that property owners have the contractual right to use their land however they see fit as we watch the larger natural environment becoming so stressed that an estimated half of all the species on the planet now face extinction over just the next several decades.[10] This so-called sixth extinction will be particularly dire for the human species, its primary cause, because we depend on so many other species to meet our needs—more than any other animal on the planet.

As the cause of this extinction, humanity also has the capacity to reverse it if we change our behavior quickly and dramatically enough. In other words, present actions need to happen in the context of future consequences; this requires, as the United Nations World Commission on Environment and Development has said, "development that meets the needs of the present without compromising the ability of future generations to meet their own needs."[11] That seems fair enough, although knowing what future generations will need and determining what might compromise their ability to meet those needs has proven difficult, in part because the human population continues to grow at an unprecedented pace and our expectations about what constitutes a good life are expanding just as rapidly. How can we meet our needs and not compromise the ability of future generations to meet theirs, and what incentive exists for us to do so?

Pragmatic or utilitarian ethics can help sort out such questions. Pragmatism, as the philosopher Charles Sanders Peirce defined it, holds that the "the sum of [the practical] consequences constitute the entire meaning" of an idea or action. This suggests that we never fully know something until after we have had a chance to judge its effects.[12] In terms of the natural environment, pragmatism means that we should act with great restraint and in incremental and experimental ways so that we—or, more likely, future generations—can assess the consequences of our actions before continuing. This runs counter to the popular idea of pragmatism as equivalent to practicality. The real meaning of pragmatism, the sum of its consequences, suggests that the only true practicality arises from considering the long-term effects of what we do on everyone and everything—other people, future generations, and diverse species.

Utilitarianism goes in a slightly different direction. First promulgated by Jeremy Bentham in the eighteenth century, utilitarian ethics takes a quantitative and hedonistic view of doing the right thing: we should strive to maximize pleasure and minimize suffering for the greatest number.[13] Subsequent thinkers like John Stuart Mill qualified Bentham's "hedonistic calculus" by arguing that some pleasures—like friendship and personal accomplishment—have a higher value than the carnal variety, and others, like Peter Singer, as already mentioned, have expanded Bentham's calculus to include the greatest good of all animals, not just humans.[14] But all of these varieties of utilitarian ethics confront the same questions: How can we measure the greatest good, and how do we know which action we take now will maximize the good in the future? And does pleasure—or practicality for that matter—offer the only way or even the best way of measuring the value of what we do now in order to ensure a better future for ourselves and others on this planet?

THE VIRTUOUS LANDSCAPE

These three approaches to the landscape have some limitations, however. Duty ethics seems well suited to idealized landscapes, from cemeteries at one extreme to wilderness areas at the other, but it offers little help for dealing with the actual landscapes that we inhabit every day. Contract ethics, in turn, appears perfectly adept at addressing how we currently divide up the landscape into public and private property, but it runs counter to—and indeed may have helped cause—the problem of climate change, which will inevitably alter the future landscapes in which we live. Utilitarian ethics offers a way of assessing the effects of our actions on the health of landscapes and of the natural world as a whole, but that ethical stance has the downside of our never knowing the full impact of what we do on future generations or evolving ecosystems.

Given those limitations, how should we move forward? One answer lies in virtue ethics, which encompasses the other three and expands on them in new and old ways. At least in the West, virtue ethics is among the oldest ways of thinking about our responsibilities to others. It rests on the idea that before we can change the world around us, we need to change ourselves. This ancient idea probably reflected the reality of the human condition for most of our history as a species, in which we lacked the means to alter the landscapes around us to any great degree. We thus developed an ethics around the idea of adaptation, with a focus on virtues such as justice, courage, prudence, and temperance. Taming human nature wisely took precedence over taming nonhuman nature.

Virtue ethics fell out of favor in the modern era as our technological prowess enabled us to alter the world around us with increasing speed and efficiency. Modern ethics has focused more on our actions than on our character and depended more on our reason than on our values, addressing the right thing to do rather than the right way to be. This parallels our treatment of the landscape, in which we have gone from adapting to the natural world as we find it to shaping it according to our will and for our convenience. While that ability to command and control nature has certainly made human life more pleasant, it has also brought us to the point where the resources on which the human species has always depended—clean water, clean air, healthy ecosystems—have begun to erode at such a rate that our very existence is threatened.

Virtue ethics has made a comeback over the past half century or so, as philosophers have regained an appreciation of virtuous behavior as the basis for living a good life.[15] We need to do the same with how we relate to the natural world and take responsibility for the landscapes around us. Rather than viewing nature as ours to use as we see fit, we need to ask what sort of beings would undermine what they need for their own existence as well as the existence of so many other species. Given current trends, the climate will force us to ask this question if we haven't already done so.

This chapter was first published in a slightly different form as "The Ethics of the Landscape" in the Chinese journal *Landscape Architecture Frontiers* (2013).

[1] Clive Ponting, *A Green History of the World* (New York: Penguin, 1991), 141–60.

[2] Peter Singer, *Animal Liberation: A New Ethics for Our Treatment of Animals* (New York: New York Review, 1975).

[3] W. H. Davis, "The Land Must Live," *Rodale's Environment Action Bulletin* 3 (1972): 4–7.

[4] Thure E. Cerling, Jonathan G. Wynn, Samuel A. Andanje, Michael I. Bird, David Kimutai Korir, Naomi E. Levin, William Mace, Anthony N. Macharia, Jay Quade, and Christopher H. Remien, "Woody Cover and Hominin Environments in the Past 6 Million Years," *Nature* 476 (August 4, 2011): 51, http://www.nature.com.

[5] William Cronon, "The Trouble with Wilderness; or, Getting Back to the Wrong Nature," in *Uncommon Ground: Rethinking the Human Place in Nature,* ed. William Cronon (New York: W. W. Norton, 1995), 69–90.

[6] Immanuel Kant, *Fundamental Principles of the Metaphysic of Morals,* trans. Thomas Kingsmill Abbott (Chicago: University of Chicago Press, 1952).

[7] Bill McKibben, *The End of Nature* (New York: Random House, 2006).

[8] Thomas Hobbes, *Leviathan* (Chicago: University of Chicago Press, 1952).

[9] Jean-Jacques Rousseau, *The Social Contract or Principles of Political Right,* G. D. H. Cole, trans. (Chicago: University of Chicago Press, 1952).

[10] Richard Leakey and Roger Lewin, *The Sixth Extinction: Patterns of Life and the Future of Humankind* (New York: Doubleday, 1995).

[11] United Nations World Commission on Environment and Development, *Our Common Future* (New York: United Nations, 1987), http://www.un-documents.net/wced-ocf.htm.

[12] Peirce, *Pragmatism as a Principle and Method of Right Thinking.*

[13] Jeremy Bentham, *An Introduction to the Principles of Morals and Legislation* (Garden City, N.Y.: Doubleday, Doran, 1935).

[14] John Stuart Mill, *Utilitarianism* (London: Parker, Son and Bourn, 1863).

[15] Roger Crisp and Michael Slote, *Virtue Ethics* (New York: Oxford University Press, 1997).

12

VIRAL CITIES

If Frederick Law Olmsted, one of America's great public intellectuals, were alive today, I suspect that he would speak out not only about issues like climate change and species extinction but also about something that he saw firsthand: the vulnerability of human beings to perhaps our greatest predator, viruses. In the digital age, *going viral* has come to refer to an infectious idea that replicates itself, like a real virus, spreading rapidly through online networks.[1] We have seen the power of this phenomenon in everything from the marketing of products and services to the mobilizing of like-minded people for political causes as disparate as Barack Obama's presidential campaign and Tea Party protests. The metaphor of the digital virus can help us understand, in new ways, the growing threat of actual viruses in the real world. Rapidly rising human populations living in increasingly unsanitary conditions have combined with transcontinental air travel to greatly increase the likelihood of a viral pandemic—one that would have profound impacts on daily life and the global economy.[2]

We have only begun to assess how such a pandemic might affect us. One early effort to do so was an exhibition held in 2010 at the Storefront for Art and Architecture in New York City. Curated by Geoff Manaugh of BLDGBLOG and Nicola Twilley of Edible Geography, *Landscapes of Quarantine* brought together eighteen architects, artists, and designers whose work engages this issue in various ways. While many zones of quarantine are located, for obvious reasons, in isolated settings, some have been sited in cities—for instance, the now inactive quarantine islands in Venice's lagoon and in New York City's harbor. As the exhibition's curators note, "The practice of quarantine extends far beyond questions of epidemic control and pest-containment strategies to touch on issues of urban planning, geopolitics, international trade, ethics, immigration, and more." They also recognize the long history of quarantine: "The practice dates back at least to the arrival of the Black Death in medieval Venice, if not to Christ's 40 days in the desert."[3]

A turning point occurred in London in 1854, when the English physician John Snow traced a cholera outbreak in Soho to contaminated water in a public well on Broad (now Bushwick) Street; Snow's landmark work spurred the creation of the field of epidemiology and the profession of public health.[4] Snow's discovery not only dispelled the then-common miasma theory of disease, which attributed illness to "bad air," but it also made illness a geographic issue, connecting epidemics to particular causes in specific places. All at once city design and infrastructure mattered in both the conveyance and the prevention of disease.

Snow's findings soon influenced urban architecture and engineering. In New York City in the 1860s, cholera and malaria outbreaks led to the establishment of the Metropolitan Board of Health—the first municipal health authority in the United States—and to building and zoning codes that controlled overcrowding, mandated better sanitary conditions, and propelled infrastructure investments that have influenced city systems and services to this day.[5] Indeed, those codes have served us so well over the past century and a half that we have possibly become complacent about new public health threats in cities around the world. As Manaugh and Twilley write, "Quarantine has re-emerged as an issue of urgency and importance in today's era of globalization, antibiotic resistance, emerging diseases, pandemic flu, and bio-terrorism."[6]

THE GEOGRAPHY OF ILLNESS

First, some statistics. The United Nations has recorded a one-third increase in global epidemics in just one year, 2004–5, and an eightyfold increase in pandemics over the course of the twentieth century.[7] The UN data also show that the geography of illness remains highly uneven. The number of people killed by biological illness in 2004–5 was one-third more in the least developed countries than in developing nations and 160 times more than in the most developed parts of the world. But given the speed with which viral infections can be transported around the globe, geographic differences matter less and less. In the twenty-first century all of the world's human population will likely become almost equally exposed to pandemic disease.

To be sure, the relative mildness of the 2009 H1N1 influenza outbreak might lead us to dismiss the severity of the threat. Many did die from H1N1—nearly five thousand globally, according to the World Health Organization—but not enough to prompt a real increase in preventive measures.[8] We may not be so lucky next time. Viral infections like the Ebola and West Nile fevers kill quickly, and no vaccines yet exist to fight them.[9] And North Americans have only to read the history of their continent for evidence of how viral infections can devastate populations: Native Americans declined in number by as much as 80 percent after their encounter with unfamiliar and incurable European illnesses, although scholars still debate the methods and rates at which this occurred.[10]

What does it mean to design with viruses in mind today? We might take cues from how we protect ourselves in the digital environment.[11] A computer virus can cripple hardware and subvert software, preventing us from working or communicating. To avoid this, we have at least three options. First, we can go to the source of the virus and try to stop its spread; second, we can erect digital firewalls and install virus detection software to halt its arrival; and third, we can try to prevent infection by distancing ourselves from it and not opening e-mail attachments. While such efforts rarely ensure complete protection, they do reduce the likelihood of harm from a virus. These precautions also suggest how we might design our cities to respond to viral diseases let loose around the globe.

The first line of defense involves attacking the source of a pandemic. Viruses can mutate and spread almost anywhere, but some environments facilitate this more than others. The rapid increase in overcrowding in cities and so-called informal settlements in impoverished regions has pro-duced unhealthy living conditions that can generate and spread deadly zoonoses—that is, diseases that transfer from animals to humans in close proximity.[12] With fast-growing slums now accommodating more than one billion people—a number expected to double in the next three decades—the chance of an outbreak of zoonotic disease has gone up rapidly.[13]

Further, we can't assume that the development and spread of disease will necessarily be unintentional. Slums can breed not only disease but also despair, and some observers worry that this will provoke bioterrorism. In *Planet of Slums,* Mike Davis argues that "the 'feral, failed cities' of the Third World—especially their slum outskirts—will be the distinctive battle space of the twenty-first century. Pentagon doctrine is being reshaped accordingly to support a low-intensity world war of unlimited duration against criminalized segments of the urban poor. This is the true 'clash of civilizations.'"[14]

Whether for humanitarian, public health, or geopolitical reasons, im-provement of the urban conditions that give rise to viral outbreaks is urgent. The challenge—helping the billion people who live in poor shelter in unsanitary districts—might seem overwhelming, but addressing it might

120 be the wisest, and most cost-effective, investment we can make. The U.S. Centers for Disease Control and Prevention estimates that the economic impact of a pandemic could range from $71 billion to $166 billion, excluding the cost of disruptions to commerce and society.[15] Compare that to the $16 billion lent by the World Bank for shelter improvement in ninety countries over the past thirty-four years, and it's clear that the level of investment has come nowhere close to acknowledging the risk involved.[16]

But even if the developed nations start right now to commit more money to ameliorating global poverty, progress will be slow, given the scale and diversity of needs. And that leads us to the second strategy: building firewalls and detection methods to prevent viruses from spreading. The place to start is at international airports. Airline travel—which can speedily send viruses against which we have no defense around the world, causing the infection of millions of people before we even know what's happened— has unintentionally become the most efficient means of transferring disease ever invented. Researchers studying the H1N1 pandemic detected a high correlation between the disease's spread and airline flights from Mexico in March and April 2009. They found that "international air travelers departing from Mexico were unknowingly transporting a novel influenza A (H1N1) virus to cities around the world."[17] This highlights the fact that while some associate contagious diseases with isolated or impoverished places, viruses become pandemic first in the most economically active and globally connected cities, which have the busiest airports and the most flights to and from the greatest number of other cities.[18]

Cities have a long history of fighting disease at ports and other points of entry. In the fifteenth and sixteenth centuries, when Venice suffered a series of outbreaks of bubonic plague, the government quarantined sailors and cargo for forty days on Lazzaretto Vecchio, a small island about two miles from the Piazza San Marco.[19] In the nineteenth and early twentieth centuries, New York City quarantined boat passengers on Hoffman and Swinburne Islands to halt the spread of cholera and other illnesses.[20] And during the 1918 influenza pandemic, some U.S. cities required that visitors present health certificates before they were allowed to enter.[21] In the age of global air travel, efforts to slow the spread of disease through quarantine seem inconceivable. But this process has already begun, as many experienced during the 2009 H1N1 outbreak. The U.S. government warned

VIRAL CITIES

arriving air passengers that "their travel may be delayed" and that they might have to " pass through a scanning device that checks your temperature" and "be quarantined for a period of time if a passenger on your flight is found to have symptoms of H1N1 flu."[22]

The risk of disease transmission may eventually change not only how we travel but also how we work and relate globally. The old adage "Think globally, act locally" may be more pertinent than ever since mobile video technology has matured to the point where we can communicate seamlessly in real time with almost anyone, almost anywhere. And as we become more knowledgeable about the larger environmental costs of air travel, global commuting might seem increasingly irresponsible and wasteful. Global citizenship might mean being less physically but more electronically interconnected.

In the digital environment we try to evade viruses by avoiding the unfamiliar; in the physical environment we try to evade viruses by practicing what public health physicians call "social distancing"—another form of avoiding the unfamiliar. "In the event of a serious pandemic," write Jeanne Lenzer and Shannon Brownlee, school closings and voluntary and even mandatory quarantines "will require . . . widespread buy-in from the public. Yet little discussion has appeared in the press to help people understand the measures they can take to best protect themselves."[23]

Social distancing has architectural and urban implications. It can take extreme and even inhuman form, as Daniel Defoe recounts in his novel *A Journal of the Plague Year,* first published in 1722. The novel takes place during the Great Plague of 1665, when British officials imprisoned whole households in their own homes if even one family member showed signs of disease. As we saw during the SARS outbreak of 2002–3, and in the reaction to H1N1 in 2009, people do alter their behavior in response to the possibility of contracting disease, changing how they relate to others and how they use public space: wearing masks, installing hand sanitizers, avoiding contact, shunning strangers, staying indoors, and even fleeing cities.[24]

THE CHANGES PANDEMICS BRING

Pandemics can usher in enormous cultural change. During the plague year of 1665, when Cambridge University was temporarily closed, Isaac Newton left Cambridge, where he'd been a lackluster student, and retreated to the rural isolation of his family home in Woolsthorpe, where he proceeded to make key discoveries regarding gravity, planetary motion, optics, and calculus.[25] But most of us will need more personal interconnection and institutional support to remain productive in the event of the social distancing that an infectious outbreak might demand. Telecommuting is an option, and in fact by 2007 nearly one-quarter of Americans in the workforce were already regularly performing some part of their jobs from home, and 62 percent wished they could do so.[26]

With telecommuting comes the need for more mixed-use neighborhoods that can provide a range of services to people working close to home. This might seem to counter the tactic of social distancing, but it reminds us that in earlier eras, before global travel became an easy option, most people lived in comparatively small and stable communities with others who shared exposure and immunity to the same diseases. This made it essential that most daily needs be provided for within a relatively small geographic area—which also served to limit interactions mainly to those who had diseases in common. In this sense, membership in a community offered more than a social and economic benefit; it was literally a matter of life and death, since traveling too far away from their own viral communities made people both threats to others and vulnerable to infection.

The prospect of pandemic, then, should spur us to rethink one of the prevailing divides in urban design—that between those who envision a high-tech metropolis of global connectedness and those who call for a return to traditional, small-scale, mixed-use settlements. We will actually need both the high-tech metropolis and the small-scale settlement. The digital environment will connect us globally, while the mixed-use settlement will provide us with the diverse local goods and services we will need in a less mobile future.

There is also much we can do within communities and in individual buildings to protect people from viral infection. This might include rethinking the smallest details of urban life, such as the innocent but potentially hazardous gestures of shaking hands and passing papers between people. And it may involve our paying more attention to those elements of buildings—doorknobs, light switches, restroom faucets, and the like—that we now know are points of contact for transmitting disease. Here, too, both old customs and high tech are relevant. Hand shaking used to be a sign of solidarity among members of the same (viral) community—something we would do well to remember when we greet strangers. And motion detection and remote sensing technologies—now often viewed as offering convenience—may become necessities as we seek ways of operating the designed environment without coming in physical contact with it.

By approaching architecture and urban design with pandemics in mind, we can make our cities healthier and more sustainable. Moving bits rather than bodies, increasing the mix of uses in local communities, and reducing the degree of contact we have in the physical environment will not only increase our chances of surviving a pandemic but also decrease our ecological footprint. These are related phenomena. One of the great worries in the epidemiological community is that infectious diseases will arise because of climate change, and so the more we can do to stem the latter, the more we will do to prevent the former.[27]

This gives new meaning to Marshall McLuhan's idea of the "global village."[28] McLuhan envisioned electronic media as making the globe more like a village, with the whole planet able to communicate and connect as easily as a local community. What McLuhan couldn't see half a century ago, but what seems likely in our virally vulnerable world, is that we may have to live, literally, in more village-like ways; we may all inhabit a digitally connected globe and at the same time live physically separated in our own viral communities.

That prospect will surely raise objections—it goes against the expectation of freedom that has come to characterize modern life, especially in highly developed nations. Won't a globe of physically isolated village-cities return us to a more "primitive" existence, haunted by tribal conflicts, ethnic prejudices, and fear of strangers? Won't barriers to travel impose unacceptable restrictions on our ability to experience other places and understand other cultures, and won't such limitations constrain our ability to grow intellectually and socially beyond the bounds of our home communities?

These are precisely the questions we need to raise; it makes no sense to protect our physical health if political repression and social oppression are the results. To help prevent such unintended consequences, we might take advantage of another type of virus: the cultural virus that biologist Richard Dawkins, in *The Selfish Gene,* first called a "meme"—a compelling idea that can replicate in the minds of others, increasing the intellectual

124   diversity of a community while also "killing off" an existing concept or unexamined assumption.[29]

One challenge in fighting actual viruses is that we cannot see them, and so we downplay their importance. Thus it becomes especially useful to make viruses somehow more visible. In this process the meme of "viral cities" might play a key role. We can transform our cities in large and small ways to protect us from pandemics—and such transformations might have the added advantage of making the threat real, making it immediate and tangible in ways that abstract public pronouncements or warnings simply cannot.

This gets to the heart of a debate among those who study memes, "meme-ticists," as cognitive scientist Douglas Hofstadter calls them.[30] Memetic "internalists" focus on the cognitive aspects of ideas, paying little attention to the physical environments that give rise to the ideas, while "externalists" argue that physical contexts can both encourage and reflect changes in our thinking. From my reading of this literature, the internalists appear to have won the debate, with neuroscience and cognitive psychology dominating the field. But when it comes to applying the meme of biological viruses as a significant shaper of human life in the twenty-first century, the externalists may have the edge. It may be that the physical environment—even with all the electronic gadgetry that can help us discover and transfer knowledge—will once again become fundamental to how we conceptualize and respond to the real viral threat. Only through changes in our actual behavior—in our travel expectations, work habits, living patterns, social customs, and self-conceptions—will we be able to slow a pandemic long enough to develop vaccines and strengthen immunity.

This puts us in a race of sorts: Which virus will embed itself? Will it be the conceptual meme of "viral cities" that spurs us to rethink our daily activities and our responsibilities to others? Or will it be the virulent gene in some actual virus for which we have no cure that arrives stealthily via an infected airline passenger and spreads faster than we can react? Let us hope it is the former and not the latter, although the history of cities suggests otherwise. History suggests that we rarely act against an invisible threat until we have suffered the pain of ignoring it, as happened in Venice in the fourteenth century and in London in the seventeenth and nineteenth centuries. But maybe this time we will behave differently. If we take the current threat seriously and do not dismiss it as too remote a possibility for worry, we may beat the odds and avoid the worst of the pandemics headed our way. Should we bet on it?

This chapter was first published as "Viral Cities," *Places* (October 18, 2010), http://places.designobserver.com/feature/viral-cities/13948.

[1] Alan Montgomery, "Applying Quantitative Marketing Techniques to the Internet," *Interfaces* 31, no. 2 (March/April 2001): 90–108.

[2] Michael T. Osterholm, "Preparing for the Next Pandemic," *Foreign Affairs*, July/August 2005.

[3] Storefront for Art and Architecture, *Landscapes of Quarantine*, curated by Geoff Manaugh and Nicola Twilley, March 10–April 24, 2010, http://www.storefrontnews.

[4] Steven Johnson, *The Ghost Map: The Story of London's Most Terrifying Epidemic—and How It Changed Science, Cities, and the Modern World* (London: Penguin, 2006).

[5] Stephen Sussna, "Bulk Control and Zoning: The New York Experience," *Land Economics* 43, no. 2 (May 1967): 158–71.

[6] Storefront for Art and Architecture, *Landscapes of Quarantine.*

[7] See United Nations Office for Disaster Risk Reduction, International Strategy for Disaster Reduction, accessed December 11, 2015, http://www.unisdr.org.

[8] See World Health Organization, "Pandemic (H1N1) 2009," August 10, 2010, http://www.who.int.

[9] Paul Farmer, "Social Inequalities and Emerging Infectious Diseases," *Emerging Infectious Diseases* 2, no. 4 (October–December 1996): 259–69.

[10] Russell Thornton, "Aboriginal North American Population and Rates of Decline, ca. a.d. 1500–1900," *Current Anthropology* 38, no. 2 (April 1997): 310–15.

[11] See Microsoft, "Tips for Protecting Your Computer from Viruses," accessed December 11, 2015, http://windows.microsoft.com.

[12] See World Health Organization, "Zoonoses and the Human-Animal-Ecosystems Interface," accessed December 11, 2015, http://www.who.int.

[13] See United Nations Human Settlements Programme, *The Challenge of Slums: Global Report on Human Settlements, 2003* (London: Earthscan, 2003).

[14] Mike Davis, *Planet of Slums* (New York: Verso, 2006), 205.

[15] Martin I. Meltzer, Nancy J. Cox, and Keiji Fukuda, "The Economic Impact of Pandemic Influenza in the United States: Priorities for Intervention," *Emerging Infectious Diseases* 5, no. 5 (September/October 1999): 659–71.

[16] Robert M. Buckley and Jerry Kalarickal, eds., *Thirty Years of World Bank*

Shelter Lending: What Have We Learned? (Washington, D.C.: World Bank, 2006).

[17] Kamran Khan, "Spread of a Novel Influenza A (H1N1) Virus via Global Airline Transportation," *New England Journal of Medicine* 361 (July 9, 2009): 212–14.

[18] Alexandra Mangili and Mark A Gendreau, "The Transmission of Infectious Diseases during Commercial Air Travel," *The Lancet* 365 (2005): 989–96.

[19] Maria Cristina Valsecchi, "Mass Plague Graves Found on Venice 'Quarantine' Island," *National Geographic,* August 29, 2007.

[20] Sharon Seitz and Stuart Miller, *The Other Islands of New York City* (Woodstock, Vt.: Countryman Press, 2003).

[21] Robert Kenner, dir., "Influenza 1918," *The American Experience,* Public Broadcasting System, 1998.

[22] See Centers for Disease Control and Prevention, "Fact Sheet: Screening and Monitoring Travelers to Prevent the Spread of Ebola," November 10, 2015, http://www.cdc.gov.

[23] Jeanne Lenzer and Shannon Brownlee, "Does the Vaccine Matter?," *Atlantic,* November 2009.

[24] Bobbie Person, Francisco Sy, Kelly Holton, Barbara Govert, Arthur Liang, and the NCID/SARS Community Outreach Team, "Fear and Stigma: The Epidemic within the SARS Outbreak," *Emerging Infectious Diseases* 10, no. 2 (February 2004): 358–63.

[25] Richard S. Westfall, *The Life of Isaac Newton* (Cambridge: Cambridge University Press, 1994).

[26] Chris Kanaracus. "Telecommuting: A Quarter of U.S. Workers Do It Regularly," *PC World,* November 27, 2007.

[27] Paul R. Epstein, "Climate Change and Infectious Disease: Stormy Weather Ahead?," *Epidemiology* 13, no. 4 (July 2002): 373–75.

[28] Marshall McLuhan, *The Gutenberg Galaxy: The Making of Typographic Man* (Toronto: University of Toronto Press, 1962).

[29] Richard Dawkins, *The Selfish Gene* (Oxford: Oxford University Press, 1976).

[30] Douglas R. Hofstadter, *Metamagical Themas: Questing for the Essence of Mind and Pattern* (New York: Basic Books, 1996), 65.

PART V

POLITICS

We often do not see politics as something we design, which makes the many failures of our political system and its unwillingness to tackle the problems we face all the more frustrating, because we could avoid them if we took a design approach. This part of the book considers the redesign of our politics from a few different perspectives. The first chapter explores the value that design thinking and abductive reasoning might bring to our political discourse, enabling us to see the world in less ideological and more nuanced ways and helping us recognize the unintended consequences of our poorly designed politics and the unseen connections between costs and benefits, which our political culture too often views as unrelated.

Chapter 14 reviews the consequences of political opposition to change of almost every sort. This "politics of no" has become too easy for individuals and communities to use as a wedge to stop things that they might even acknowledge that they need—as long as it doesn't happen in their own backyard. This chapter describes two situations that highlight the perverse nature of this oppositional politics: an aborted attempt to build affordable housing in a community that desperately needed it and a frustrated effort at stopping gun violence in a city that certainly wanted it. The ability of design to find win–win solutions to major problems stands in contrast to the lose–lose nature of this resistant political culture.

The final chapter in this part steps back to look at the politics of planning and urban design and at how they also reflect the oppositional nature of our thinking. That way of thinking has a long history in Western culture, but this chapter ends with a plea for another, equally strong tradition: the "opposable" thinking that enables us to hold seemingly opposite ideas in our minds at the same time and to imagine solutions that embrace apparently opposite goals. The abductive nature of design epitomizes such opposable thinking, and we would all benefit if it had a stronger role in our politics.

13

DESIGNER
POLITICS

The redesign of societal systems invariably encounters political opposition, since many individuals and organizations have vested interests in the way things work now, however poorly they perform, and see any change as a threat to their position and power. And that is why our political system itself needs redesigning. In Congress, vested interests and their lobbyists have shown how effectively they can halt a change agenda in almost every area of our economy, harming the ability of the United States as a nation to move forward on almost any front.

Design becomes especially valuable in such situations. Clients and communities often seek out design help when they encounter some degree of dysfunction in their lives, their businesses, or their environments that calls for new products or services, new buildings or houses, or new organizations or operations. In every case, they begin by embracing the need for change, something that politicians could learn from.

Although often dressed in a lot of black and white, designers generally see the world in shades of gray as they continually try to find win–win solutions to design problems—solutions that will accommodate different needs—and creative resolutions for seemingly irresolvable conflicts. Because of that, many in the design community, like many in the general public, view the "I win, you lose," polarized nature of the current political culture in the United States with dismay. In such a black-and-white world, belonging to one political party seems to mean that you can't agree with anything advocated by the other. To his credit, President Obama, who once aspired to be an architect, has tried to find middle ground in this polarized culture and to seek win–win solutions to the challenges we face as a nation, but in the process he has had to endure the slings and arrows of both the political left and right. Those who see things as black or white apparently do not like shades of gray.

I realized that years ago when I served as an expert witness in a court case. A group of people peacefully protesting the killing of animals to make fur coats had gathered legally on the sidewalk outside a department store in the downtown area, and yet they were arrested for doing exactly the same thing in front of the same department store chain's location inside a major shopping mall. The prosecution saw this as a black-and-white issue: one protest occurred in the public domain and the other on private property. But I testified that, from a design perspective, how we define property legally does not always align with the nuanced way we experience property in our daily lives. While legally private property, shopping malls serve public purposes in our communities.

The differences between legal definitions of the world and our daily experience of it confront us all the time. Think about the space in front of the typical single-family house. While a property line exists between public and private ownership, that space really consists of a gradation of mostly public, semipublic, semiprivate, and mostly private space. Even inside houses, we have various rooms, more or less private, to accommodate visitors, acquaintances, friends, and family of different levels of intimacy.

We all live, in other words, in shades of gray in both our private and our public lives. So why do we have such a hard time accepting the same in our political life? It may be because of the temptation to mistake reality for our abstractions of it. The mathematics of political decision making, with statistics, polls, and data surrounding almost every issue, can cause even the most down-to-earth politician to forget the reality that those abstractions represent. And that, in turn, can lead our elected officials to see things in absolute terms, as if reality has somehow come to conform to our statistical portrait of it. A refusal to compromise may seem normal in that black-and-white world, but it seems surreal and even nonsensical in the real one.

Some might dismiss such black-and-white thinking as just politics, rationalizing something that has become increasingly irrational. Accepting such thinking, though, may be as dangerous as the thinking itself. In environmental design, we have learned that pushing any structure or system to an extreme can lead to its catastrophic failure, as happens when excessive loads or earthquake tremors lead to the collapse of bridges or buildings. Most people, however, don't see that the same applies to invisible structures like our political system. Look at the collapse of the regimes in places like Egypt, Tunisia, and Libya, where the outrageous behavior of dictators and the extraordinary gap between rich and poor led to rapid political implosion.

Here in the United States, the more extreme our politics and the more unequal our economy become, the more we risk stressing our system to the point of collapse. No one wants that to happen, and so it remains up to the electorate—up to all of us—to start demanding that our representatives remember the world in which the rest of us live, among shades of gray.

Some of the black-and-white thinking in American politics has also come from parties' adopting some of the worst aspects of corporate branding, so that adhering to their parties' brands seems to matter more to some public officials than solving our country's most pressing problems. Politicians who want to think for themselves can also encounter the kind of resistance sometimes seen in large companies: the "brand police" are on the lookout for anything that might muddy the ideological purity of the party.

While designers often help organizations clarify and visualize their brands, the design process runs completely counter to this branding mentality. Design involves experimentation and the use of prototyping as a way to explore as many different responses to a problem as possible in order to find what works the best. And, as every designer knows, the best solutions rarely exist within the boundaries of the existing brand, which often created the problem in the first place. Our political culture could learn some of those same lessons.

OUR POLITICAL BATTLE OF THE BRANDS

I recently attended a gathering of civic leaders who met to grapple with some of big challenges headed our way: climate change, disruptive technologies, the obesity epidemic, the aging population, and so on. The meeting made two things immediately clear. Despite the diversity of the group, no one questioned the reality of these challenges, and no one—whether on the political left or right—disagreed with the goals of a resilient infrastructure, a vibrant economy, a healthy community, and a productive workforce.

The event generated a wide range of creative ideas about how to deal with these challenges, which made me wonder why we have so much difficulty doing the same at the national or even at the statewide level of government. The problem comes, I think, from confusion in our political culture between means and ends. The vast majority of people—and politicians—seem to agree on the ends; who doesn't want security, prosperity, and health? Our political gridlock arises from disagreements over the means of achieving those ends: through more government regulation or less, more economic stimulus or less, more control of individual behavior or less.

Unfortunately, the two dominant political parties in the United States have branded themselves with the conflicting means that they advocate rather than with the ends about which most of us seem to agree. This makes it almost impossible to move forward, since any compromise over the means appears to threaten both parties' brand identities and leads too many politicians to resist reaching across the aisle. But when we start with the goals we agree on rather than the means over which we disagree, it becomes much easier to find common ground.

The design thinking used at the civic leaders' workshop helped make that happen. By having diverse groups of people wrestle with big challenges, devise as many different ways as possible to address them, and present their proposals to others for comment, the organizers of the meeting set up a creative and iterative process that led to new solutions, many of which defied the conventional categories of political left and right. In several cases, the most creative ideas came from the inversion of the typical way in which we think of challenges. One group, for example, argued that we need to see an aging population not as a problem but as an asset that can help us tackle other challenges, with elders providing services such as mentoring and tutoring of underprivileged children or sharing memories of how previous generations lived in more sustainable ways.

Another idea emerged from the conversation that bears on all of this. We like to speak about the "American Experiment," but we seem to have a hard time experimenting with diverse ways of doing things and then assessing the results of these tests. This difficulty comes not only from rigid adherence to the brand on the part of our political parties but also from the apparent desire of each party to have its way of doing things prevail in statehouses across the country as well as in Congress. We confuse our real differences over means with an illusory disagreement over ends, and we also mistakenly think that there should be only one means—the Democrats' means or the Republicans' means—to achieve a common end.

For example, it makes no sense to advocate for tax cuts or at least no tax increases as the solution to every problem, as the Republican brand seems to assert. The design community learned long ago that applying the same answer to every problem leads to a lot of terrible solutions that not only don't resolve the problems but also often make them worse. Instead, we need as many different experiments as possible going on. Raise taxes high in some places and lower them significantly in others, and let's see what happens. Will the better schools and services in the high-tax localities compensate for the likely loss of tax-sensitive individuals and corporations?

And will economic growth in the low-tax locations outpace the effects of their decaying schools and infrastructure?

At the same time, it makes little sense to refuse to consider changing any aspect of federal entitlement programs like Medicare and Social Security, as the Democratic faithful seem to insist is crucial. Here, too, the design community can provide plenty of examples in which something designed under one condition or set of expectations needs renovation or rethinking in light of changing needs or demands. With people living longer and staying healthier further into old age, programs devised in an era of shorter life spans and more rudimentary medicine probably need revision. Let's see what happens when different states or regions tweak one aspect or another of these entitlements and then rigorously assess the results after a set period of time. Will funds freed up with lower benefits lead to other investments that enhance quality of life, or will older people flee such places, leading to declining tax bases that negate any entitlement savings? Performance-based design, which looks at how we respond to environments and systems, offers methods for answering such questions, including querying people before decisions are made and assessing people's behavior under various conditions.

Above all, we need to stop the battle of our political brands and take more advantage of the opportunities to try different approaches to problems that federalism gives to each state. And we need to remember what made the American Experiment the envy of the world. We did not get here by arguing endlessly over untested ideologies but instead by experimenting and then pragmatically embracing the ideas that produced the best results.

In doing so, we also have to accept the fact that not all problems lend themselves to simple solutions or, sometimes, any solution at all. Some of the challenges we face involve paradoxes whose "solutions," while well-intentioned, can have unintended consequences. Design deals in paradoxes all the time. People come to designers with dilemmas, often wanting more than their budgets allow or desiring some likely unachievable goals, and the design process becomes a way of adjusting ideas to the reality of a situation.

INCREASING COSTS BY CUTTING SPENDING

Too many voters seem to believe that by reducing expenditures on social programs, we can permanently reduce the size and cost of government.

On its surface, that argument seems to make sense: spending less will cost us less. When we look more carefully at what that actually means, however, we can see that this is not necessarily so, depending on the nature of the program in question.

Take homelessness, for example. The widespread incidence of homelessness in the United States has many causes, including the recent wave of foreclosures that sent many former home owners into precarious housing situations. But cutbacks in governmental funding remain among the primary causes of homelessness in this country. The problem goes back decades, to the Community Mental Health Act of 1963, which had the admirable goal of deinstitutionalizing long-term mental health patients and moving their care to community mental health centers. When the government did not fund these centers, large numbers of mentally ill people ended up on the streets.[1] When President Reagan cut the budget of the Department of Housing and Urban Development by three-quarters over the course of his administration in the 1980s, the number of homeless people again jumped dramatically.[2]

Some may think that such reductions in governmental aid give the homeless an incentive to get jobs and pull themselves up by their bootstraps. I won't address that argument here, except to say that, as the son of a psychologist who had homeless patients, I find it profoundly naive to expect people with schizophrenia or depression or who have been victimized by domestic violence to just pull themselves up by their bootstraps.

In reality, cutting government funding for programs to address homelessness increases the cost of government. Research bears this out. One study has shown that providing subsidized or supportive housing costs the government less—sometimes more than a third less—than the amount spent on emergency room services, hospitalization, and incarceration of the homeless.[3] We often don't see how spending cuts and costs are related because costs are spread across different levels of government, from local to federal, and across types of allocations, such as public safety, health care, and criminal justice. But the evidence is clear and undisputable: cutting government spending in areas that prevent problems from occurring in the first place can cost taxpayers more over the long run.

We need a much more nuanced sense of how to cut government expenditures if we want to reduce the cost of government, and design can help

137   with this, given its method of seeing the connections among seemingly
unrelated things and approaching the world from the point of view of
ordinary people. First, as designers do in understanding the totality of a
problem, we need to think about government spending as a whole and
stop making cuts at the federal and state levels that only increase costs
at the local level.[4] Taxpayers have to pay one way or the other, and simply
shifting expenses—especially when doing so leads to increased costs—
makes no sense. Second, we need to recognize the relationships among
different kinds of government expenses, as designers distinguish between
short-term savings and long-term costs. When we start to envision the
world from the perspective of a person in need of public assistance as
opposed to that of the policy makers who make funding allocations, we
can see how savings in one area (cutting funding for supportive housing,
for example) can lead to increased expenses in others (such as increased
health care and criminal justice costs).

Finally, as in every design project, we need to account for indirect as
well as direct costs. The direct savings that came with the rapid closing of
many mental institutions in the early 1960s and the dramatic reductions
in HUD's budget in the 1980s brought with them huge indirect costs to
communities that went far beyond increased spending on policing and
hospitalization. These costs included the perception of cities as unsafe,
which in turn helped fuel a drop in urban tax bases as people abandoned
inner-city neighborhoods, an increase in infrastructure costs as development began to sprawl, and a rise in living expenses as people needed more
cars and other equipment in order to conduct their lives.[5] Were we to tally
all of these indirect costs—accrued, in part, as a result of reduced funding
for housing the poor and mentally ill—we would see how much cutting
the government dramatically increased not only the cost of government
but also the cost of living for us all.

So, as we look for ways to cut the cost of government, we need to see
that the best way to do so often involves increased spending on prevention.
We know this has worked in the health care arena. Spending more on
prevention can reduce the impacts of disease, as demonstrated by the
campaign against smoking, which significantly lowered the incidence of
tobacco-related illnesses, and the costs related to them, among some sectors
of the population.[6] Prevention also works in education, where investment

138 in early childhood development saves society money in the end.[7] We need to examine every other area of governmental activity to determine where spending on prevention would be beneficial.

Designers understand this. Good design anticipates the future and invests more up front to prevent problems and reduce later costs. One of the heroes of the pull-yourself-up-by-the-bootstraps crowd is Benjamin Franklin, who, in addition to his worthy advice about frugality, industry, and moderation, cautioned us that "an ounce of prevention is worth a pound of cure." There is no better motto to guide us through the difficult decisions we will need to make as we slim down our government while preventing the social dysfunctions that led to its added weight in the first place.

139   Portions of this chapter were previously published in "What Politicians Might Learn from Designers," *Huffington Post* (August 29, 2011), http://www.huffingtonpost.com/thomas-fisher/what-politicians-might-le_b_937658.html; "Our Political Battle of the Brands," *Huffington Post* (April 24, 2013), http://www.huffingtonpost.com/thomas-fisher/our-political-battle-of-t_b_3140720.html; and "How Cutting Government Spending Can Increase the Cost of Government," *Huffington Post* (October 5, 2011), http://www.huffingtonpost.com/thomas-fisher/government-spending-_b_995955.html.

[1] David A. Rochefort, "The Community Mental Health Revolution," in *From Poorhouses to Homelessness: Policy Analysis and Mental Health Care,* 2nd ed. (Westport, Conn.: Auburn House, 1997).

[2] Hannah Bell, "How Reagan Created 'the Homeless' and Why Charity Can't Fix It," Democratic Underground, April 4, 2008, http://www.democraticunderground.com.

[3] National Alliance to End Homelessness, "Cost Savings with Permanent Supportive Housing," March 1, 2010, http://www.endhomelessness.org.

[4] Mike Bostick, Matthew Ericson, and Robert Gebeloff, "How the Tax Burden Has Changed," *New York Times,* November 29, 2012, http://www.nytimes.com.

[5] Mike Davis, *City of Quartz* (New York: Vintage, 1990).

[6] American Cancer Society, "Tobacco: The True Cost of Smoking," 2015, http://www.cancer.org.

[7] Steffanie Clothier and Julie Poppe, "New Research: Early Education as Economic Investment," National Conference of State Legislatures, accessed November 23, 2015, http://www.ncsl.org.

14

THE POLITICS OF NO

Resistance to change and a tendency toward extremism can happen as much in our communities as in our politics. Indeed, the latter often just mirror the former, and so the redesign of our national political system needs to involve a reexamination of how politics works on the local level. Much of the NIMBY (not in my backyard) mentality that exists in many communities comes from a fear of change and from expectations that any project or proposal will result in the worst possible outcomes. Design can help defray some of the pessimism and suspicion that lead to NIMBYism, but only if communities give design a chance.

Although statistics are hard to come by, NIMBY opposition to projects, especially those that serve poor or minority people—seems to be on the rise. The architectural and design communities are understandably frustrated by NIMBYism, since it can cause them to lose commissions as projects die or are put on hold. But communities are also affected, as unthinking opposition to anything new often proves profoundly self-defeating.

An example of such NIMBYism occurred in an effort I was involved in many years ago to build affordable housing in a predominantly African American neighborhood in Williamsburg, Virginia. Highland Park, an area of about one hundred modest single-family homes, stands on a rise in the land near the center of Williamsburg but carefully screened from tourists' view. Colonial Williamsburg (CW) developed the neighborhood in the 1940s and 1950s, in part as a residential area for people displaced by the Rockefeller-funded restoration of the city's historic core; relatively little new construction had occurred there since then.

When Williamsburg built Highland Park for the community's displaced citizens, NIMBYism hardly existed; as far as I could tell from the historical record, the uprooted residents of Williamsburg held no organized protests against what had happened to their town and literally in their backyards. Compensating people for their property and letting them build what they wanted on new land—lessons too often forgotten these days—probably helped the city quell any opposition. Still, for better or worse, people appear to have been more accepting of big development projects forty or fifty years ago; such acquiescence now seems hard to understand. Even though the Rockefeller family's sponsorship of CW remained a well-kept secret as property was amassed for the community, it also seems surprising that this process didn't encounter more property owners refusing to sell. During the

142 course of this project, however, we did discover old wounds between CW and the residents of Highland Park, wounds that had taken a long time to heal.

CW owned a fourteen-acre piece of land in the northeast corner of Highland Park, and it wanted to build affordable housing there because the average price for a house in Williamsburg had risen well above what lower-wage CW employees could afford. Having recently built two affordable houses for its employees, CW saw the Highland Park property as an opportunity to build more. As the project developed, though, it became clear that it would have to be bigger than was first thought. The site could accommodate up to sixteen clustered units without a special-use permit. However, once a developer was brought in—the Hampton Roads Community Development Corporation—and had made a detailed financial analysis, the number of units increased to between twenty-five and thirty. The developer arrived at that number by calculating the absolute minimum of site development costs, a total unit cost, and a 5 percent contingency, with CW and others picking up the soft costs. Based on those assumptions, the developer would need to build twenty-five or more houses to reach the cost-per-unit goal, and building that many units would require a special-use permit from the city.

At first, obtaining the permit didn't seem to present a problem, as the city initially supported the project. But the proposal met with a very different reaction from the moderate-income residents of Highland Park. At a neighborhood meeting, the development team encountered a great deal of resistance from most residents. Although a few people in the audience spoke about the need for affordable housing, the majority saw only trouble. An apartment complex had been built near the site a few years before, and, as one Highland Park resident put it, "the project brought a lot of undesirable elements into the neighborhood." Several people in the audience expected this project to do the same, even though the houses would be owner occupied and not rented. Others objected to the density of a cluster development and to the increased traffic, and still others complained about the fact that the new development would have improvements such as curbs and drains that the existing streets did not.

We commonly think of NIMBY as a middle- or upper-class phenomenon, where people with money, power, and time work to keep "undesirable" projects out of their communities for fear that certain kinds of facilities will lower property values, detract from community cohesiveness, or (as is often thought but rarely mentioned) bring in the "wrong sort" of people. The response of the Highland Park residents, however, showed that NIMBYism cuts across classes and races. Here was a moderate-income minority population using the same words ("undesirable elements") and expressing the same fears ("it produces clutter and makes the area slummy") often heard in affluent suburbs.

I could understand some of the suspicions of the Highland Park residents. Like many minority communities, this one seemed somewhat neglected by local officials; part of the neighborhood meeting was devoted to how residents could get debris removed from the swamp near the neighborhood's main entrance after their repeated but vain efforts to get the city to act. The opposition to the new development also had a fatalistic quality, as if the memory of the community displacement years ago remained fresh in some people's minds. As one woman asked, "Will Colonial Williamsburg go ahead and build anyway, no matter what the community says?"

The answer was no. The development team did not want to build a project against the will of the local community. Also, without the support of the neighborhood, the city would not grant the project a special-use permit, and without that, the numbers no longer worked. The developer met again with the residents to see whether they could reach a compromise, but without success, and the team decided not to pursue the project.

The development group learned some lessons from this failed effort in Williamsburg. For example, listening carefully to the comments of the Highland Park residents, they heard not just the catchphrases of NIMBYism but also the very words that the design community might use when analyzing a community plan: "Will a feasibility study be done?" "How many more people can Highland Park absorb?" "Will the new homes have a problem with flooding?" "Will there be another entry to the neighborhood?" Such questions indicate how the design community has, perhaps unwittingly, helped to feed the NIMBY phenomenon.

NIMBY ON THE LEFT AND THE RIGHT

Consider the ideas central to NIMBY, such as the empowerment of local communities, the opposition to large-scale development, and the reinforcement of the character of a place. Those concepts emerged in the 1960s and

1970s, when the design community reacted against urban renewal and embraced such things as neighborhood preservation and participatory planning. NIMBY has become a kind of distortion or exaggeration of those ideas, as opposition to large-scale development has evolved into opposition to development of any kind, as incremental planning has come to mean every neighborhood for itself, and as preservation of the character of a place has become code for keeping outsiders out.

Did the design and planning professions, in attempting to correct one wrong, sow the seeds for another? Did urban designers prepare the ground for NIMBY by giving people the tools to fight all development? Have we now become victims of our previous successes? The answer to all three questions is probably yes, although we cannot blame NIMBY solely on the architectural community. The most reactionary form of NIMBY has roots much deeper than anything planted by architects and planners.

NIMBY blossomed in the 1980s, during the era of free market government. Its nourishment, however, came as much from the political left as from the right. If the right wants to empower the individual, the left wants to empower the group, especially all groups it considers marginalized for one reason or another. The right argues for self-interest, the left for special interests, and both arguments lead to essentially the same place. In Williamsburg, many of the Highland Park residents opposed the project because they saw that it would run counter to their self-interest of maintaining property values and preserving the neighborhood's existing density. At the same time, local officials, while professing support for the project, placed restrictions on it in response to various special interests— wetlands requirements for wide setbacks and expensive drainage systems, zoning requirements for wide streets and a lot of off-street parking.

Amid such a thicket of specific interests, the common good often gets lost. Too few people, least of all politicians, seem willing to stand up to NIMBY, to argue that everyone would be better off if everyone were to share equally in making sacrifices. Although an official of the city of Williamsburg did attend one of the development team's meetings with the Highland Park residents, not one political leader showed up to ask the residents to set aside their self-interest to help the entire community achieve something it needed.

Such absence of leadership, while frustrating to many people, also creates opportunities for architects and planners. Almost every case of NIMBY, for example, has been preceded by bad planning, with some neighborhoods having been neglected or dumped on too many times and other communities so often exempted from sacrifice that they think they are immune. As such, NIMBY offers us a chance to reassert design and planning as preventive measures: proper planning now can help eliminate NIMBY in the future. In the case of Highland Park, had its streets been brought up to modern standards and had the existing multifamily housing in the neighborhood been better designed and managed, objections to further development might not have been so severe.

NIMBY also offers designers a chance to use the skills they've honed in resolving the conflicts in clients' programs to help conflicting interests within a community find common ground and to develop a plan on which everyone can agree. This means not just designing buildings that fit into the context but also employing the problem-solving methods of design within the political process.

This, of course, is easier said than done. In Williamsburg, the development team came too late to change some of the bad planning of the past and did not get far enough into the project to resolve, through design, some of the community's concerns about the future. Still, architects and planners have within their hands the tools to fight NIMBY. They helped set the stage for it as far back as the 1960s, and they have the means to help undo it, showing communities how to construct viable common ground that can make people look further than their own backyards.

CONFLICTING RIGHTS

For all of our willingness to speak up about not wanting undesirable projects in our own backyards, many Americans—at least those of a certain ideological bent—appear amazingly blasé when it comes to accepting something as undesirable as bullets passing over or through our backyards. We seem almost fatalistic about ballistics. The constitutional right to bear arms has made it almost impossible for communities besieged by gun violence to get firearms off the streets, so let's think like designers and look at the problem from a very different perspective.

On a Monday after Christmas in my city, a bullet left a firearm and traveled across two streets, a front yard, and a vacant lot before striking a house and hitting the head of a three-year-old boy, who was climbing the stairs with his three brothers to hide in a closet because they had heard gunshots.[1] The boy died the next day. Had the bullet's trajectory taken it a little farther to the east, it would have missed the house and struck a neighboring elementary school.

As Senator Daniel Patrick Moynihan once put it, "Guns don't kill people, bullets do."[2] The problem of gun violence begins and ends with bullets, and if we are to protect the right of all American citizens to live safely in their homes, free of the fear of projectiles invading their space, then we need to focus not on guns per se but on the real killer: ammunition. Handgun bullets are relatively cheap, but the real cost of that one stray bullet is enormous.

A study published in the *Journal of the American Medical Association* calculated the mean medical cost per gunshot injury in the United States in 1994 to be about $17,000 (almost $25,000 in today's dollars), producing $2.3 billion in lifetime medical costs, of which $1.1 billion or nearly half was paid by U.S. taxpayers. The researchers concluded: "Gunshot injury costs represent a substantial burden to the medical care system."[3]

Add to that the cost of police work related to gun violence and the cost of bringing to trial and possibly incarcerating shooters, which averages $31,286 annually, and a conservative estimate of the cost of that one stray bullet borne by our health and judicial systems is $68,000 the first year and roughly two-thirds that every year for as long as the perpetrator sits behind bars.[4] If we include the loss of projected lifetime earnings—$1.2 million for high school graduates and roughly double for college grads—and the indirect costs of gun violence on people's stress levels and home values, the long-term costs skyrocket.[5]

For those who shrug and say that this is the price we have to pay for our right to bear arms, let's look at that stray bullet in terms of another cherished freedom: our property rights. Designers spend a lot of time working within property boundaries and ensuring that home owners receive the level of safety and security required by building codes. But bullets respect no property rights. The bullet that killed that boy flew across four pieces of private property and two public rights of way before it hit him. One bullet, in other words, can negate all that we have put in place to protect people and their property, and, as such, it represents an abrogation of our freedom as much as a protection of it.

147   In 1993, Senator Moynihan proposed that the federal government tax ammunition, with a 10,000 percent tax on the deadliest projectiles.[6] The gun lobby called his proposal laughable, and it went nowhere, but it is an idea worth revisiting. Instead of taxing ammunition, we might consider a more market-driven alternative: charging the ammunition industry for the costs incurred when its products are used to kill or maim people.

We know which companies make bullets, and we know how much it costs us when criminals use their products to harm others. If we were to charge them for these expenses, companies would have an incentive to put in place better precautions to prevent their products' misuse. This would also reduce the costs to taxpayers while saving lives and improving the quality of life for the millions of people who live in fear of gun violence.

The Constitution may give us the right to bear arms, but it doesn't guarantee us the right to have cheap bullets. Nor does it give some the right to violate the property rights of others with ammunition that makes us unsafe in and around our own homes. By making the deadliest bullets cost prohibitive, we would do a lot to protect the constitutional right of all of us to peaceably assemble, as the First Amendment guarantees, in our homes and on public or private property.

Portions of this chapter were previously published in "NIMBY," *Progressive Architecture* (September 1993); and in "Guns Don't Kill People, Bullets Do," *Huffington Post* (January 11, 2012), http://www.huffingtonpost.com/thomas-fisher/guns-dont-kill-people-bul_1_b_1193760.html.

[1] Matt McKinney and Randy Furst, "Stray Bullet Kills Minneapolis 3-year-old," *Star Tribune,* December 27, 2011.

[2] Daniel Patrick Moynihan, "Guns Don't Kill People. Bullets Do," *New York Times,* December 12, 1993.

[3] Philip J. Cook, Bruce A. Lawrence, Jens Ludwig, and Ted R. Miller, "The Medical Costs of Gunshot Injuries in the United States," *Journal of the American Medical Association* 282, no. 5 (1999): 447–54.

[4] Christian Henrichson and Ruth Delaney, *The Price of Prisons: What Incarceration Costs Taxpayers* (New York: Vera Institute of Justice, 2012).

[5] Jennifer Cheeseman Day and Eric C. Newburger, T*he Big Payoff: Educational Attainment and Synthetic Estimates of Work-Life Earnings,* Current Population Reports P23-210 (Washington, D.C.: U.S. Census Bureau, July 2002), https://www.census.gov.

[6] Moynihan, "Guns Don't Kill People."

15

LEFT, RIGHT, AND WRONG

Those who engage in NIMBYism and deal in the politics of no often blame the design community and especially the planning community for many of their discontents rather than see urban designers and planners as allies in coming up with more creative solutions to problems. That hostility to design and planning should concern more than just those who do such work; it should worry us all, since we all suffer from the lack of planning and the poor performance of systems that some of the most extreme advocates of laissez-faire capitalism justify as simply the market-place at work.

Despite this political resistance, however, public planning agencies and private planning firms continue to do their work, devising zoning codes and policies, developing land-use and transportation plans, and directing physical and economic growth. And the private sector thrives not despite this work, as some capitalistic fundamentalists might assert, but because of it. At the same time, some of the responsibilities previously assigned to the public sector are now handled increasingly by the private sector. While the design community debates the aesthetics and relevance of New Urbanism, for example, we sometimes overlook the fact that this movement has in many places represented a shift in responsibility for planning to private developers, whose designers now envision whole towns rather than just parts of them. At the same time, other tasks of planning now occur at the local level, where neighborhoods establish their own priorities without concern for a larger vision.

Urban design and planning, at their best, help us see past local self-interests to a greater good, so why the apparent aversion to them? Our political culture holds at least a partial answer. Over the past few decades, both the political left and the right have attacked planning, but for very different reasons. Since the 1960s, the left has often viewed planning as a tool of those in power, a means of maintaining a repressive order. While that criticism has had some benefit—sensitizing planners to the needs of the powerless, for instance—it has taken its toll on the confidence and expansiveness of planners. Many planning documents now focus so intently on limited, small-scale interventions that they fail to give us a sense of the whole.

In contrast, since the Reagan era, the political right has seen planning in a different light—as something akin to socialism, a drag on free markets. This attitude, too, has brought some needed change. Most planners have

150 given up on old forms of command and control and have learned to act in less bureaucratic and more entrepreneurial ways, combining private-sector management ideas with their public responsibilities. Nevertheless, the criticism of the political right has led some planners to take a pseudoscientific stance that is content with analysis rather than synthesis—that is, they describe problems rather than design solutions to them.

The views of the political left and right related to planning seem opposed, but as political scientist Mark Lilla has argued, both are products of our age of reaction, in which left and right adhere equally to the idea of individual liberation, whether it be liberation from social convention among those on the left or from economic constraint among those on the right.[1] If nothing else, our country has been busy building that utopia of liberation, be it with single-family homes that physically isolate us from our neighbors, free-plan commercial buildings that minimize the constraints on change, or signature works of architecture that hold up the designer as the model of the liberated loner.

Defined as the art of finding and creating common ground, planning has not fared well in a political climate that favors complementary extremes rather than consensus. Yet we need planning now more than ever. Without planning, the left ends up defeating through fragmentation what it most wants—the empowerment of communities and interest groups. Not only is a city more than the sum of its neighborhoods, but also neighborhoods can go nowhere unless their city has a coherent identity and direction, which planning helps create.

At the same time, without planning, the right endangers the very free markets it seeks to protect. As leaders in the business community—from management guru Peter Drucker to multibillionaire investor George Soros—have pointed out, capitalism needs social ballast, or what some have called "social capital," to keep it from destroying what it depends on for its long-term viability: healthy workers, safe communities, and sustainable resources. Planning helps build that social capital, without which capitalism itself would crumble.

What might we do to support the idea of planning in a political culture hostile to it? First, we should insist that those we vote into office insulate planning from partisan politics. That may sound politically naive, but it isn't if we recognize planning for what it really is: not a service of govern-

151 ment or a tool of politicians but an oversight and watchdog activity more akin to the accounting or judicial activities of government. We would not tolerate a politician telling a judge how to decide a case or deciding what a government accountant can and cannot look at, nor should we accept elected officials dismissing judges or accountants based on unpopular decisions or an unwillingness to take orders. Planning is no different. If it is to serve us well, it must be independent, able to look out for the common good apart from the myriad public and private interests that want to gain some advantage through it.

Second, we should embrace the common good that planning seeks to protect. The problem, of course, is that most professionals work for private clients who want their own needs addressed first, which creates a built-in tension that we too often overlook. Many professions have become—and have come to be perceived by the public as—pawns for their private clients, all too willing to do whatever is asked of them within the limits of the law. Such behavior can kill a profession. Planning remains one of the few professions that works almost entirely in the public sector, and for good reason. It serves as a kind of "metaprofession," reminding every other profession of its responsibilities to the public. We need planning, in other words, to protect us from ourselves, and we can perform no greater act of self-interest than to demand that planning remain independent of all self-interest—including our own.

AUTHORITY AND FREEDOM

At the heart of the hostility toward planning lies the peculiar fear of authority many people have along with a near obsession with freedom—a dichotomy apparent in the work of two of the most important urban designers of the twentieth century, Le Corbusier and Frank Lloyd Wright. Both envisioned cities based on their divergent beliefs about the relationship between freedom and authority.

Le Corbusier saw human freedom as dependent on and inseparable from authority, and most of his work, especially his urban design schemes, explored that idea in physical form. In his various plans for Paris, for instance, he called for the demolition of most of the city's historic fabric and its replacement with superblocks of apartments and high-rise office buildings accommodating as many as fifty thousand people. He wanted to liberate the ground for parkland and for spaces where people could freely interact.

We now understand the downsides of this kind of urban renewal, which critics such as Jane Jacobs have rightly recognized as antiurban.[2] But how one sees it depends on one's view of freedom and authority. Le Corbusier, in condensing Paris into towers, saw himself as enhancing urban life and human freedom, not detracting from it. Were he to see what eventually became of his urban design ideas, with automobiles rather than people occupying much of the land on which our cities' towers stand, I suspect he would attribute the failure not to his idea but to the authorities who are unwilling or unable to assert the control necessary to make it work.

The juxtaposition of authority and freedom takes a different form in Le Corbusier's proposals for Rio de Janeiro and São Paulo, Brazil, and for Montevideo, Uruguay. In those schemes, the physical order comes not from the geometry of the plan, as in his Paris proposals, but from the continuous structural frame within which apartments of varying configurations could be built. The sheer size of the structure would have required the coordination and control of a central authority. But the use of that authority to build such a structure also would have given individuals much more freedom in the design and arrangement of their living spaces than would ever have been possible at such densities otherwise.

This idea of freedom through authority prompted Le Corbusier to support syndicalism, a trade union movement popular in France that espoused union control of the means of production. While syndicalism appeared anarchistic in its empowerment of workers and its rejection of parliamentary democracy, many of the supporters of this political movement also backed fascist leaders, reflecting a belief in the coexistence of individual freedom and a strong central authority.

That idea has a long history. From the *Republic,* in which Plato saw the absolute rule of philosopher-kings as essential to individual freedom, to *Leviathan,* in which Thomas Hobbes advocated the absolute rule of a central authority as necessary to civilized life, political theorists have long seen authority as the basis for freedom. While Le Corbusier may not have been fully aware of the idea's lineage, he certainly gave it physical form in his work.

Frank Lloyd Wright's work reflects a very different political vision. Wright's Broadacre City proposal, for example, gave form to the agrarian ideal of people living close to and at least partly off of the land. Wright associated freedom with the autonomy of having access to nature, to one's own land, and to the mobility that technologies such as the automobile, airplane, and helicopter could provide. That ideal led to a very decentralized city, and just as critics lambasted Le Corbusier for promoting the destruction of city centers, they excoriated Wright for encouraging suburban sprawl.

While Le Corbusier saw freedom as occurring within a strong authority, Wright saw individual freedom as necessitating an intimacy with nature and the small-scale institutions of family and community. For Wright, as for Thoreau, that government was best that governed least. And yet, unlike Thoreau, Wright emphasized the importance of community, especially communities on the scale of a few families. In his Quadruple Block Project of 1902, for instance, he had four houses occupying the corners of a square block, each with its own driveway, entrance, and backyard, but with a low wall that enclosed the backyards into a single space and linked the houses, distinguishing the community of four families from the surrounding neighborhood.

The good society, Wright thought, would emerge from such small-scale, consensual communities. Wright's vision, like Le Corbusier's, had a considerable ancestry. Jean-Jacques Rousseau, for example, idealized life lived close to nature and societies in which consensus, rather than an absolute authority, ruled. Similar ideas motivated the democratic and agrarian thought of Thomas Jefferson and the transcendentalism of Emerson and Thoreau. While Wright never systematized his social ideas into a coherent theory, he seemed conscious of their roots, especially among American thinkers. That his vision was later distorted in the mass-produced suburbanization of the United States after World War II does not diminish the importance or power of what Wright saw, any more than the large-scale urban renewal in American cities after the war diminishes the compelling nature of what Le Corbusier envisioned.

OPPOSITIONAL OR OPPOSABLE THINKING

Despite their differences, Le Corbusier and Wright both represented a tradition of seeing reality in oppositional terms, something that we saw plenty of in the twentieth century. But in recent decades in the United States, we have begun to shift from that oppositional way of thinking to more integrative habits of mind. Oppositional thinkers perceive situations in binary terms and often see conflict in an adversarial, win-or-lose way. Such thinkers also tend to view conflict in terms of unattractive trade-offs, to consider situations sequentially or as independent parts, to simplify the possible causes, and to limit the consideration of alternatives. Oppositional thinking frequently uses sports or military metaphors to frame discussions, and it often has the combative tone of trial law or partisan politics, where winning can become an end in itself. At the same time, such thinking had a formative role in shaping cities in the past, where communities were divided in a binary way, between public or private property ownership.

Not to sound too oppositional about it, but the inverse of oppositional thinking is what Roger Martin has called "opposable" thinking. In his book *The Opposable Mind,* Martin defines this mode of thought with a quote from F. Scott Fitzgerald, as "the ability to hold two opposing ideas in mind at the same time and retain the ability to function."[3] In comparison with oppositional thinking, integrative or opposable thinking includes a much larger set of variables when addressing a problem, considers multiple and nonlinear causes, visualizes the whole as well as the parts, and searches for creative, out-of-the-box solutions. Such opposable thinking, in contrast to the oppositional kind, takes a both/and rather than an either/or approach to problems, seeks win–win rather than win–lose solutions to them, and does so through cooperative rather than competitive relationships. Instead of the black-and-white world of the oppositional mind, integrative or opposable thinkers see the world in shades of gray.

Opposable thinking has become increasingly dominant as an approach to public problems, many of which have resulted from oppositional thinking. For example, in the United States we no longer accept racially segregated or "redlined" communities, which stemmed from an oppositional way of looking at how people should live. And as we watch the ideological battles and listen to the combative tone of politicians in Congress and our statehouses, we can see how oppositional thinking tends to lead, in the end, to gridlock. In the ever-more interconnected, global reality in which we live, we have no choice but to become more integrative and opposable in our thinking: embracing diversity, welcoming differences, and keeping seemingly opposed perspectives in mind at the same time.

Oppositional thinkers may see those with a more opposable mind-set as lacking clarity or logic, but that perception arises from a misunderstanding of the rigor of opposable thinking. While oppositional thought tends to use inductive or deductive logics, opposable thought favors the abductive kind, making lateral connections among seemingly disparate ideas in order to create something new and better than we had before. Such reasoning continually crosses boundaries in search of innovative and creative ideas; thus it runs counter to every effort to divide reality into dichotomies.

Opposable thinkers look at issues from multiple scales, in both space and time, to make sure they have accounted for all of the likely consequences of their actions. Too many decision makers in the past have addressed challenges at one scale or in one time frame, paying little attention to history or context, and the results have been a lot of unintended and sometimes undesirable consequences. To reduce the likelihood of unanticipated results, opposable thinkers work at several scales at once and try to anticipate the many possible outcomes of decisions over long time frames and in far-removed places.

A related characteristic of opposable thinking is the use of an iterative, critical process. Too often, we try to solve the wrong problem or implement a decision without prototyping and testing it. Opposable thinkers start by trying to define the real problem, which is often not the one we think it is, and then explore multiple schemes, subjecting the work to a number of peer reviews and critiques before anything is implemented. If we are going to solve a problem, it might as well be the right one, and we should select a solution that we know will work.

Opposable thinking also involves aesthetics. Most people see aesthetics in terms of the appearance and the appeal of things, and that is certainly a part of it, but aesthetics also represents a powerful way of overcoming the often-false polarities and reductive tendencies of oppositional thought. Aesthetics shows us how to deal with simplicity and complexity at the same time and in an integrated way, as we see in every well-designed product and environment.

Aesthetics also tolerates differences of opinion. Unlike the oppositional idea of convincing others that we are right and they are wrong, the opposable mind often uses aesthetics to embrace the diverse opinions of others and to find a way to work with them rather than against them, something that we need to learn to do in our politics as well as our civics.

Finally, aesthetics appeals to our emotions as well as to our reason. Factual information may convince us to take a particular course of action or to agree to a specific narrative about a situation, but rarely does it move most people to change their beliefs or alter their views of the world. For that, we need aesthetics. The major religions understand this and orchestrate words, images, sounds, and spaces in ways that cause people to transform themselves and their lives. Secular culture—both the private and public sectors—should consider doing the same, focusing less on the bottom line or the latest poll numbers and more on the experiences, values, and emotional needs of people.

Portions of this chapter were previously published in *Architecture Minnesota* (July/August 1998); "Architecture and Social Vision," *OZ* 9 (1987), published by Kansas State University College of Architecture and Design; and "Public Value and the Opposable Mind: How Multiple Sectors Can Collaborate in City Building," *Public Administration Review* (2014).

[1] Mark Lilla, "The Truth about Our Libertarian Age," *New Republic*, June 17, 2014, https://newrepublic.com.

[2] Jane Jacobs, *The Death and Life of Great American Cities*. New York: Random House, 1961.

[3] Roger Martin, *The Opposable Mind: How Successful Leaders Win through Integrative Thinking* (Boston: Harvard Business School Press, 2007), 7–8.

PART VI

ECONOMICS

Like our educational and political systems, our economy (a system equally designed) does not work for most people nearly as well as it should. As often happens in a redesign process, we might begin by returning to the original intentions of the designer—in the case of capitalism, Adam Smith. In 1776, Smith asked why we value diamonds, which have so little use, and don't value water, without which we cannot live.[1] He saw capitalism as a way of resolving that paradox of value, with the invisible hand of the marketplace enabling us to do good while doing well. Yet, after a few centuries of growth, capitalism still has not resolved the wicked problem of our overvaluing diamonds and undervaluing water.

The first chapter in this part looks at our built environment, in which we spend huge amounts of money on the diamond-like baubles of lavish materials and excessive space while wasting the things we cannot live without: freshwater, clean air, and healthy ecologies of plants and animals that we need to remain healthy ourselves. The move toward sustainability and resilience represents one way of resolving Smith's paradox, and this chapter looks, abductively, at how that has and hasn't worked.

The second chapter considers the next stage in capitalism's development, the rise of what economist Jeremy Rifkin calls the "third industrial revolution," and what it implies for how we will live and work, how our cities will change, and how economic activity will respond to the new ways in which we will make things and deliver services.

Chapter 18 explores what social psychologist Richard Farson calls "metadesign," the application of design thinking to big-system problems, like creating an economy that provides for everyone's hierarchy of needs, starting with the most basic necessity of all: shelter.

[1] Adam Smith, *An Inquiry into the Nature and Causes of the Wealth of Nations* (Chicago: University of Chicago Press, 1952), 12.

16

AN OPPOSABLE ECONOMY

Economics has tended to follow an oppositional way of looking at the world.[1] We see that not only in the idea of competition, with winners and losers, but also in the way we view the designed world as being in opposition to the natural one, with the latter serving as something to exploit for the former. Economics did not start this way. For example, its name shares the same root as ecology: *eco* means home, and economics involves the management of our planetary home and ecology the study of it. Originally, when people inhabited relatively small communities, the "home" meant not just our dwellings but also the natural and designed environments, and "eco-nomics" and "eco-logy" related to the scale at which most people lived. The oppositional view that has tended to pit economics and ecology against each other over the past century or so stems not from something inherent in the two ideas, since they share a common focus on "the home," but instead from the scale at which we now conceive of them.

We now understand ecology and economics at both small and large scales, locally and globally, but the suffixes of the two words suggest a fundamental difference in how they proceed. In its study of our planetary home and all of the ecosystem patches within it, ecology utilizes Martin's "opposable" way of thinking, which keeps large and small scale in mind at the same time, knowing that ecosystems at one scale depend on and affect those at other scales.[2] Economics should do the same, but it has not yet managed to do so very well. Instead, it looks at resources in isolation from their human and natural ecosystems, and economists, rather than dealing with the damage and waste this causes, tend to view these as "externalities" that fall outside their cost-benefit calculations. This represents an oppositional way of thinking, with winners and losers, rather than an opposable one in which winners also lose when any system continually creates losers. Just as we might have a hard time managing a home that is too large, humanity has not managed the planet very well. When it comes to economics—the management of our home—scale matters, and the smaller the scale at which it operates, the better.

Adam Smith realized this in his economic vision. He saw capitalism as working best at a local scale, where "moral sentiment" would serve as a check on the desire of some people to exploit other people and other places.[3] We would not pollute the river that we also drink from or harm neighbors we must deal with on a daily basis. Thought of as an ecosystem patch, capitalism works well. It husbands supplies, stewards resources, and curbs demand to fit with what a local economy can produce and manage. At a global scale, however, Smith's idea of moral sentiment breaks down. Because we can exploit people we will never know and damage places we will never see without a sense of personal responsibility or moral duty, global capitalism is different in kind and not just in degree from local capitalism.

That difference in kind suggests that the real distinctions among economic systems have to do with their scale and not their type. We have long thought of communism as the economic opponent of capitalism, but both became large-scale, bureaucratic systems, and, as such, they had many of the same faults. And despite their obvious differences, the twentieth-century economies of the United States and the former Soviet Union tended to suffer from similar failures, as big initiatives and poorly designed incentives led to the bursting of economic bubbles. At the same time, those two large-scale economies produced similar built environments, with destructive urban renewal, faceless office towers, arid public housing projects, and soulless cities—and all of it damaging to ecosystems.

Reaction to the idea of large-scale, bureaucratic governments and businesses emerged in the United States in the 1980s. Supply-side economics held out the false promise of shrinking the government and unleashing the private sector by cutting taxes and distributing political power to state and local levels. Yet just the opposite occurred. The U.S. government proved very difficult to shrink, and, indeed, its obligations continued to grow faster than its revenues, leading to periods of large deficits. At the same time, corporations such as the auto companies and the investment banks became "too big to fail," requiring bailouts by the federal government that displeased many on the political left and right for different reasons.

In hindsight, postmodern design of the 1980s showed that something had gone wrong. Despite claims of contextualism, much of the historicist work of that period seemed to get bigger and glitzier as the decade wore on, with ornament stretched across the facades of buildings in great displays of ostentation and with developments and individual structures that grew in size and scale. Our designed environments often mirror our unstated desires, and the ugliness of the former should cause us to wonder about the latter.

In response to the failure of both postwar and supply-side economics, a growing number of critics have begun to see our problems as stemming from the sheer scale of our economy and the sheer size of big business and big government.[4] A redesigned economy would return to the term's original meaning and see economics and ecology as inseparable, understanding global impacts but always acting locally. Such an economy would operate not according to the current system of constant growth, resource depletion, pollution, and waste but rather as "a steady-state economy," as critic Kirkpatrick Sale puts it in *Human Scale*—diverse, balanced, and well adapted to the local habitat. Sale argues for an economy that "minimizes resource use, sets production on small and self-controlled scales, emphasizes conservation and recycling, limits pollution and waste, and accepts the finite limits of a single world."[5]

The designed environments in which we live and work should reflect this economic idea. They should conserve energy, use renewable or recyclable materials, reduce our dependence on fossil fuels, create more intimately scaled communities, and construct buildings using local materials and labor as much as possible. This represents not left-wing utopia but simply a recognition of the obvious: that we cannot continue to exploit finite resources until we have nothing left for ourselves or others, nor can we continue to pollute the air and water on which we all depend. Many in the design community have begun to create built environments that acknowledge these facts, but there remains a lot of resistance on the economic side, in part because we still lack a sense of how to get from the exploitative and unsustainable economy we now have to a new one.

It's as if we have become addicts, hooked on the power and pleasures that a carbon-based economy has created for us over the short term. The psychologist Anne Wilson Schaef argues in her book *When Society Becomes an Addict* that our social system sometimes behaves in an addictive manner not unlike that of a drug abuser, an idea that certainly seems to apply to how reliant the U.S. economy has become on oil.[6] When our supply of oil seems threatened by conflicts in other countries, the United States fights with the intensity of an addict deprived of a fix. Our military support of oil-producing nations feels like we are protecting our dealers to ensure our drug supply. And as the continual supply of our drug has started to appear vulnerable because much of it comes from other countries, the United States has started to "frack" for oil within its territory, like an addict desperately looking for the last few veins to tap.

164   Many may reject this analogy, but such denial is also part of addiction. Besides, the United States has already admitted to having a dependency problem, back during the oil crises of the 1970s. Unfortunately, we did not set our goals high enough then; rather than attempting to end our reliance on oil, we accepted a reduction in demand. But addictions can prove difficult to control, and in the 1980s we suffered a relapse, increasing our oil use and helping our dealers in the Middle East—both friend and foe—to rearm themselves. As we look back on the past several decades, the wars we continue to wage seem almost inevitable. Addiction breeds violence, as we know at the local level, with drug-fueled conflicts seen in the streets of many cities.

Still, today we have even more cause to end our oil dependence than we had years ago. By doing so, we could not only partly defuse the situation in the Middle East but also begin to curb the even more ominous threat of the changes to the earth's climate that have come to light. The widespread combustion of oil and gasoline has become a major suspect in the mounting evidence for climate change.

In addition to denial, our frequent response to such threats has been to seek out (or hope for) technological solutions: creating more fuel-efficient automobile engines, for example, or designing less wasteful mechanical equipment for buildings. But just as methadone provides only a palliative to heroin addiction, such technical "fixes" leave intact our seemingly unlimited craving for oil, a finite and increasingly vulnerable resource.

Instead of seeking technological solutions, we should begin to address the underlying reasons for our oil dependence, first by examining the way we live. Here, the design community can make a real contribution. While the professions of architecture and urban design cannot change the world, they can begin to offer visions of what an existence much less dependent on oil might be like. The weaning of the West away from oil must be accompanied by a broader questioning of mass production and consumption, large-scale bureaucratic organization, and natural resource exploitation. As with most addictions, our dependence on oil will not be cured unless we make changes in our way of life.

Such talk may seem, to some, either hopelessly idealistic or outright un-American. That criticism, however, stems from a nearsighted view of history. The West's absolute dependence on oil is less than a century old and the result of conscious choices to pursue certain technologies, such as the gasoline engine and fossil-fuel-driven heating, rather than others, such as the electric engine and solar heating. With enough conviction and the right leadership, we can begin to make other choices.

One such choice would be to rescale and revalue our economy. What does that mean and what might it entail? In design, when a problem seems unsolvable, it is usually because we are thinking about it at the wrong scale; when we look at the issue from a larger scale or try to address it at a more manageable scale, we can often make a lot more progress. The economy, as a designed system, would benefit from the same way of working.

The national scale of most economies has proven increasingly problematic. On one hand, many corporations have become global players, making it harder for any one nation to regulate or even tax these businesses and making it easier for some companies to evade meeting their home countries' environmental standards or even their workplace safety standards and taxation requirements. On the other hand, many communities find themselves at odds with and frustrated by national economic policies that run against local interests and values, be it the subsidization of rural communities by prosperous metropolitan ones or the imposition on urban communities of the more conservative values of rural ones.

As we overcome our addiction to oil, either by choice or as the result of the eventual depletion of its supply, we will need to look at more local ways of fueling economic activity. That will likely involve not just the use of more local sources of energy—solar power in sunny regions, hydro in coastal areas, wind in higher elevations—but also local economies' utilization of local material resources and talent. One of the fastest ways of rescaling our economies to become more local and more in line with the scale of ecosystem patches is through the use of local currencies, something that has become more common in recent years. A local currency gives a community leverage to incentivize what it values and disincentivize what it doesn't want or can't sustain.

The rise of local currencies and local economies will demand that we employ an opposable way of thinking, forcing us to accept seemingly contradictory economic strategies and public policies among adjacent communities and regions. If a rural community values guns and the livelihood that hunting allows and an urban community bans guns in response to the human and economic toll of gun violence, so be it. Likewise, if an urban community values treating same-sex couples as equals to heterosexual couples and a rural community sees this as contrary to its beliefs and its faith traditions, then also so be it. Economic activity will follow such policy decisions, as will the demographic profiles of particular regions as people migrate to those places that align with what they value.

That kind of migration already occurs, of course, as individuals and families move to where they feel more at home. While that mobility has transactional costs to those who make such changes in their lives, it comes at a lower price than the political dysfunction that has resulted from our not accommodating the profound regional differences across the United States.

The notion of national economies withering and regional economies emerging has gained credence in recent years, with advocates such as Bruce Katz at the Brookings Institution, and it also has a fairly long history, dating back at least as far as Jane Jacobs's 1969 book *The Economy of Cities*.[7] In the context of this book, the regionalization of economic activity also has a design component to it. Local economies and currencies will force communities to create the systems and incentives that they want to see. This will help each place recognize that it has the capacity to design its economy to fit its values and its capacities, and will almost guarantee that whatever a community devises, it will have to avoid becoming addicted to some unsustainable or highly vulnerable outside resource and learn to depend, instead, on the creativity of its own people in utilizing and stewarding what is readily at hand. For most of human history communities have managed to do this, and we can learn to do it again.

Portions of this chapter were previously published in "Our Oil Addiction," *Progressive Architecture* (March 1991).

[1] Smith, *The Wealth of Nations,* bk. 1, chap. 4.

[2] Martin, *The Opposable Mind.*

[3] Adam Smith, *The Theory of Moral Sentiments* (Indianapolis: Liberty Fund, 1984), pt. 4, chap. 1.

[4] The desire to reduce the scale of organizations, public and private, cuts across political lines, with organizations like the Center for Sustainable Economy sharing some views with the Tea Party faction of the Republican Party.

[5] Kirkpatrick Sale, *Human Scale* (1980; repr., Gabriola Island, B.C.: New Society, 2007), 330–31.

[6] Anne Wilson Schaef, *When Society Becomes an Addict* (New York: HarperCollins, 1987).

[7] Bruce Katz and Jennifer Bradley, T*he Metropolitan Revolution: How Cities and Metros Are Fixing Our Broken Politics and Fragile Economy* (Washington, D.C.: Brookings Institution Press, 2013); Jane Jacobs, *The Economy of Cities* (New York: Random House, 1969).

17

A THIRD INDUSTRIAL REVOLUTION

169   Local economies cannot exist in isolation from global effects, any more than ecosystem patches can exist apart from global climate change. So even as economic activity becomes more locally distinctive, global economic and technological changes will still affect it. One such change involves the rise of what the economist Jeremy Rifkin has called a "third industrial revolution."[1] Rifkin's argument has profound implications for our daily lives and for how we will occupy the planet in the future. Enabled by digital media, mobile devices, and micromanufacturing technologies like 3-D printing, the third industrial revolution, like its two predecessors, "will fundamentally change every aspect of the way we work and live," writes Rifkin. With it will come a shift, he argues, from the "top-down organization of society . . . to distributed and collaborative relationships," from "fossil-fueled" industry to a "green industrial era," and from "hierarchical power" to "lateral power."[2]

Industrial revolutions have long affected design fields like architecture. The modern architectural profession emerged in the nineteenth century, during the first industrial revolution, as the mechanization of manual labor led to the need for new types of buildings and as technology allowed for larger and taller structures. The global profession of today arose in the twentieth century with the mass production and consumption of the second industrial revolution, which saw the rise of specialized architectural firms able to mass-produce big buildings all over the world as well as star architects able to create signature structures suitable for mass consumption via the media.

Although the second industrial revolution is ongoing and will remain with us for some time, it has entered what Rifkin calls its "end game," burdened by its unsustainable dependence on fossil fuel and its unsupport-able levels of debt.[3] Meanwhile, the third industrial revolution has come on at a rapid pace, evident in the speed with which, for example, social media has transformed the news business, iTunes has upended the music industry, and Google has become the world's third most valuable company in just fifteen years.

Evidence of the speed of its adoption, the third industrial revolution has become the theme of the World Expo 2017, to be held in Kazakhstan. Rifkin has consulted on the event, which has embraced his "five pillars" of this new economy:[4]

1. Shifting to renewable energy
2. Envisioning buildings as power generators
3. Using hydrogen to store energy
4. Sharing power via an Internet-enabled grid
5. Switching to electric vehicles

As Expo 2017 brings international attention to this revolution, we will feel the real impact of it on our daily lives as we shift from an economy of mass production and consumption to one based on mass customization, in which everyone may become a producer as well as a consumer of goods and services.

Designer Alastair Parvin has shown what this might mean.[5] He and his Wikihouse team have developed an open-source design for a small, extremely low-cost house that ordinary people can download, fabricate on a CNC machine, and erect themselves in a day without the need for tools or even construction skills. If the twentieth century "democratized consumption," says Parvin, the twenty-first century will "democratize production" through mass customization efforts like Wikihouse.

The third industrial revolution will also have a tremendous effect on the forms of cities. Most of us still occupy the unsustainable shell of the second industrial revolution: living in residential areas, commuting to work in commercial districts, and buying goods often produced at a large scale in faraway places. The third industrial revolution may turn all of that on its head. For instance, the people who staff many of the software and digital fabrication companies that have sprung up in cities all over the United States increasingly live, work, and make things—and even grow things—in close proximity to one another.

Fostering this new economy may require a rethinking of policies written in the twentieth century and still largely enforcing the old economy of mass production and consumption. The separation of residential, commercial, and industrial zones, for example, has become a barrier to innovation, which increasingly depends on the maximization of interactions among diverse people and human activities. This may, in turn, put New Urbanism in a new light. More walkable communities and denser mixed-use and mixed-income neighborhoods will now have economic benefits as well as social and environmental ones.

The third industrial revolution may lead as well to new kinds of buildings, as happened in the previous two industrial eras. Just as we separated cities in the twentieth century into single-use zones, we have constructed a lot of buildings for singular purposes, full of special-use spaces. That made sense in the old economy based on disaggregation and specialization, but in the new economy—characterized by a fluidity of living, working, and making—purpose-built structures can become quickly obsolete.

To see what lies ahead, we might look at where many businesses of the third industrial revolution have gone: to the warehouse districts of cities. They have done so not because entrepreneurs like exposed brick but because older warehouses often have the spatial flexibility and structural capacity to accommodate a wide variety of uses. This suggests that the buildings that will do the best in the new economy will have a switchable character, with high ceilings, hefty construction, and open plans that allow people to mass-customize their own spaces.

NEW KINDS OF PRACTICES

Professional design practice may also change in dramatic ways. For example, public-interest design, now a marginal practice in the architectural profession, seems likely to grow and thrive in the third industrial revolution. That will stem partly from the mass customization that will come with seeing all seven-plus billion people on the planet as potential "clients" and providing them with open-source, easily fabricated systems that they can download and adapt to their particular needs, as Parvin has done.

But public-interest design also prompts a type of practice ideally suited to the collaborative and distributed quality that Rifkin sees as characteristic of the new economy. The need to develop extremely low-cost, culturally appropriate solutions has led public-interest designers to form nonprofit firms like MASS Design Group and IDEO.org, often in partnership with other nongovernmental organizations (NGOs) and universities.[6] In contrast to the medical model of practice that the design community has long followed, providing custom responses to individual needs, public-interest design has begun to evolve a public health model of practice, mass-customizing architecture for large populations of people.

Rifkin sees businesses morphing in the third industrial revolution "from primary producers and distributors to aggregators" able to "manage the multiple networks that move commerce and trade."[7] For instance, in the second industrial revolution architects became the primary producers and distributors of building designs. But in the third industrial revolution, as managing flows becomes more important, the specialization in building design has marginalized architects, at least in the minds of many clients, who face all sorts of design problems that do not involve the creation or renovation of buildings.

While a growing human population will still need a lot of buildings, design firms may morph along with the rest of the business world to become more the managers of networks and aggregators of expertise, with building design becoming just one of many services. Indeed, given the expense of erecting them and the impact they have on the planet, buildings may also become solutions of last resort, after architects have explored every other alternative to meet their clients' needs. And construction, when it occurs, may have to be more noninvasive, like modern surgery, minimally disturbing sites and allowing for the rapid healing of people and places.

This may, in turn, bring changes to the composition of firms. As Rifkin suggests, the second industrial revolution encouraged monocultures in everything from how we grow food to how we organize businesses. While monocultures create efficiency and predictability, in the case of architecture they also make it hard for clients to tell the difference between one firm and another, with all firms offering similar services, standard practices, and, at least to some clients, indistinguishable results.

Rifkin sees the third industrial revolution rewarding those who create polycultures and permacultures instead of monocultures. That may lead architectural firms, long dominated by the design disciplines, to cultivate richer and more diverse ecologies of staff and consultants from a wider range of backgrounds and fields, people who are able to embrace what Rifkin describes as the dominant values of the new economy: "empathy" and "biosphere consciousness."[8]

Polyculture firms have begun to emerge as architects partner with physicians to meet the needs of people with particular health conditions, with chemists to devise new recyclable and biodegradable products, and with anthropologists to understand the beliefs and behaviors of people in different cultures. Such firms may serve niche markets, but they also have very little competition and, in a globally connected world, large numbers of potential clients.

POLITICS OF THE NEW ECONOMY

The third industrial revolution has equally profound implications for economic policy. The twentieth century defined an era in which capitalist and communist governments competed, militarily as well as economically. The face-off between those two systems, however, obscured more important shifts within capitalism itself as it went global and, more recently, as the digitally driven third industrial revolution has started to overthrow old business models and transform capitalism from within. Governments need to get ready for this new economy, which combines elements of capitalism and communism and represents one of the great opportunities of our era.

Those who work in the public sector know all too well that they can no longer keep going as they have, cutting budgets and squeezing services while continuing, year after year, to try to do all that they have done in the past with less and less money. We might wish things could go back to the way they were, but that won't happen for one primary reason: the economy in which we work has changed in fundamental ways. Hoping or pretending that this isn't so will only delay the inevitable and make it harder for us to adapt when we find ourselves forced to change.

To understand how the current economy differs from the one we have known, consider just one statistic: analysts who follow small businesses estimate that the proportion of "contingent" workers—the self-employed, freelancers, and "accidental entrepreneurs" laid off from full-time positions—in the workforce will grow to 40–45 percent by 2020 and will become a majority by 2030.[9] The recent economic downturn has fueled some of that growth, with a sizable number of people forced into contingent work with the slowdown in hiring in many parts of the global economy. As such, the increase in the number of involuntarily unemployed workers represents a lot of personal hardship, with a lost generation of workers too old to learn the skills needed for the new economy and yet too young to retire from the last one. Helping that part of the population remain productive workers and engaged citizens presents a real challenge for the public sector.

The rise of a large contingent workforce also has a more optimistic side to it, however, since it reflects the emergence of an economy in which workers will have much more flexibility in terms of how, when, and where they work. They will have, over the course of their careers, many "gigs" and maybe even several careers rather than the long-term, relatively permanent employment of the old economy. Global competition has driven this shift, in part, by forcing employers to keep fixed costs low and to staff up or down quickly, whenever and wherever needed. But equally important has been the ability of people in the Internet age to work from their homes, with colleagues locally or around the world, offering products or services that they believe in and get satisfaction from providing.

Much of the political discussion in the United States seems oblivious to this tectonic shift in the economy. Apart from leaders such as former secretary of labor Robert Reich, who has written insightfully on this topic, most American politicians talk as if we were still in the last century.[10] For example, efforts by the federal government to enhance manufacturing jobs, while very much needed, seem focused on boosting an older model of large-scale, "heavy" industry. In the next economy, "manufacturing" may more often occur at a micro scale, with freelancers 3-D printing in their back bedrooms or the self-employed laser cutting products in their garages. The skills that such workers need will be less about manual labor and more about operating computer-controlled equipment or developing craft abilities.[11]

Meanwhile, the opposition to universal health care among some in the business community also misreads the new economy. Self-employed workers will increasingly depend on durable, reliable infrastructure as they communicate with and ship products to customers globally. They will need affordable health care equal to what large companies provide their employees, and they will have the option of living wherever they want, which will likely be places with high quality of life and added convenience.

Other countries understand this all too well. My colleagues in Canada talk about their country being well positioned to attract the best and brightest entrepreneurs from the United States and abroad because of its universal health care coverage, its openness to immigrants from all over the world, and its extensive public investment in quality-of-life features ranging from safe, affordable neighborhoods to clean, accessible natural areas. In other words, public efforts that are often dismissed in Congress as "socialism" and voted against because they represent "big government" have become critical factors in the global economic competitiveness of the United States. Those places that respond to the needs of the new economy first will thrive, and those that don't will fade along with the old economy they continue to cling to.

The economy, in other words, will demand not only a greater amount of public investment than conservatives seem to want but also a different kind of public investment than what at least some liberals have in mind. Much of the infrastructure discussion in both parties, for instance, seems to extrapolate trends from the last century, based on the old economy of people commuting to work nine to five, Monday through Friday. In the next economy, that commuting pattern may largely disappear as people's travel needs become less time-bound and more dispersed. As a result, we may find ourselves with more highway capacity and transportation infrastructure than we need, enabling us to reduce expenditures in this area. At the same time, we may need a much more robust data infrastructure and a much more resilient electrical grid, powered by as many different sources as possible to ensure its reliability.

Indeed, resilience, affordability, and quality of life may become three of the public sector's most important economic development strategies in the future. Because contingent workers can often live where they want, they seem ready to choose to live in places that can provide them the access and flexibility they need to do their work, along with the features that make a place hospitable for such workers, who often lack offices to go to or colleagues to work with. It may become more important, for example, for a community to provide high-bandwidth wireless service and good quality of life than to offer the traditional economic incentives of tax breaks, financial incentives, and minimal regulation. What worked in the old economy can completely backfire in the new one.

This postindustrial, post-Gutenberg world is not a new idea. But the growing fluidity of the global economy, the dramatic disruptions of the digital revolution, and the radical empowerment of individuals through mobile computing and micromanufacturing have all made that idea a reality for an increasing percentage of the workforce. If this new economy is to thrive, we will need the same degree of flexibility, adaptability, and

176 creativity in the public sector. It seems likely, for example, that the public sector will experience the same growth in contingent workers, able to do specific tasks at lower cost without the long-term commitment of full-time staff. Many communities, of course, utilize volunteers for a number of activities, and that practice will likely grow as the number of retired people increases. But a contingent workforce in the public sector will also open up opportunities for greater flexibility in how citizens engage with their government. People who have more time than they do cash, for example, might be able to perform work in lieu of paying some taxes or, in a barter arrangement, provide some kind of services in exchange for others.

We can already see the impact of this economy in the retail sector, with the advent of iTunes leading to the closing of many record stores and the success of Amazon.com prompting the bankruptcy of many bookstores. Growing at double-digit rates and expected to account for more than $2 trillion in sales in the United States in 2016, e-commerce has given many individuals and small businesses access to a global marketplace for specialized products and services that the old economy never could have sustained.[12] The trend of e-commerce replacing activities that once occurred in brick-and-mortar locations does not mean that we won't need buildings anymore, but it does suggest that we will increasingly use buildings primarily for what we can't get any other way, such as face-to-face conversation in the company of others. Indeed, coffee shops and similar places may become even larger and more pervasive as growing numbers of the self-employed use the consuming of beverages as an excuse to get out of their home offices to be with and work among others.

To see the new economy in action, go to the nearest coffeehouse and observe the number of people who sit there for hours, working on their laptops and tablets. So how do we embed the fact of this new economy into day-to-day public decision making? One rule of thumb might be useful here. If a public investment involves continuing to do what a community has done for decades—extending roadway infrastructure, expanding bridges and highways, approving more suburban tract developments, enforcing single-use zoning codes—we need to stop and ask if the way things have been done in the past will serve people well in a future that already looks so different from what we knew in the last century. Will we need the same kind or level of investment if half the workforce is at home, with more flexible time constraints, greater need of a social safety net, and higher quality-of-life expectations? Where might we need more investment, and where can we do with less? If nothing else, pausing to ask such questions will enable communities to do what we all need to do these days: think more creatively and imaginatively about a future that will increasingly reward those who think in exactly that way.

The Great Recession, in some ways, signaled the ending of the second industrial revolution and the beginning of the third. And while many workers have suffered greatly in the process and have yet to recover fully from that downturn, we need to see the enormous opportunity that the new economy has put in front of us. Industrial revolutions, as we know from the previous two, prompt the redesign of almost everything. And if we can cast aside some of our old practices and assumptions about what work entails and recognize the vast array of design problems that our civilization now faces, we will see no end to the work we have to do. While these problems remain serious and in some ways threatening to our survival, their solutions will emerge from what Rifkin calls "deep play . . . the way we experience the other, transcend ourselves, and connect to broader, ever more inclusive communities of life."[13] Let the play begin.

Portions of this chapter were previously published in "Architecture in the Third Industrial Revolution," *Architect* (February 2014); and "The Contingent Workforce and Public Decision Making," *Public Sector Digest* (March 16, 2012), http://www.publicsectordigest.com/articles/view/980.

[1] Jeremy Rifkin, *The Third Industrial Revolution: How Lateral Power Is Transforming Energy, the Economy, and the World* (New York: Palgrave Macmillan, 2011).

[2] Ibid., 5.

[3] Ibid., 13–14.

[4] Justine Testado, "Adrian Smith + Gordon Gill Wins Kazakhstan Astana World Expo 2017 Competition," Archinect, November 1, 2013, http://archinect.com.

[5] See Alastair Parvin, "Architecture for the People, by the People," TED Talk, http://www.ted.com. See also Parvin's website, http://www.wikihouse.cc.

[6] See the websites for MASS Design Group, http://massdesigngroup.org, and IDEO.org, http://www.ideo.org.

[7] Rifkin, *The Third Industrial Revolution,* 120.

[8] Ibid., 150.

[9] Small Business Labs, "The Structural Shift to a Contingent Workforce," June 3, 2010, http://www.smallbizlabs.com/2010/06/the-structural-shift-to-a-contingent-workforce.html.

[10] Robert Reich, "Entrepreneur or Unemployed?," *New York Times,* June 1, 2010, http://www.nytimes.com.

[11] Adam Davidson, "It Ain't Just Pickles," *New York Times Magazine,* February 19, 2012, 14–17.

[12] "Global B2C Ecommerce Sales to Hit $1.5 Trillion This Year Driven by Growth in Emerging Markets," eMarketer, February 3, 2014, http://www.emarketer.com/Articles.

[13] Rifkin, *The Third Industrial Revolution,* 268.

18

METADESIGN

One way to think about design as "deep play" entails what Richard Farson, president of the Western Behavioral Sciences Institute, has called "meta-design." A former public member of the American Institute of Architects' board of directors, Farson mused on this when he stepped down from the board in 2003:

> I sometimes wonder what an American architect would say if approached by the leader of China (or the eight hundred million ill-housed, struggling Chinese) seeking his or her help. "Well, the way we believe residential architecture should be practiced is that each home should be custom designed. The architect should be an integral part of the process for each structure, from beginning to end, carefully surveying the site, designing a structure that is particularly suited for that site, working intensively with the client to understand that individual's special needs, making sure that the contractors are performing, and that the project is completed on budget. Normally it takes us about a year or so to finish such a project, and we can undertake perhaps ten a year. We don't condone selling stock plans. But we could bring a thousand architects to work with you." The leader would shake his head, concluding that such a program, even if China could afford it, would take eight hundred years.[1]

Farson ended his talk by calling for a new type of professional, the meta-designer, focused less on the design of individual projects and more on orchestrating a wide range of other disciplines to help address the problems of the built environment. Even more controversially, he argued: "Architecture should be publicly supported in the same way that education and medicine are. Our professional strategies should include making a case for major public funding, to the tune of trillions of dollars over time."

Large-scale public funding of the design profession will not likely happen soon, but Farson's observations show how the dominant mode of design practice may no longer align with what the world needs. The designer–client relationship parallels the doctor–patient relationship in medicine, in which individual needs get addressed one at a time by the professional. But medicine has also evolved another model—public health—to address the needs of large groups of people. The design community has long had a relationship with public health (as we saw in chapter 10), but rarely has it looked to public health as a model for practice. Most practitioners in the design fields work in small businesses, like physicians, rather than in industry and government, like the public health community, even though health, safety, and welfare stand as central justifications for our status as professionals. As a result, we have not built the institutions and agencies that can help us bring our knowledge to large numbers of people who need our expertise and yet cannot, individually, pay for it.

As was evident after the flooding of New Orleans, the devastation of broad swaths of coastline along the Gulf of Mexico and the Indian Ocean, and the leveling of millions of homes in northern Pakistan, the design community lacks a clear way of addressing the large-scale threats to public health that can occur in the built environment—threats that will become increasingly pressing in the future as intense weather events are brought on by global climate change. As MIT scientist Kerry Emanuel has shown, tropical storms now last half again as long and generate winds 50 percent more powerful than storms of just a few decades ago, the result of ever-warmer tropical seas.[2] With rapidly increasing populations living in vulnerable areas, we could see a whole new category of the homeless, "environmental refugees" as Oxford scientist Norman Myers calls them, with "as many as 200 million people overtaken by disruptions of monsoon systems and other rainfall regimes, by droughts of unprecedented severity and duration, and by sea-level rise and coastal flooding."[3]

How should we respond to such a sobering prospect, affecting developed, developing, and undeveloped countries alike? It may be, at least in the short term, that designers can work best as independent, creative entrepreneurs in partnership with the public and nonprofit entities dedicated to helping the growing numbers of people rendered homeless or placeless because of environmental or economic dislocation. Some designers have begun to do just that. They have addressed different aspects of the sustainability and equity problem: the infrastructure needs of slum dwellers, the shelter needs of the homeless, the material needs of those with few resources, and the habitation needs of those on the move.

Such work clearly represents an economic opportunity. But it also raises an ethical question: What obligation do we have to protect people from the elements, provide for their basic needs, and promote their well-being and sense of belonging to a community of other people? Do people, in other words, have a right to shelter? To answer that question, let's begin with the shelter part. Archaeological and anthropological evidence shows that human beings have always had the ability to construct shelter for themselves. Obviously, some people are more skilled at such construction than others, but every human community has possessed the ability to shelter itself, just as we have long had the ability to feed and clothe ourselves. If we didn't, we would not have lasted long as a species, and so securing shelter remains a core part of what it means to be human.

Indeed, when we look at the diversity of shelter that humans have evolved over many thousands of years, we can only marvel at its sophistication: its cultural appropriateness and climate responsiveness. And the fact that we have largely built such shelter with what we have had at hand and have left almost no trace of it behind speaks to the superiority of indigenous shelter to much of what we build today.

For further evidence of our ability to secure shelter, we have only to look at the millions of people living in informal settlements in cities around the world. Drawn by economic opportunity or pushed by rural poverty, the residents of these favelas, barrios, and slums (their very names evocative of their dismissal by the formal economy) have shown great initiative and imagination in the use and reuse of the materials at hand in creating shelter for themselves and their families.

We should not romanticize these environments. As Katherine Boo shows in her book *Behind the Beautiful Forevers,* life in the "undercity" of a Mumbai slum is extremely difficult.[4] What is most inhuman about these places is not the shelter itself but the lack of basic infrastructure—clean water, adequate sanitation, and safe power—as well as the residents' lack of ownership of the land, which makes life there tenuous.

We all depend on governments and nongovernmental organizations to establish the infrastructure and the legal frameworks that allow us to occupy land in a safe and sanitary way, something rarely provided to the residents of informal settlements. That has made the provision of "sites and services" by entities like the World Bank an important strategy in such communities, ensuring stable land tenure and dependable infrastructure on which people can build shelter for themselves.[5] The failure of many governments to provide such things in informal settlements brings us to what we mean by the word *right.*

PROPERTY RIGHTS AND WRONGS

Most governments will say that squatters "have no right" to settle on the land that they occupy. People may have the ability to construct shelter for themselves, but where they build it becomes a matter of property rights, the withholding of which enables those in power to control those without power. Indeed, the image so often seen in global cities of informal settlements pushing right up against formal—and frequently quite expensive—housing makes this conflict between those who have a "right" to their property and those who have no such "right" all too visible.

In the seventeenth century John Locke wrote, "There can be no injury, where there is no property."[6] One way to deal with the inequalities and "injuries" that come from owning or not owning property is through the dissolution of private property, something that utopian writers have envisioned since the time of Plato. This seems unlikely in a world dominated by capitalistic thinking, which upholds private property rights as almost sacrosanct. But the rise of informal economies (which, according to the World Bank, amount to between 25 and 40 percent of the annual economic activity in developing countries in Asia and Africa)[7] suggests that another option has already taken hold: people building their shelter on whatever land they can, regardless of who owns it.

We often see the rise of informal settlements and the informal economies they depend on as a sign of impoverishment, but it may also signal something else: the decline of the nation-state and the ineffectiveness of central governments in controlling what ordinary people do to meet their needs. The people living in such informal communities may not have the "right" to be there, but they do have the responsibility to take care of themselves and their families, and they take on that responsibility with great energy and often a lot of imagination.

Even asking the question of whether people have a right to shelter reveals a terrible skew in how we think about and organize our world. Of course people have a right to protection from the elements; unlike other animals, humans cannot live for very long outdoors, and denying the right to shelter constitutes a denial of what makes us human, something that no one has the right to do. Even criminals who commit the most heinous crimes against humanity still have the right to shelter in the form of a prison cell. That we even ask the question of whether such a right exists suggests that we have somehow lost touch with fundamental aspects of our humanity.

The question also shows that we don't understand a fundamental paradox: the best way to help oneself is to help others. Or, put another way, we only hurt ourselves—economically as well as psychologically—when we refuse to help those in need of something so basic as shelter. Research has shown that people who live in mixed-income communities have better health outcomes than those who live in uniformly poor neighborhoods. Wealthier communities may think that they are protecting their real estate values by forbidding the building of "affordable" housing, but the well-to-do in those communities ultimately pay a much higher price, for two reasons: first, mixed-income neighborhoods have, on average, higher real estate values than those with properties all of one kind, and second, we all pay for higher health care costs through higher premiums and copays when a sizable segment of the population has poor health. By disassociating costs and keeping different areas of human activity artificially separated, we end up making costly—and foolish—mistakes that harm ourselves as well as others.

DESIGN IN THE HIERARCHY OF NEEDS

These costly errors result from our organizing modern societies in ways that cause us to remain stuck on the first two levels of Abraham Maslow's hierarchy of needs.[8] Those first two levels involve basic needs like food, water, warmth, security, stability, and freedom from fear; as Maslow argues, we cannot satisfy higher-order needs like a sense of belonging (Maslow's third level), self-esteem (fourth level), and self-actualization (fifth level) if we remain constantly worried about satisfying the needs of the first two levels. Poor people, of course, face this dilemma, unable to fulfill their higher-order needs because they do not know where their next meals will come from or whether they will be safe when they next leave their homes.

But first- and second-order needs seem to preoccupy almost everyone in our commercial culture, rich and poor. By focusing our attention on what we desire rather than on what we need, commerce has made the quality of our (often imported) food, the convenience of our (often bottled) water, the ubiquity of our (often fossil-fueled) warmth, and the invincibility of our (often electronic) security so much of an issue that people work long hours and aspire to high-paying jobs so that they can afford luxury versions of the most basic needs, and they end up having no more time than the poor for activities that lead to self-actualization.

Maslow does not list shelter in his hierarchy of needs, although warmth, security, and stability are clearly related to having a home. Shelter also seems to be a part of the higher-order needs, involving a sense of belonging, self-esteem, and self-actualization. A life without shelter and a community of some sort is, in a fundamental sense, not a human life. So why do we even need to ask if there is a "right" to shelter? Because the withholding of shelter may be a way to control or defeat others, such as when dictators in countries like Libya and Syria attempt to remove rebels by leveling the buildings and settlements they inhabit or when warring tribes in places like Rwanda or Darfur engage in ethnic cleansing through the elimination of entire neighborhoods or villages. The withholding of shelter through violence becomes a way of dehumanizing enemies.

This leads us to ask, as we deal with homelessness in the United States, what motivates the withholding of shelter for every one of our citizens? Does this constitute our own form of economic cleansing, our own violence against those who suffer from mental illness, addiction, or simply bad luck? Do we so fear the possibility of such hardship in our own lives that we wish the homeless would simply go away, so that we don't have to address their lack of shelter? Does the question of the "right" to shelter say more about those who would deny that right than it does about anything else?

The denial of a right so basic to human well-being as shelter ultimately raises the most fundamental question about ethics: Does anyone, from the most embattled dictator to the most hard-line capitalist, have the right to deny others such a right? In the West, there are four fundamentally different approaches to answering the question of rights, and all four lead us to the same conclusion, although they take divergent paths.

In terms of virtue ethics, it takes but a second of reflection to see that those who would withhold the right of others to have at least a minimum of shelter are not fair, just, or prudent. All human beings have a right to have their most basic needs met, and any society that would deny that right undermines the very basis on which human societies have any role at all. Nor is such denial prudent, since a population without shelter quickly becomes a population that will seek to overthrow those who would deny such a basic need. Here architects and the design community generally have a central part to play not only in the design of housing but also in revealing what happens when such housing is denied.

Social contract ethics leads to a similar conclusion. This ethics holds that all societies have a "contract" with their people to meet their needs, and while different societies meet this contract in different ways, ranging from central authoritarian to minimal, laissez-faire governments, all have (as Hobbes and Rousseau both argued) a contractual responsibility to ensure some degree of shelter for their people. Violation of that social contract, again, becomes a reason for the people to overthrow those in power and establish a new government that meets its contractual obligations. Architects and designers, too, are a part of that social contract, and their professional obligation to enable people to have access to shelter equals the obligation of medical professionals to ensure that people have access to health care or of legal professionals to ensure that they have access to justice.

Duty ethics takes a more reciprocal path to the same point. Kant argued not only that we should treat others as ends and not means to our ends but also that we should act as if everything we do is to become universal. With that categorical imperative in mind, clearly the absence of shelter for even a few cannot become a universal, since that would mean we would accept the absence of shelter for all. So, unless we are all willing to be without shelter—hardly something any person would want—we cannot let any one of us be without it. Here, too, professional duty comes into play. Architects and designers cannot provide architecture for a few without assuming some responsibility for ensuring that all people have at least the minimal shelter available to them. In other words, the design community has as much of an obligation to the poorest among us as to the wealthiest, who can pay design fees; anything less than honoring that obligation represents an absolute abrogation of professional duty.

Finally, consequentialist ethics takes us on yet another path to the same end. It argues that we should attend to the greatest good for the greatest number, a utilitarian calculus that forces us to ask what the greatest number of people need and what actions would lead to their greatest good. In attempting to answer these questions, some may argue that as long as the greatest number of us has shelter we need not concern ourselves with the minority who don't, but that misunderstands the consequences of such thinking. The greatest good has to include the need of all people to have access to shelter, and the greatest number—all people, in other words—have a right to that good. Which is to say that we have not only a right but also an obligation to assert the right of all people to shelter, at least in its most basic form, and anyone who would deny that such a right exists is, in the end, simply wrong.

This chapter first appeared, in different form, as "The Ethics of Housing the Poor," *Journal of Home Economics Institute of Australia* 13, no. 3 (2006).

[1] Richard Farson, comments upon his retirement from the American Institute of Architects board, 2003.

[2] Kerry Emanuel, *Divine Wind: The History and Science of Hurricanes* (Oxford: Oxford University Press, 2005).

[3] Norman Myers, "Environmental Refugees: An Emergent Security Issue" (paper presented at the 13th Economic Forum, Prague, May 2005), 1, http://www.osce.org.

[4] Katherine Boo, *Behind the Beautiful Forevers: Life, Death, and Hope in a Mumbai Undercity* (New York: Random House, 2012).

[5] Stephen K. Mayo and David J. Gross, "Sites and Services—and Subsidies: The Economics of Low-Cost Housing in Developing Countries," *World Bank Economic Review* 1, no. 2 (January 1987): 301–35.

[6] John Locke, "On Property," in *Second Treatise of Civil Government* (Chicago: University of Chicago Press, 1952).

[7] World Bank, "Labor Markets: Workers in the Informal Economy," accessed November 23, 2015, http://web.worldbank.org.

[8] Abraham H. Maslow, *Hierarchy of Needs: A Theory of Human Motivation*, Kindle ed. (n.p.: All About Psychology, 2011).

PART VII

BELIEFS

Much of the poor performance we find in our systems stems from the dysfunctional ways in which we see the world and the beliefs we have about it. Take the idea of competition. While it now dominates much of our thinking about our relations with other people and even other species, human beings have long survived because of the opposite: an altruistic desire to help others, which no doubt arises at least in part from our ability to imagine what we would want others to do for us in similar situations. But it matters greatly how we help. Doing things for others that they have the capacity to do themselves simply debilitates them and reinforces our own sense of power and superiority, however altruistic our intentions. It is far better to help people help themselves by enabling them to do what they already know how to do.

The first chapter in this part looks at how that might happen in informal settlements that lack basic building codes and safety standards because governments and the communities' formal economies do not have the ability or desire to enforce such standards. Rather than provide safe buildings to the millions of people who need them, something that no amount of humanitarian aid could ever fully accomplish, designers could use abductive methods to leverage the capacity of people in such settlements to ensure the safety of their environment themselves, using the same means that they use to build other aspects of their communities.

The second chapter generalizes this approach, looking at how it represents a larger shift in Western culture away from the two prevalent mythologies of the past that allowed us to dominate nature for either theological or technological reasons and toward a new mythology that sees human communities evolving in ways similar to the rest of the animal world.

The final chapter describes how that evolution may occur: through the organization of our knowledge of the world according to how the world is organized—spatially rather than disciplinarily. Ecosystems exist as spatial wholes, as integrated patches, and we will never understand (or stop damaging) such systems until we conceive of them in the same way. Only then may our species finally grow up and join the others with whom we share this planet.

19

COMMUNITY RESILIENCE

Economically impoverished communities, especially the informal settlements that have arisen on marginal or undesirable land in rapidly developing cities around the world, seem to lack any sort of design. Families
frequently build wherever they can, with whatever scrap materials and
discarded products they can scrape together. While these abodes often
represent opportunity and hope for their inhabitants, who have escaped
even worse situations, the living conditions in many informal settlements
are perilous for the people living in and among them, with sometimes
unsanitary dirt floors, unsafe electricity (if they even have electricity), and
unstable structures that are liable to collapse when stressed by hurricanes,
earthquakes, or monsoons.

The physical poverty of such slums, however, often obscures the
wealth of social and cultural capital that can exist within them. And while
the design community has much to contribute to informal settlements in
terms of better housing and infrastructure, the inability or unwillingness
of governments to improve such places makes traditional design methods
rather ineffective. Here, the design of the invisible may have more to offer.
In organizing and educating a community's inhabitants and deploying
unconventional strategies that leverage their rich social networks, designers
can help people make even the most marginal housing and precarious
neighborhoods safer places in which to live. Since such informal settlements rarely have code officials to enforce building standards or the
political support and public capability of building infrastructure, designers
need to engage the core of these communities: parents and their children
and neighbors and their friends.

This approach has become particularly important in an era in which
natural disasters have taken a great toll; according to the Emergency
Events Database, more than 100,000 people have died and more than 200
million have been rendered homeless by disasters each year since 2001,
with an estimated annual economic impact of approximately $90 billion.[1]
The destruction of buildings by tremors or floods has been responsible
for much of the homelessness and death. As the saying goes, earthquakes—
and, by extension, tsunamis—don't kill people, buildings do, and so the
rapid increase in mortality and homelessness in postdisaster situations
is directly related to where and how humans build.

How, then, might we design systems that enable the inhabitants of informal settlements to protect themselves from such hazards as well as to become more resilient to external shocks? The following ten strategies by no means exhaust the possible answers to that question, but they begin to convey the way in which the design community might approach such a challenge. These ideas may seem unconventional in the context of developed countries, where more effective code enforcement and governmental regulation are in place, but design always reflects its context. These ideas try to respond to where the real wealth lies in many emerging countries, with the people themselves, their cultural traditions and personal bonds. Resilient social systems typically evolve over long periods—indeed, their longevity is partial proof of their resilience—and tapping into their durability offers some of the greatest opportunities to make a real difference in the lives of people in need.

One system firmly in place and highly valued, although often horribly underfunded, in many poor countries is the educational system. The fact that kids in Haiti managed to go back to school relatively soon after the 2010 earthquake, often meeting in makeshift classrooms, is an example of the resilience of the educational system in many countries, despite disasters. So how can we use this system to ensure better building safety? One answer might be to teach children the basics of building safety in school, teaching those who live in disaster-prone regions especially about the threats they and their families face when living and working in buildings inadequately reinforced against earthquakes and tsunamis. This might entail the development of simple school curricula, adapted to particular cultures and climates, that would instruct both teachers and pupils on building safety. This may sound odd, but we have evidence that this approach works from our experience in the United States, where educating children about the hazards of smoking helped curb tobacco use among adults as well. Children can be not only great agents of change but also harsh critics of adults, so why not use that force for the good of creating safer buildings and communities?

A second and related strategy involves the use of peer pressure among the social networks of communities. The smoking example is also relevant here. When Americans came to understand that secondhand smoke can be as deadly as smoking itself, we started to see rapid changes in behavior and in the laws regulating smoking, as people saw the actions of others affecting their own health and safety. A similar use of informal social networks might work in the case of promoting building safety; informal information channels could be employed to reveal the ways in which one person's poorly built and inadequately reinforced structure can negatively affect the stability and safety of the structures of others. This is most direct in informal settlements, where people have some personal control over the structures they inhabit, but it could also apply to larger buildings that are badly constructed and potentially unsafe. Peer pressure against those who design, develop, and build unsafe buildings can be a very effective way of achieving a safer environment without resorting to government regulation or enforcement. And in a world with increasingly widespread access to the Internet, social media may lead to something rarely seen before: crowdsourced constraints on those who would act illegally or unethically.

A third idea, with a more positive spin, might be to introduce games. Imagine a game, for example, in which people in high-risk seismic zones compete for desired rewards by seeing who can install the most metal strapping to cross brace buildings in a given time frame. Part of teaching people the rules of the game would, of course, involve instructing them as to where the cross bracing would do the most good—that is, in the process of engaging in the game, they would be educated about the problem and its solution. Similar safety games could be devised to address other disaster threats; for instance, people living along coastlines could compete to see who can get to high ground the fastest, in preparation for when a tremor occurs in advance of a tsunami. Using competition to prepare people for possible disasters and making safety education a social event through the use of games—something we might consider in the United States as well, given the amount of time American youth spend playing computer games—are ways of improving people's quality of life while building their knowledge and sense of community.

This leads to a fourth and related idea: conveying information through cell phone networks. There are, by some counts, five billion cell phones in use around the world, accessed by more than two-thirds of the human population, and many of the users of these cell phones otherwise may have very little money and few possessions. As we saw in the early days of the Arab Spring, cell phones can become critically important tools for even the most impoverished or oppressed, who can effect change through the use of these devices. What if we took advantage of that existing communication infrastructure to improve our physical environment and the safety of buildings and communities? The organization Worldchanging has already developed an open-source website with public-interest design ideas available to anyone with a computer or cell phone.[2] It would not take much more effort to use such a site to begin to convey, in a visual and nonlinguistic form, the basic practices of building safety and structural reinforcement relevant to the material conditions of diverse communities around the world. Never before has it been easier to convey lifesaving information to people by cell phone, as the public health community has discovered. We could take advantage of this technology to promote our own lifesaving building and zoning strategies.

The strategy of using games, whether physical or digital, brings us to a fifth approach: aesthetics. We prefer some games and some phone apps over others because of their aesthetic qualities: how easy they are to learn, how clearly they lead to a goal, and how beautifully they fulfill their objectives. Aesthetics is a powerful tool in affecting human behavior, and while we often separate aesthetics and technics in the developed world, we have an opportunity to reunite them in the developing world in order to enhance safety, creating new safe building practices that are aesthetically pleasing as well. The vernacular architecture in many parts of the world has long done this, revealing the way in which it was built, often with adaptations to the climate and culture of a place. There is a great deal of resistance in developing countries to the idea of returning to vernacular traditions. In Haiti, for instance, the lightweight, wood-framed, thatched-roofed shelters native to the island were remarkably resistant to earthquakes, light enough not to kill people if they fell, and easily rebuilt if tremors or floods destroyed them. But such vernacular building traditions have become aesthetically unacceptable in countries yearning to be more modern. The challenge then becomes one of creating, with the participation of the local residents, modern versions of the vernacular traditions that served them so well in the past. What might the modern equivalents of lightweight, easily assembled structures in a place like Haiti be like? This isn't about going backward but about moving forward to imagine an aesthetically acceptable future that is safer as well as more culturally and climatically appropriate.

Design offers one way of achieving this; advertising offers a sixth possible approach. The public health community has recognized the power of advertising to incite unhealthy behaviors in populations by making things that are hazardous—eating high-fat food, driving fast cars—seem normal and desirable, and so it has learned to fight fire with fire by using advertising images to convey the unhealthiness of such habits and the ugliness and heartache that come from hazardous behavior. Developing countries are awash in Western images promoting things that we have recognized as unhealthy—smoking, for example, remains all too common in such countries. Why not use the medium of advertising to address the unhealthy and hazardous environments in which people live? Given the enormous cost of rebuilding places and people's lives after natural disasters, the cost of advertising what to look for in safe buildings might be well worth it; such an expense would represent only a tiny fraction of the amount of money relief organizations and governments pump into post-disaster settings. This, in turn, suggests a reversal in how people might perceive the design professions—not as a cost too expensive to afford but instead as a form of preventive health care, an investment in which will reduce much greater costs somewhere else.

A seventh strategy might be to leverage consumer behavior in altering unsafe building practices through information campaigns. Communities in most developing countries include myriad small shopkeepers who set up along streets or in the ground floors of buildings, with location close to their customers a key to their success. That locational sensitivity offers an opportunity to put pressure on the owners of unsafe buildings. An information campaign identifying those buildings most vulnerable to collapse could influence the decisions not only of consumers in terms of where to shop but also of store owners in terms of where to locate. This in turn could put a great deal of financial pressure on building owners to get their buildings off the list of unsafe structures. This strategy uses consumer choice rather than regulation as the basis for building safety, with the idea that economics often trumps enforcement.

Indeed, economic strategies may hold the greatest promise for making progress on improving building safety, especially when they utilize existing economic networks. One of the most direct ways to create safer environments is to pay people to monitor and report on the unhealthy activities of others. Health organizations have learned that an effective way of getting people in impoverished communities to take their medications is to pay people to go house to house to ensure the medicines are taken. While that sounds cumbersome and expensive, it turns out not to be so, given the comparatively low cost of employing people in poor communities. Also, this approach uses the social networks and local knowledge of the people in the communities—information that outsiders do not have. The same strategy might work for ensuring building safety: people in local communities could be trained to observe the construction going on in their areas and report on—or, even better, offer advice to—those who are building in hazardous ways. If governments cannot afford enforcement, maybe NGOs can offer direct payments for such observation and reporting.

A ninth idea, and a variation of this economic strategy, would involve the use of barter or micro-lending systems. We have seen how ingenious the people in developing countries can be in leveraging very small loans to start businesses and raise their living standards. What if a similar system were applied to the improvements people make to their living situations, a kind of micro-mortgage system in which people could receive small loans to improve the safety of their dwellings? They could use the cash to pay for building materials and barter for the construction skills necessary to reinforce structures or improve their safety and security. The loans could be considered "repaid" when evidence of the improvements made is produced. The funding for this could come from the pools of disaster relief and emergency response money on which governments and NGOs draw after catastrophic events, with the micro-mortgages viewed as a kind of insurance against the much greater expense likely to be incurred if nothing is done to ensure safer buildings.

A related and final strategy involves using building safety as a key criterion for property ownership in impoverished countries. The economist Hernando de Soto has argued, persuasively, that the best way to stabilize communities, encourage development, and grow the formal economy in informal settlements is to give the residents title to the property on which they have squatted and built.[3] While that has merit as an economic strategy, it often does too little to leverage the granting of title to require that people meet reasonable building safety requirements. This utilizes one legal process that even in the poorest of countries remains relatively intact—title to property and records of ownership—to achieve a public good: safer buildings. As in more developed countries, the possession of title to a property can bring with it an obligation to ensure that the property is safe enough to protect the health, safety, and welfare of those who live and work there.

Facing up to the instability, inequity, and absolute unsustainability of modern technological society, we find ourselves in a situation in which we have not only a lot to offer the developing world but also a lot to learn from it in terms of how to be more resilient and to do more with less, achieving the maximum effect with a minimum of resources. From that perspective, informal settlements may be far behind in terms of their development needs, but they are way ahead in terms of their dependence on social capital in a world where that may become the main source of wealth for us all as other resources dwindle and more systems fail.

This chapter originated as a talk that I delivered at the conference "The Campaign for Safe Buildings" at Yale University's School of Architecture (November 2011).

[1] Centre for Research on the Epidemiology of Disasters, Emergency Events Database, accessed November 30, 2015, http://www.emdat.be/database.
[2] Worldchanging, http://www.worldchanging.com.
[3] Hernando de Soto, *The Mystery of Capital: Why Capitalism Triumphs in the West and Fails Everywhere Else* (New York: Basic Books, 2000).

20

EVOLUTIONARY
TRANSFORMATION

Among the more religiously minded, the word design brings with it an association with the concept of intelligent design, which sees God—or whatever deity or deities a faith community believes in—as the ultimate designer, giving form and shape to every living thing and to the planet itself. In defiance of the scientific consensus around evolution and the slow adaptation of species to their environments, intelligent-design adherents see in the complexity of life-forms and the ecosystems they occupy the hand of a supreme being, drawing an analogy to the environment-shaping work of human designers.

The debate between evolution and intelligent design may seem far removed from and maybe even irrelevant to the issues that the design community deals with. The creation of the built environment, one project at a time, happens at a much faster pace than the evolution of species and in a much more confined space than, say, God's creation of the universe as described at the beginning of the Bible. But this argument between science and religion can shed light on the nature of design, especially as it has expanded to include "invisible" phenomena of human and nature interactions. Evolutionary science reminds us that, when it comes to living things, change often involves small adaptations to environments over very long periods, and these small adjustments can have enormously beneficial effects. At the same time, intelligent design reminds us of the limits we face in trying to fully understand a world we did not create and in creating a world the consequences of which we do not fully understand.

We can learn from this debate, in other words, two very different ways in which humans have related to the natural world, at least in Western culture. As the literary critic Northrop Frye observes, "There have been two primary mythological constructions in Western culture. . . . [In the older mythology] Man was a subject confronting a nature set over against him. Both man and nature were creatures of God, and were united by that fact." Starting in the eighteenth century, the old mythology, Frye argues, found itself usurped by a new mythology rooted in science and technology and based on "the conviction that man had created his own civilization." Frye recognizes that "a major principle of the older mythology was the correspondence of human reason with the design and purpose in nature which it perceives." In the new mythology, "design in nature has been in-creasingly interpreted by science as a product of a self-serving nature. . . . The rational design that nature reflects is in the human mind only."[1]

According to Frye, "Contemporary science, which is professionally concerned with nature, does not see in the ancient mother-goddess the Wisdom which was the bride of a superhuman creator. What it sees rather is a confused old beldame who has got where she has through a remarkable obstinacy in adhering to trial and error—mostly error—procedures."[2] Both of these mythologies are still very much alive, as the debate between intelligent design and evolution shows. Rather than one mythology replacing the other, though, as Frye suggests, the two have become more or less dominant at different times, with the first serving as the basis for resistance and a place from which to counter its opposite.

What Frye's observations reveal, and what often gets lost in the debate between intelligent design and evolution, is that both of these mythologies assume that human beings occupy a special place on this planet, which allows us to dominate, control, and exploit nature, whether through the license that theology gives or through the power that technology provides. Intelligent design and evolution, in other words, while opposed in fundamental ways, offer two competing versions of the same idea: that humanity represents a culmination of a process—whether via divine blessing or intellectual prowess—that allows us to rule the planet, an idea that looks increasingly unsustainable at the beginning of the twenty-first century.

In a study titled "Changing Images of Man," compiled by the Center for the Study of Social Policy/SRI International, several authors, including the historian of mythology Joseph Campbell, describe the Western idea that we humans have the right to use nature and other people as we see fit, leading to what they call a "technological extrapolationist" future.[3] Given our current trajectory, they see a deeply divided and unsustainable future characterized by an increasing concentration of economic and political power in the hands of a few and a growing accumulation of scientific and technological knowledge controlled by "knowledge elites," with most people living in rapidly expanding, unhealthy "megapolitan" cities.

The authors further argue, however, that the seeds of an alternative future exist in the rise of a "postindustrial" economy, an ecological sensibility, and an ethic of self-realization for everyone. These factors could lead to an "evolutionary transformational" future featuring a deconcentration of economic and political power, social constraints on technological progress, more participatory decision making, a stabilized population, and decentralized and more diverse ways of living. The ideas in this report, written in 1973, are echoed by those who now advocate, some decades later, more equitable, ecologically friendly development, although clearly "technological extrapolationists" are still in control of global corporations and major political parties.

Design offers a way beyond this impasse, pointing us in a more sustainable—and more humble—direction than that of the two previous mythologies that have driven civilization. To follow this path, however, we need to understand design in a new way. Most nondesigners see what designers do as the act of giving form or shape to something outside themselves; the designer is envisioned as a transcendent figure who stands outside or above a situation. That notion of the designer plays to the Western idea of humanity standing outside or above nature and justified in shaping it to our will. However, every working designer knows that is generally not how design happens.

While designers do experience transcendent moments—when a solution to a problem comes almost out of the blue or when a problem's place in a much bigger picture becomes clear—they spend most of their time, so to speak, inside of a problem, working within the constraints of a situation, viewing it from the perspective of those who will use the design, and attending to myriad details about how it will get made and withstand use. Design, in other words, involves seeing the world from the inside out more than from the outside in—as immanence more than transcendence.

THE PERENNIAL POSSIBILITY

The author Aldous Huxley would have understood this. In *The Perennial Philosophy,* he argues that all of the major religious traditions have at their core the ideas of both transcendence and immanence.[4] Drawing from the Roman philosopher Plotinus, Huxley urges us to see that "each being contains in itself the whole intelligible world."[5] The divine, in other words, lies not just out there but in each of us, as well as in everything that is not us.

Huxley also suggests that this perennial philosophy leads to an altered view of our relationship to nature. Echoing the "evolutionary transformational" future already mentioned, Huxley writes: "The desire to bully Nature into serving ill-considered temporal ends [is] at variance with . . . the Perennial Philosophy. . . . Compared with that of the Taoists and Far

Eastern Buddhists, the Christian attitude towards Nature has been curiously insensitive and often downright domineering and violent . . . regard[ing] animals as mere things which men do right to exploit for their own ends."[6]

Huxley recalls here the ancient Greeks, who "believed that hubris was always followed by nemesis, that if you went too far you would get a knock on the head to remind you that the gods will not tolerate insolence on the part of mortal men. . . . The Greeks . . . regarded Nature as in some way divine; they felt that it had to be respected and they were convinced that a hubristic lack of respect for Nature would be punished by avenging nemesis."[7]

Modern design has helped facilitate this hubristic lack of respect for nature by providing us with the means not only to separate ourselves from nature in our fossil-fueled homes, offices, and automobiles but also to disconnect ourselves from the consequences of our actions. We have only lately begun to ask: Where do the materials we use come from? What affects have our designs had on nature? Where will the things we make go once we no longer need them? What other uses might they have, and who will be deprived of their benefits in the future once we've exhausted finite resources? Modern design has also served the technological extrapolationists well by using the persuasiveness of well-designed objects and environments to normalize our hubristic behavior in ways that people just a few generations ago would have seen as irresponsible and unsustainable.

But if design is part of the problem, it can also be part of the solution. "The doctrine that God is in the world," Huxley notes, "has an important practical corollary, the sacredness of Nature, and the sinfulness and folly of man's overweening efforts to be her master rather than her intelligently docile collaborator. Sub-human lives and even things are to be treated with respect and understanding, not brutally oppressed to serve our human ends."[8] In terms of design, this means seeing ourselves as an integral part of the natural world, valuing all beings and working with nature as collaborators rather than as controllers. Some will view such principles as impossible to achieve, since we cannot help but affect the material world when we act, needing to consume food and resources in order to live and work. Others will find them harmful to people because achieving them requires constraining the economic growth that people depend on for their livelihood and security.

All such reactions are normal and part of the incredible skill with which we delude ourselves into thinking that we can avoid the fate we bring upon ourselves through our own lack of humility and prudence. Such delusion is not unique to our culture or our time. As the environmental historian Jared Diamond documents in *Collapse: How Societies Choose to Fail or Succeed,* isolated cultures such as the Maya, the Anasazi, and the Easter Islanders pushed their use of key natural resources (such as timber) to the point where their civilizations collapsed in the wake of widespread starvation. Diamond asks: "What did the Easter Islander who cut down the last palm tree say while he was doing it? Like modern loggers, did he shout 'Jobs, not trees!' or 'We don't have proof that there aren't palms somewhere else on Easter, we need more research, your proposed ban on logging is premature and driven by fear-mongering!'"[9]

Vernacular design offers myriad examples of how to avoid such a fate. Cultures that embraced Huxley's perennial philosophy, including pre-eighteenth-century Western culture under the sway of Frye's first mythology, used objects mostly derived from locally available materials and local labor. Built of local materials that could be reused or were bio-degradable, their habitable structures used shade and cross ventilation for cooling, passive solar and renewable resources for heating, and flexible, multiuse interior space for living, working, and sleeping. Such cultures' settlements remained condensed in size, modest in scale, and close to agricultural land and open space, where the natural resources they depended on were carefully stewarded.

From the vantage point of our fossil-fueled, nonrenewable, massively wasteful, artificially heated and cooled built environment, such vernacular strategies may seem too difficult to adopt, too much about regressing to some primitive state. But modern architecture is full of threads with which we can weave a more "perennial architecture," one that does not simply reinforce our prior beliefs but helps people envision an "evolutionary transformational" future, demonstrating higher evolution and more intelligent design. In that sense, the perennial path involves not a radical departure for Western culture but rather an honest interpretation of it.

From that perspective, a perennial way of designing would try to meet our needs with the lightest impact, the fewest resources, and the least hubris. Such values underscore the notion of invisible design: before we manipulate the physical world to address a situation, we should see if we can solve the problem without altering existing human and natural ecologies, at the lowest cost and with a minimum of materials and energy. The sustainability movement in design reflects those values and shows that an evolutionary transformational culture has already begun to take root, as Joseph Campbell and his colleagues argued, even as forces exploiting nature and other cultures continue to thrive. The design community needs to pick up these threads, draw them out wherever we find them, and make a newly designed fabric that will, like Huxley's perennial philosophy, last a long time and have meaning across many cultures.

What might that fabric look like? What principles should guide us as we go forward? Such questions lead to others:

- What if we perceived everything and everyone as sacred, treating each, to paraphrase Immanuel Kant, as an end and not a means?
- What if we gave equal care and attention to every action, every material, every person, and every other species, cherishing all and wasting nothing?
- What effect would design rooted in such values have on those in our culture who produce things mindlessly, consume things quickly, and desire things constantly?
- What if we served others—especially the neediest among us, who benefit most from design—without concern for receiving anything in return?
- What if Mies van der Rohe's dictum that "less is more" applied not only to buildings but to the people we serve: the less they have, the more they need, and the more valuable design becomes?
- What if we saw design as primarily about connecting people to each other and to the natural world in every way possible?
- What if, in addition to the physical and visual connections designers make all the time, we focused on making social and spiritual connections as well, as Huxley's perennial philosophy suggests?
- What if design helped every one of us do without and do as little as possible?
- What if design accommodated not only those who have the most, who consume far more resources than they need or the world can afford, but also those who make up the rest of the world's population, who have learned, out of necessity, to live with much less?

207 In the context of modern commercial culture, hooked on growth, these ideas may sound impractical or even a bit crazy, but they simply express, in design terms, the perennial ideas that every sustainable human culture has embraced in order to thrive. We can ignore them, dismiss them, mock them, and continue on the "technological extrapolationist" path we're on, but our way of life will not survive long if we do. The task we all face is how to use design to prevent that from happening. If it does happen, and if, in a couple of generations, we go the way of the Maya, then those who have taken these ideas to heart and learned to live by them may be the ones to start the perennial world over again.

This chapter first appeared as "The Perennial Way of Design" in the journal *Center 15: Divinity, Creativity, Complexity* (April 2010).

[1] Northrop Frye, *The Modern Century* (Oxford: Oxford University Press, 1967), 106–11.

[2] Ibid., 111.

[3] Joseph Campbell, Duane Elgin, Willis Harman, Arthur Hastings, O. W. Markley, Floyd Matson, Brendan O'Regan, and Leslie Schneider, "Changing Images of Man" (Policy Research Report 4, prepared for the Charles F. Kettering Foundation and published by the Center for the Study of Social Policy, May 1974).

[4] Aldous Huxley, *The Perennial Philosophy* (New York: Harper & Row, 1944).

[5] Ibid., 5.

[6] Ibid., 77–78.

[7] Ibid., 76.

[8] Ibid.

[9] Diamond, *Collapse,* 114.

21

SPATIALIZING KNOWLEDGE

The dysfunctional systems that pervade our designed world mirror an unfortunate characteristic of modern life: our disconnection from the people and places that immediately surround us. That disconnection reflects the ways in which we have abstracted the world into separate fields, deconstructed it into distinct disciplines, and organized our knowledge of it into categories that have nothing to do with the integrated way in which places actually exist. Libraries offer the key to how this has happened and what we might do about it.

In Victor Hugo's *The Hunchback of Notre Dame*, the archdeacon holds up a book before the cathedral and says, "This will kill that. The book will kill the edifice."[1] Of course we know that the printing press did not "kill" buildings. We still have cathedrals and books, and, indeed, most books wouldn't survive very long unless stored in buildings. But we also know that the advent of books changed cathedrals, which had been thought of as "books in stone," with the stories of the Bible depicted in their statuary and stained glass. We still have cathedrals today, but they no longer have to serve also as books, and so they have changed in fundamental ways, becoming more abstract in form, more diverse in function, and largely shorn of their didactic ornament.

I mention this because we find ourselves at a moment in time where we could hold up a digital device—a laptop, smartphone, or e-reader—and declare, in front of either a book or a building, that "this will kill that." While we know that such devices will not "kill" books or buildings, we are also deep enough into the digital revolution to sense that digital media—including spatially oriented media like geographic information systems (GIS)—seem destined to have the same kind of effect as the printed book did beginning some five hundred years ago.

This brings to mind Marshall McLuhan's observation that each new technology "turns its predecessor into an art form."[2] Physical books will indeed survive the onslaught of downloadable e-books, but as we depend less and less on books for information or even as the most convenient way to access information, we will increasingly value them as an art form, as McLuhan put it, as beautiful objects and works of great craftsmanship.

And what about Victor Hugo's claim that books ultimately trump buildings? Downloadable e-books have not "killed" the library as a building type, but as happened with the cathedral after the widespread adoption of the printing press, libraries have increasingly become places where people go to have experiences that they cannot find anywhere else. Like the modern cathedral, the modern library going forward will likely have a greater array of functions, playing a more social and less didactic role in people's lives; it may, at least partly, lose the primary purpose it once served, of storing large quantities of books. It may be that in the future we will go to libraries to admire the craftsmanship of books and to interact with others about what we have learned through the information we have downloaded on mobile devices.

The biggest effect of the digital revolution, however, may be less material and more metaphorical. As McLuhan also argued, the "medium is the message," with major changes in media leading to changes in our metaphors and to the meanings that we ascribe to the world.[3] The mass-produced book led to a view of the world as a kind of machine, a metaphor that reflected the very thing that made this new media possible: the printing press. And that change in metaphor, in turn, led to many of the revolutions that followed: the Protestant revolution in the sixteenth century, the scientific revolution of the seventeenth century, the democratic revolutions of the late eighteenth century, and the industrial revolution of the nineteenth century.

OUR WEBLIKE REALITY

The machine metaphor lasted well into the twentieth century and paradoxically gave rise to the very technology—computers—that would ultimately overturn that metaphor. In the early twentieth century, people were still talking about the world in mechanistic ways, with intellectuals like Leo Tolstoy calling the body "a living machine" and Le Corbusier calling the house a "machine for living in."[4] Later in the century, such mechanistic analogies were still being drawn, with physicist Stephen Hawking, for example, regarding the "brain as a computer."[5]

Computing, though, also gave us the Internet. And with that, along with the miniaturization of computing in mobile devices, we have gradually realized that computers represent not just a faster form of computation but also an entirely new medium that has brought with it a new metaphor that increasingly dominates our view of the world. It took machines, in other words, to move us from a mechanistic view of reality to a networked one. We no longer view the brain as a kind of computer, but instead as a neural network; we no longer speak of society as a well-oiled mechanism, but instead as a social network; and we no longer see the human body as a machine, but instead as part of the web of life.

This shift in metaphor matters even more than the media that have prompted it. We will, of course, continue to use machines just as we will continue to use books, and so our material world will remain layered with technologies of the past as well as the present. But when we start to think of ourselves and see the world differently, big things begin to happen, as we saw in the wake of the printing press. Human relationships and social structures change, as we have seen in the Arab Spring revolutions in North Africa, fueled by the crowd-sourcing capabilities of cell phone technology; in the micro-lending revolution in the developing world, enabled by the financial transfers possible through social networks; and in the green revolution going on around the world, empowered by access to information formerly out of reach of ordinary people. The metaphor may ultimately be the message that matters.

This metaphor of the world as a network or web is altering our intellectual lives as well. The old machine metaphor privileged physics, mechanics, and engineering—three of the fields most closely associated with mechanisms. The new web metaphor, in contrast, draws from fields like biology and ecology, seeing in their understanding of how natural ecosystems work a parallel to the networked world we now occupy and informing us about human ecosystems and how they relate to each other in particular places.

The increasingly weblike way of seeing the world, in turn, has profound implications for how and in what form we seek information. The printed book offers us a linear way of doing so. We begin at the beginning—or maybe at the end, with the index—and work forward or backward through a book or at least parts of it to find the information we need. Digital media, in contrast, operate in networked ways, with hyperlinked texts taking us in multiple directions, social media placing us in multiple communities, and geographic information systems arranging data in multiple layers. No one starting place, relationship, or layer has privilege over any other in such a world.

FROM THE TEMPORAL TO THE SPATIAL

The linearity of the book compared with the multiplicity of the web leads to an even more fundamental shift in how we assess reality, moving from a temporal view to a spatial one. As with reading a book, we see time as an arrow, a linear path with starting and ending points. While we learned from Einstein that we can slow time down depending on how fast we accelerate, we cannot reverse time or occupy different speeds of time simultaneously.

But that is not the case with space. As with the web, we can manipulate space, move in multiple directions within it, and reverse it—tear a space down, for example—if we choose. The World Wide Web, of course, often seems aspatial. It connects us to people and places not in, and often far from, the actual spaces we occupy. Indeed, this new weblike way of engaging in the world appears to have collapsed both time and space, making everything that ever existed anywhere in the world immediately available to us, as if temporal and spatial distances no longer matter. Such effects, however, disguise the essentially spatial nature of digital media. The laterally linked and complexly networked nature of the web gives it a spatial form, conceptually if not always physically. And the layering of data and simultaneity of information through the web make it place based, even if that "place" exists in virtual space.

This line of thinking, in turn, suggests that the ways we currently store information (in digital documents and files) and distribute it (through e-mail, e-books, e-zines, and the like) may represent a transition stage in this technology. Such formats mimic the forms that emerged from the printing press and paper technology, and because of their familiarity, they have enabled us to adapt to accessing digital information. But they also reinforce a linear way of thinking about information that is inherently at odds with the web metaphor through which we increasingly see the world.

Geographic information systems will eventually become a major way—perhaps the dominant way—in which we access information because of the essentially spatial nature of GIS software. Rather than seeing information as discrete bits accessed linearly and temporally, as though moving along a necklace of data, GIS layers information spatially, linking it according to its relevance to other data on a given layer and according to its relevance to all the other layers in a given place. It allows us to "map" information, and such mapping may become the primary way we organize, access, and distribute knowledge in the future.

This use of spatial tools to match the spatial nature of a web will have a profound effect on how we think about information itself. The book led us to see information in highly discrete ways. By packaging related content between two covers, the book encouraged us to see knowledge as a set of distinct disciplines, each with its own discourse and eventually its own set of assumptions and use of language that made it increasingly hard for anyone not in that discipline to understand. By sorting information according to disciplines, books enabled us to think of knowledge as divorced from any particular physical or conceptual space. As a result, we can take almost any subject—say, water—and find that topic addressed in myriad ways by many disciplines—the sciences and social sciences, literature and history, art and poetry—all located in different places in libraries and all addressed in different ways through different disciplinary lenses.

That way of organizing knowledge has served us well over the past several centuries as we have sought to understand and control the world around us. But it has gotten in our way in recent decades, as we have come to realize the damage we have done to the world and the threat that poses to our civilization and to us. By dividing information into discrete disciplinary units, we have created what we might call the paradox of knowledge, in which we have vast information about the world and yet remain ill informed about our effect on the world.

This suggests that we may need to arrange knowledge differently in the future, not according to disciplinary categories but instead according to the way in which the world is organized: spatially. GIS offers one way of doing so. While the data-rich digital mapping of GIS was initially developed to ease geographic analysis and enhance spatial decision making, it has the potential to organize knowledge in ways that align more closely with the ecological patches that characterize ecosystems.

Such a method of organization might seem suited for spatially oriented fields, like geography, forestry, and planning, but how, you might ask, does it make sense for fields that appear to have no spatial equivalents: philosophy or pharmacy, history or histology, literature or linguistics? It's a good question, but maybe the wrong one to ask. It may be that we need to stop asking how to preserve our disciplines, which, for all their value, remain abstractions of or at least partial views of the world, and instead start asking how to preserve what remains of the natural world, which our disciplines, if they have any value, need to serve.

SPATIALIZING KNOWLEDGE

How might we spatialize knowledge? Rather than organizing knowledge by type or discipline, we could use GIS to embed all of the knowledge relevant to a place in the myriad layers of information about it. And as we scroll over a place, we could select the pertinent layers and begin to see the relationships among disciplines and the connections among data. Many talk about the need for interdisciplinarity, but as long as we organize knowledge in disciplinary silos, the connections among disciplines will continue to elude us. When we instead begin to organize knowledge spatially, the connections will come to the fore, as we focus less on the layers and more on the overlay of them and on their relevance to particular situations.

This, of course, may seem too much to ask: the reorganization of knowledge and the spatializing of education. We have, however, managed over the last couple of centuries to temporalize education. Every field has a history, and almost every one requires that students of the discipline study that history. Indeed, historical understanding has become such a part of what we define as an educated person that we take it almost for granted, but this wasn't always the case. It wasn't until the nineteenth century that we began to believe that, as Hegel argued, we cannot fully comprehend anything without knowing its history.

In the first decades of the twenty-first century, we need to see that the same holds true for space as much as it does for time. We cannot fully understand any field without also spatializing it, without also seeing how it relates to all other disciplines as they come together in particular places, with given groups of people, in specific social and environmental contexts. We need to know how disciplines have evolved over time, but we also need to know how they constitute the whole of particular places and of the people there.

This does not mean that we should see such spatial analysis as an end in itself. With the exception of historians, scholars rarely study temporal phenomena—history—as an end in itself. In most fields, the study of history serves as a means to an end, as a way of better understanding how the present came to be and what the future might hold. The same is true for a spatial understanding of the design fields. Except for a few, like my own field of architecture, which does study space as an end in itself, most disciplines will likely see this weblike, spatial turn in our thinking as a means of understanding their subjects in new ways. Space represents, like time, an "a priori" condition, as Kant argued, a precondition to everything else, and so having a sense of the relationship of space and time—how a field evolved spatially as well as temporally, what happened where as well as when—will increasingly become necessary if we are to fathom how we have done so much damage to so many places and to the cultures of so many people on the planet even as we purportedly know more about them.

The spatializing of knowledge via its mapping onto places has another advantage as well: it becomes a visual way of conveying information across the barriers of language and to the growing percentage of the human population that remains illiterate. The book divides the literate from the illiterate and, as such, has helped reinforce the power of the former over the latter. Victor Hugo understood that when he had the archdeacon hold up the book as killing the building. The medieval cathedrals spoke to both the literate and the illiterate, and, in some respects, the book made large stores of knowledge inaccessible to the latter.

The digital divide threatens to do that as well, with the wealthier parts of the world having much more access to information than the poorer parts. The web and cloud computing may help end that division by making most of what we need to know available at low cost, with "dumb" devices able to access information anywhere in the world. But there remains the problem of literacy, as well as translation, and so eliminating the digital divide through such devices will only partly close the gap that exists between those who have access to knowledge and those who don't.

We may never close that gap until we spatialize knowledge through the use of visual tools like GIS. Enabling people to see the information relevant to their lives, whether or not they can read, and to map it to the places they know in order to understand the conditions that affect their lives could have a transformative effect in empowering those who have been left behind by the book and even by the early incarnations of the computer.

GIS may represent the leading edge of computer mapping and visual-ization technology, but it also signifies, in some respects, a return to the world that Hugo's archdeacon saw as threatened. This brings to mind an observation of the novelist and semiotician Umberto Eco: that modernism represented a premedieval condition, which suggests that our post-post-modern world may have more characteristics in common with the medieval world than we have recognized.[6]

If the medieval cathedral tells stories in stone and glass, GIS tells them through layers and overlays. Both do so visually and spatially, both speak to viewers whose language or even whose literacy may not matter, and both reveal relationships and meanings that no book could ever capture. At the same time, the medieval cathedral and digital cartography both have the power to move us to action, to help us see things with our own eyes and without the interpretation of an author who might want to edit what we know or affect what we think.

Just as the book helped give rise to the Protestant revolution, in which people wanted to read the Bible for themselves and make up their own minds, so too might the visual and spatial power of GIS someday give rise to a secular version of the same, in which people, protesting the power of a few to control so much of the knowledge about the world, will want to see that information for themselves and make up their own minds.

This leads to my final point about the spatializing of knowledge. The temporalizing of knowledge has, through the agency of history, helped us understand the past and possibly comprehend how the present came to be, but rarely does it enable us to venture very far into the future. We call that science fiction or fantasy, setting such future-oriented thinking apart from what we can reliably know about the world as it is or as it once was. And we tend to see such work as somehow of lesser quality or validity than the work of the sciences, social sciences, and humanities.

But spatial understanding has a different relationship to the future, as well as to the past and present. Spatial knowledge recognizes place, rather than time, as the ultimate continuity in our lives. And while none of us can see the future as a temporal idea, we continually imagine the future of places, projecting possible spatial arrangements based on what we see around us.

The design disciplines do this all the time, using spatial means to imagine what could be, envisioning the future of a place, product, or environment, and depicting that visually for others to see. We commend or criticize a design and accept or alter it to fit our idea of what should happen in a particular place or with a particular product. We don't consider design a lesser discipline—it is simply a different one, operating according to its own criteria and assumptions.

The leading edge of GIS rests with the idea of "geodesign," the use of geographic analysis of what is as the basis of making design decisions about what could be. Rather than seeing future-oriented thinking as somehow fiction or fantasy, geodesign allows us to connect what we know about the world with what we might want the world to be. Just as GIS can serve as a means of organizing knowledge spatially, geodesign might serve as a means of projecting that knowledge into the future, and of assessing its merits based on what we know about a place.

Why does this matter? Because we stand on a precipice similar to that experienced by Hugo's archdeacon, with even more drastic implications. We might well say that "this will kill that," but in our case, "this" represents modern civilization and "that," the natural world. Since the rise of the book, although not necessarily because of it, the Ponzi scheme with the planet that we have developed over the last couple of centuries exploits natural resources, other species, foreign cultures, and even future generations in order to keep those at the top of the pyramid enriched.

And as we know from the collapse of other Ponzi schemes, such frauds cannot last. They tend to collapse suddenly and without warning, and those—like us—who have been most enriched by the schemes have the furthest to fall. The only way we can avoid such a fate is by realigning our relationship with the natural world, reorganizing our considerable knowledge about it in order to reveal the forces that lead to our unsustainable practices, and relearning how to steward what remains of the planet we have so altered. If we don't make these changes, we have only to alter the terms of Hugo's observation slightly. This—the collapse of our Ponzi scheme—will kill that—the civilization we have built up over two hundred years.

The spatializing of knowledge, in other words, isn't just an academic exercise or the result of some arcane interest of a few spatial thinkers or GIS specialists. With it, we can begin to set the foundation for a more sustainable future for ourselves as we see the impacts of our actions and the relevance of our knowledge to the particular places in which we live.

218 This will not kill anything except the ridiculous illusion that we can continue to live beyond the carrying capacity of our planet. And doing so is not just about space—it's about time!

Portions of this chapter were delivered as a keynote address to Big Ten university librarians in May 2013.

1 Victor Hugo, *The Hunchback of Notre Dame* (1831; repr., New York: Modern Library, 2002).

2 McLuhan, *Understanding Media*, ix.

3 Ibid., 8–13.

4 Leo Tolstoy, War and Peace (1869; repr., New York: Modern Library, 2002), 241; Le Corbusier, *Towards a New Architecture* (1923; repr., Los Angeles: Getty Publications, 2007).

5 Quoted in Ian Sample, "Stephen Hawking: 'There Is No Heaven; It's a Fairy Story,'" *The Guardian*, May 17, 2011.

6 Umberto Eco, *The Aesthetics of Chaosmos: The Middle Ages of James Joyce*, trans. Ellen Esrock (Cambridge, Mass.: Harvard University Press, 1989).

POSTSCRIPT
A PAST AND
POSSIBLE FUTURE

Although I wrote most of this book as articles during the past few years, the idea of this work took root in 1974, when I met and had conversations with the historian and critic Lewis Mumford. Most of my way through college, in a professional architecture program, I had begun to doubt my desire to follow my grandfather into the architectural profession or to join the family's architectural firm in Detroit when I graduated. I had discovered during college that I preferred writing to designing and the expression of ideas to the making of forms and spaces, and that what I liked about architecture—and design generally—had more to do with what it says about our culture and beliefs than with it as an end in itself. I felt out of place in school and unclear about what I should do—the sign, I suppose, of education at work. But in the summer of 1974, while I was working for the Historic American Building Survey in Rhinebeck, New York, I went with our supervising architect and his wife to nearby Amenia to visit Lewis Mumford's daughter, who was a friend of theirs, as well as her father and mother in their small, clapboard house.

While I had had professors who inspired me, like the architectural theorist Colin Rowe, I had never met anyone like Mumford, who wrote about architecture and cities for the *New Yorker* for several decades and also authored grand, synthesizing books about the history of cities, technology, and philosophy. I asked him that summer how I might have a career like his, and he patiently responded that I needed to know more than architecture if I wanted to write about the field; he then wrote out a list of authors—from Plato to Emerson to Patrick Geddes—whose works I should read. I did what he suggested, not only reading all of Mumford's books and those that he recommended but also going to graduate school to study the history of ideas, all with Mumford in mind.

My career has not followed a path anything like that of Mumford's, nor have I achieved anywhere near the breadth and depth of work that he produced. But I have known, since the summer of 1974, that I wanted to follow his path and to write about architecture and design in terms of what they say about our values and our ideas about the world. I did not know what form that would take, and it took me years—decades—to read enough and to even begin to know enough to write a book like this, which flies in the face of the specialization that characterizes so much of our intellectual life today.[1] "Our life has been governed by specialists," wrote

Mumford, "who know too little of what lies outside their province to be able to know enough about what takes place within it: unbalanced men who have made a madness out of their method. Our life, like medicine itself, has suffered from the dethronement of the general practitioner, capable of vigilant selection, evaluation, and action with reference to the health of the organism or the community as a whole."[2]

I know that specialization has value and specialists have an important role to play; I certainly appreciate them in medicine, despite Mumford's comment about the dethronement of the general practitioner. But I also agree with Mumford that we have too often dismissed what he called "the generalist," the person able to work across disciplinary boundaries and to make connections among seemingly disparate phenomena. Designers have many of the skills needed to play this generalist role, although many in the design community have become so enamored of specialization that they, too, have made a madness of their method.

Yet Mumford wrote about architecture, in part, because it remained for him one of the least specialized of professions, one that still valued the idea of the general practitioner. "Cut off though he is from the actual processes of building," wrote Mumford, the architect "nevertheless remains the sole surviving craftsman who maintains the relation towards the whole structure that the old handicraft workers used to enjoy in connection with their particular job."[3] Mumford was aware that this relation to the whole might not last: "It is impossible to say with any certainty whether our architects are doomed to be extruded by mechanism, or whether they will have the opportunity to restore to our machine-system some of the freedom of an earlier regime."[4]

Mumford's doubts about architecture in the age of mechanization seemed somewhat fatalistic to me in 1974. "Architecture," he wrote, "like government, is about as good as a community deserves."[5] But I now see the wisdom of his caution in a century noted for its incredibly destructive efforts on both the right and the left, on the part of the Nazis and the Soviets and the Maoists, to enact their utopian visions. While utopia plays an important rhetorical role in the envisioning of possible futures, we should never try to construct it, at least in its pure form, as some governments—and their architects—have tried to do. Mumford called these "fake utopias," and he urged us, instead, to create "eutopias," good places that "spring out of the realities of our environment."[6]

223 I took to heart Mumford's caution that the design community should not go to the opposite extreme and withdraw or become resigned to mechanization. Instead, it should reassert its ability to change the conditions within which we all live and work. Indeed, Mumford thought that the design community, which he viewed as actively engaged in the intellectual life of the early twentieth century, had become too inwardly focused and hermetic in the second half of the century. His example represented for me a path forward that the design community had neglected for too long: the idea of designers as public intellectuals, not just creating and constructing the environments that the public uses and occupies but also bringing design methods and design perspectives to the larger challenges faced by society.

Mumford put it this way:

Our architecture has been full of false starts and unfulfilled promises precisely because the ground has not been worked enough beforehand to receive the new seeds. If we are to have a fine architecture, we must begin at the other end from that where our sumptuously illustrated magazines on home-building and architecture begin—not with the building itself, but with the whole complex out of which architect, builder, and patron spring, and into which the finished building, whether it be a cottage or a skyscraper, is set. Once the conditions are ripe for a good architecture, the plant will flower by itself.[7]

In some ways, this book represents my attempt to prepare that ground and plant seeds that I hope will flower at some point.

Mumford's organic view of the world—his analogy of intellectual work to preparing soil and planting seeds—had an enormous influence on me, evident in this book. He took an ecological approach to culture, one that recognized the interrelatedness and complexity of all things, balancing our preoccupations with science, technology, and rationality with our obligations to family, community, and the natural environments in which we live. "Man is at last in a position to transcend the machine," he wrote, "and to create a new biological and social environment, in which the highest possibilities of human existence will be realized . . . for all co-operating and understanding groups, associations, and communities."[8]

He also recognized the danger that humanity faces because of our un-bridled use of technology to exploit the world's human and natural resources, and the need for us to envision a future in which we can sustain ourselves without undermining the very foundations on which civilization depends. "A fresh cultural transformation is in the making," he wrote, "one which will recognize that the money economy is bankrupt, and the power complex has become, through its very excesses and exaggerations, impotent."[9] The emphasis in this book on economic and social changes, on new modes of work and education, and on avoiding technological fixes for our problems echoes the cultural renewal that Mumford envisioned.

Looking back on Mumford's life and work, I see him as part of a dying breed of independent thinkers and writers who never became full-time academics and who continued to write for the public in accessible—indeed, beautifully crafted—prose. He was one of the last public intellectuals who used architecture and design as vehicles for communicating ideas, in part because he saw the designed world as so much a part of everyone's concrete reality and as such an accurate reflection of our values. He did more to place design front and center in the minds of a literate public than almost anyone in the design fields. Since Mumford's death in 1990 at the age of ninety-four, architecture and design have become more arcane, as academic authors have increasingly turned out jargon-laden texts, and yet also more anodyne, as slick consumer magazines have fed images of design to the public, largely bereft of ideas.

Late in life Mumford became something of a Jeremiah, predicting doom if we failed to heed his words. Although I found such writing exhilarating when I was young, I now find the apocalyptic tone of his last books some-times hard to take. His message, however, remains powerful. Mumford urged us to look at the world holistically, ecologically, and synthetically, and he continued to hope that the design community, as one of the fields that retains a "eutopian" urge, might lead such an effort, envisioning a more humanly scaled, socially responsive, and environmentally sound future, without lapsing into nostalgia on one hand or nihilism on the other.

I have tried to capture that in this book: to show how design, as a way of thinking and of being, still has the capacity to keep that eutopian tradition alive. The great value that design has to offer the world lies in the systematic way in which its practitioners develop alternative futures for a situation and then rigorously assess those alternatives to find what best meets our needs within a budget and schedule we can afford. While that skill is usually applied to the design of the environments and products we use every day, it may have even more value for finding alternatives to the designed systems that we often don't see as such and that do not function as well as they should. Design can help us find better options that, like a well-designed building, meet our goals within the constraints of time and money. Indeed, such constraints benefit this process because they put limits on what we can do, which almost always leads to more creative solutions.

Good design also benefits from the involvement of those who have the most at stake in finding a solution: the people most affected by the outcome of a design as well as those with the ability to make it a reality. Right now, such involvement doesn't always happen. Too many of those with the power to redesign a system want to keep control, and so exclude the people at the front lines of a problem, who often have some of the best ideas for changing it, or they resist changing what has benefited them personally, even when they acknowledge the need for change. A big part of the design process, then, involves making sure it includes the right people and enough diversity of voices to ensure the best results.

I hope that this book encourages others to follow a design path, to explore the role of creative thinking and abductive reasoning in addressing the wicked problems before us, far beyond the narrow confines of traditional practice. We have all the visible design we need for the top few percent of the global population who can afford to commission designers or buy what they produce. The great opportunity—and truly pressing need—lies with the invisible design that affects the lives of the rest of the human population as well as the many other species on this planet. With so much to do and so little time to do it, no designer will ever lack for important work, since the real future of design lies in its designing possible futures—more sustainable and equitable futures than the one we now face. As Lewis Mumford described the opportunity before us at the end of one of his best books: "The way we must follow is untried and heavy with difficulty; it will test to the utmost our faith and our powers. But it is the way toward life, and those who follow it will prevail."[10]

226

1 Much of the material on Lewis Mumford in this postscript is from an article I wrote about him, "What Would Mumford Say?," *Progressive Architecture* (October 1995): 70–73.

2 Lewis Mumford, *The Conduct of Life* (New York: Harcourt Brace, 1951), 181.

3 Lewis Mumford, *Sticks and Stones: A Study of American Architecture and Civilization* (New York: Dover, 1955), 106.

4 Ibid., 107.

5 Ibid., 69.

6 Lewis Mumford, *The Story of Utopias* (New York: Viking, 1962), 303, 307.

7 Mumford, *Sticks and Stones,* 94.

8 Lewis Mumford, *The Culture of Cities* (New York: Harcourt Brace, 1938), 492.

9 Lewis Mumford, *The Pentagon of Power* (New York: Harcourt Brace Jovanovich, 1970), 429.

10 Mumford, *The Conduct of Life,* 292.

INDEX

abduction, 1, 8, 21–31, 55, 58, 61, 87, 97, 155, 225
advertising, 197
aesthetics, 109, 149, 155–56, 196
apparel design, 14
architecture, xiii, xv, 10, 14, 62, 103, 110, 118, 123, 150, 164, 169, 171–72, 181, 187, 196, 205, 215, 221–24
Aristotle, 21

Bentham, Jeremy, 112
Boo, Katherine, 183
Brooks, David, 38
Brooks, Jeffrey, 38
Brown, Tim, 16
Brownlee, Shannon, 121

Campbell, Joseph, 202, 206
Central Park, 99–100, 104
creativity, x, 18, 21–31, 33, 35–41, 43, 72, 93, 166, 176–77
Cronon, William, 109–10
Cunningham, Donald, 24–25, 29

Dangermond, Jack, 38–39
Davis, Mike, 119
Dawkins, Richard, 123
Defoe, Daniel, 121
Descartes, René, 23
design education, 28, 33, 55–63
design failures, xi–xii, 8, 97
design thinking, viii, 1, 5–9, 12–19, 21–23, 26, 48, 65, 89, 93–94, 129, 134, 159
Diamond, Jared, 71, 205
digital environment, xv, 18, 33, 78, 92, 117, 119, 121–23, 169–70, 173, 175, 196, 209–13, 215–16
disaggregation, 1, 13–14, 17, 171
Drucker, Peter, 150

Echelman, Janet, 36–37
ecology, vii, 43, 123, 159, 161, 163, 172, 202–3, 206, 211, 213, 223–24
economics, vii–viii, xi–xiv, 1, 5, 51, 111, 161–63, 165–66, 169–77, 182–86, 191, 193, 197–98, 202, 204, 224
education, higher, xi, 33, 40–41, 57–63
education, K–12, viii, xi–xii, xiv, 5–7, 13, 24, 33, 35–44, 47, 49–53, 138, 194–95, 214, 221, 224
Einstein, Albert, 1, 3–10, 212
Emanuel, Kerry, 182
Emerson, Ralph Waldo, 153, 221
ethics, 107–14, 117, 186–87
evolution, 38, 43, 191, 201–6

Farson, Richard, 159, 181
Fitzgerald, F. Scott, 154
food, 13, 42, 97, 101, 103, 172, 185, 197, 204
Freud, Sigmund, 1, 3–10
Frye, Northrop, 201–2, 205
games, 195–96

Gardner, Howard, 40–41
Geddes, Patrick, 221
Gehry, Frank, 38
GeoDesign, 7, 217
GIS, 209, 212–17
Gladwell, Malcolm, 37, 39
graphic design, 14
guns, 146, 165
Haiti, 48, 194, 196

Hancock, Herbie, 38
Hawking, Stephen, 210
Hegel, G. W. F., 214
Hillis, Danny, 38
Hobbes, Thomas, 110–11, 152, 187

Hofstadter, Douglas, 124
homelessness, 51, 136, 182, 186, 193
housing, xii, 51, 70–71, 75, 100–2,
    129, 136–37, 141–42, 145, 162,
    184–87, 193
hubris, 13, 68, 80, 204–5
Hugo, Victor, 209, 215–17
Huxley, Aldous, 203–6

IDEO, 171
intelligence, 33, 40–41, 47, 94
intelligent design, 201–2, 205
interior design, 14

Jacobs, Jane, 152, 166
Jevons, William, 9–10
jobs, 42, 44, 47–49, 60, 122, 136, 174,
    186, 205
Jobs, Steve, 16–18
juvenile detention system, viii–x

Kant, Immanuel, 109, 187, 206, 215
Katz, Bruce, 166
Katzenberg, Jeffrey, 38
knowledge, vii, xiv–xv, 1, 3, 6, 14,
    23–24, 30, 33, 35–36, 40–42, 49,
    62–63, 83, 100, 109, 124, 182, 191,
    195, 198, 202, 209, 213–17

landscape, x, 80, 83, 101–5, 107–14
landscape architecture, 14, 38, 81,
    99, 102–3, 110
leadership, ix, 16, 144, 165
Lear, Norman, 38
Le Corbusier, xiii, 151–53, 210
Lenzer, Jeanne, 121
Lilla, Mark, 150
Locke, John, 184

Ma, Yo-Yo, 38
Maeda, John, 38, 43

Manaugh, Geoff, 117–18
Martin, Roger, 16, 154
Maslow, Abraham, 185–86
MASS Design, 171
McKibben, Bill, 110
McLuhan, Marshall, 17, 123, 209
medicine, 55, 99, 102, 135, 181, 198, 222
micro-lending, 198, 211
Mill, John Stuart, 112
millennials, 44, 76
Moynihan, Daniel Patrick, 146–47
Mumford, Lewis, 221–25
Myers, Norman, 182

National Academy of Environmen-
    tal Design, 48
National Collaborative on Child-
    hood Obesity Research, 48
networks, 8, 56, 92–93, 117, 172,
    193–95, 198, 211
Newton, Isaac, 121–22
NIMBY, 141–45

Obama, Barack, 42, 47–48, 117
Oldham, Todd, 38
Olmsted, Frederick Law, 97, 99–105,
    107, 117
opposable thinking, 129, 153–56,
    161, 165

panarchy, vii
pandemic, 97, 104–5, 117–25
Panek, Richard, 3–7
Peirce, Charles Sanders, 1, 21–24,
    27–30, 112
Pink, Daniel, 16
Pinker, Steven, 38
planning, 14, 75, 77–78, 82, 97, 117,
    129, 144–45, 149–51, 213
Plato, 151, 184, 221
Plotinus, 203

politics, xiv, 89, 104, 111, 117, 129, 132–38, 141, 149–50, 154–55
Ponzi scheme, 217
Popper, Karl, 21, 90
postmodern, xiii, 162, 216
product design, 14, 16
public health, xiv, 48, 55, 96–97, 99–105, 117–19, 121, 171, 181–82, 196–97
public-interest design, xiii, 7, 171, 196

Reich, Robert, 174
Rifkin, Jeremy, 159, 169–72, 177
Rittel, Horst, 14
Rontgen, Wilhelm, 4
Rousseau, Jean-Jacques, 111, 153, 187
Rowe, Colin, 221

Safdie, Moshe, 38
safety, xi, 67, 76, 108, 136, 146, 165, 177, 182, 191, 194–99
Sale, Kirkpatrick, 163
sanitation, 99–102, 104, 183
Schaef, Anne Wilson, 163
schools, xi, 6, 33, 35, 39–41, 47–52, 55, 134–35
SEED, 43–44, 51
Shank, Gary, 24–25, 29
Singer, Peter, 107, 112
sixth extinction, 111
slums, 99, 119, 183, 193
Smith, Adam, 159, 161–62
Soros, George, 150
Snow, John, 117–18
spatial thinking, 1, 3, 7, 40–41, 191, 209, 212–17
STE(A)M fields, 33, 42–44
Storefront for Art and Architecture, 117

technology, vii, 1, 9, 14–18, 33, 41–44, 60, 80, 110, 121, 169, 196, 201–2, 209, 215, 221, 223–24
third industrial revolution, 169–78
Thoreau, Henry David, 153
Tolstoy, Leo, 210
Twilley, Nicola, 117–18

United Nations World Commission on Environment and Development, 112
urban design, 14, 89, 122–23, 129, 144, 149, 151–52, 164, 232
U.S. Green Building Council, 48

Venter, Craig, 38–39
Virchow, Rudolf, 99

West, Geoffrey, 38
wicked problems, 14, 18, 33, 35, 56, 65, 79, 159, 225
will.i.am, 38
Williamsburg, Virginia, 141–45
wisdom, 35, 202, 222
Wilson, E. O., 38
Wright, Frank Lloyd, xiii, 151–53
Wulfram, Stephen, 38–39
Wurman, Richard Saul, 38, 40

THOMAS FISHER is professor in the School of Architecture, the Dayton Hudson Chair in Urban Design, and director of the Metropolitan Design Center at the University of Minnesota. He was recognized in 2005 as the fifth most published writer about architecture in the United States and has been named one of the top twenty-five design educators four times by *DesignIntelligence*. His books include *Designing to Avoid Disaster: The Nature of Fracture-Critical Design* and *In the Scheme of Things: Alternative Thinking on the Practice of Architecture* (Minnesota, 2000).